To
End of the
and Back

A Millennium Adventure

At the bus station I bought a ticket for the midday bus to Punta Arenas, Chile. I was about to enter a new country, only to leave again shortly after. To get to Tierra del Fuego I would have to take a boat from Punta Arenas. The island is unequally divided between Chile and Argentina, one of the many arguments over land between these two countries.

'Is it always so windy here?' I asked the girl behind the counter.

'Yes,' she replied, 'cold also!'

The tone of her voice suggested that she longed to be elsewhere, preferably tropical.

She then presented me with a customs form to fill in, which informs you of the various things you are not allowed to take into Chile like: animals, vegetables, fruit and semen. *Semen!* How was I supposed to help that? Perhaps I would be asked to remove it before entry. I imagined arriving at the border and being directed to join a long line of men, eventually leading to a door where a nurse would be handing out magazines.

Ian Middleton

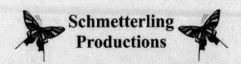

Schmetterling Productions

First published in Great Britain 2001

Copyright © 2000 Ian Middleton.

Cover design and photos by Ian Middleton © 2001
Assisted by Nathalie Speksnijder
Map by Hans van Well © 2001

Published by Schmetterling Productions
ISBN 0-9540779-0-3
email: schmetterling_productions@yahoo.co.uk

Printed and bound in Great Britain
by Cox & Wyman, Reading, Berkshire

Contents:

Map by Hans van Well © 2001

Prologue

Never Laugh at Sniffer Dogs

Getting up in the early hours of the morning is not my speciality. But when it means you have to or else miss that plane, then the only fear is that you will sleep through the alarm. This was possibly the reason for my light sleep. I hauled on my backpack, followed by the daypack then the extra bag I'd needed for all the things I had bought here in La Paz. Each bag was packed to bursting point. I pictured myself hauling this lot through customs in England.

'Anything to declare?'

'No!'

Would they believe me?

The hotel was a very dark place at four-thirty in the morning. I felt like a blind man attempting an army assault course as I fumbled my way along the landing and tried to find where the stairs began. When I reached the toilet that signified the start of the steps, I switched on its light in order for me to walk down and not fall. The main doors of the hotel were closed, so I tried the door to reception. That was locked also. Who ever heard of getting locked in a hotel? I

1

banged on the door in the hope of rousing someone. A minute or so later it opened to reveal a bleary-eyed youngster with a crooked baseball cap on his head.

'Buenos dias!' I announced, trying to sound cheerful.

'Have you paid?' he grunted.

'Yes.'

With this he allowed me through, proceeding to unlock the front door so that I could leave and he could get back to sleep.

'Is my taxi outside yet?' I asked.

He shrugged and followed me out. The street was devoid of life. We both stood there awkwardly for a moment, me wondering if the receptionist the night before had remembered to book me that taxi, and him possibly wishing he hadn't agreed to do the nightshift.

He flagged down the first taxi that shot around the corner and I got in that. My driver was extremely jolly, given the time of morning. At four-thirty in the morning speaking in Spanish was not something I found easy. In fact speaking at all was not something I found easy. But as the airport was a good half-hour ride away, I felt it would have been rude not to. We talked of my trip and of Bolivia.

'Do you like Bolivia?' he asked.

'Oh yes,' I replied, truthfully, 'it's a beautiful country. The people are so friendly, and the indigenous people are fascinating.'

'Where have you been?'

'I entered via Chile, on a tour that ended in Uyuni, then went to Potosí, Sucre and Lake Titicaca. I stayed there for ten days.'

'Did you go to Tiwanaku?' he asked, a sparkle appearing in his eyes.

Tiwanaku is Bolivia's most significant archaeological site. Very little remains of it now and it's not all that impressive. The pyramid is all but gone. All that remains are a few walls and a couple of ugly statues. If this was the best in Bolivia, then I dread to think what the others were like.

When I told the driver this, his smile fell off his face and rolled onto the floor.

'Perhaps it's because I've been spoiled by the pyramids of Mexico,' I continued, trying to counteract the bad effect this seemed to be having on our friendship.

'And what are they like?' he asked.

'Oh they're fantastic!' I exclaimed, and proceeded to waffle on about the size of their pyramids and the number of ruined cities in the Yucatan.

'Hmm!' he grunted and drove on in silence. Any attempt at conversation after that was met with indifference. At the airport I gave him an extra ten bolivianos and told him to keep the change. 'Right!' he replied, without so much as a smile, hopped in the car and sped off.

Guess he was proud of those ruins.

Once I had checked in I made my way to the departure lounge. At security the officer pointed behind me. I turned to see a suspicious-looking character beckoning me into a room the size of a changing compartment. Once inside he pulled the curtain across and stared at me.

I didn't like the look of this.

'Narcotics!' he said, quite frankly.

I shouldn't really, I thought, I'm just about to get on a plane.

He then performed a rapid body search and nodded for me to leave.

Back outside I plonked my bag on the conveyor and

started to remove my belt.

'Don't worry about that,' said the security officer, without actually removing his eyes from the screen.

'But it always sets off the metal detector,' I protested.

'It's okay,' he replied, motioning me through with his hand.

I stepped through. The alarm went off. I turned and gave a 'told you' look to the officer. He waved me on again. Their relaxed attitude to security was a bit daunting to say the least.

As I stood in the queue waiting to board the plane, I watched the sniffer dog run up and down the conveyor belt as they loaded the luggage on the plane. On occasion his back legs would fall off the side. I found this highly amusing. However this time the smile was to fall off my face and hit the floor at the sudden realisation that I had forgotten to take that bag of coca leaves out of my backpack.

My heart rate increased by double and my bowels suddenly went into spasm. For those who are unaware, the coca leaf is the substance from which cocaine is derived. It grows in Bolivia and is widely sold in the markets. The Bolivians use it for tea and for chewing. When placed in water it makes a great herbal tea. When chewed it helps combat fatigue and hunger. However in Bolivia they are legal. In other countries they are not.

As I took my seat on the plane I chided myself for forgetting such an important thing. I had constantly said to myself, 'Don't forget to get rid of those coca leaves!' but in the last minute rush to get everything and then try to fit it all into my bags, I had quite obviously neglected to do this.

So after three months of safe and relatively trouble-free travel in South America, it looked as though I could be arrested when I arrived in England, or even before I left.

Although given the carefree attitude at security I doubted if this would be the case. Even so I nervously waited for take off and hoped I wouldn't hear the following announcement: 'Would Mr Ian Middleton please come to the front of the plane.'

__1__

__THREE MONTHS EARLIER.__

__Coming of Age in Buenos Aires__

She strolled past me, shamelessly flaunting her incredible beauty. Her hair was long, soft and dark. The kind of hair that would fall perfectly back into place with just a quick flick and shake of the head. She had the kind of puppy dog brown eyes that would instantly put you under her spell. Eyes that could melt snow in Antarctica. Her skin was the colour of dark, rich coffee, and flawless. I wish she was coming on my flight! I thought to myself.

As she strolled off down the gangway and out of sight, I brought my quivering bottom lip back under control and continued to read. Then, as if my wish had been granted, she came walking back up that gangway and into the departure lounge for my flight.

'There is a god!' I muttered under my breath, as I watched her walk off and take a seat over the other side.

As we shuffled onto the plane I attempted to keep track, but lost her in the rush of people. With a bit of luck I'll be seated next to her, I thought, or at least nearby. Once seated I eagerly awaited the arrival of my travelling companion.

To my disappointment it was an old lady. As the plane taxied down the runway I looked around me in search of my dark goddess, but she was nowhere to be seen.

'Where are you going?' asked the old lady.

'Buenos Aires,' I replied. 'I'm starting a three-month trip from Buenos Aires to Tierra del Fuego, then up through Chile to Lake Titicaca.'

'Oh how wonderful!' she exclaimed, and proceeded to tell me all about Argentina and Chile, while I tried desperately to spot this girl.

She was on her way to visit her son who now lives in Santiago.

'The Chilean people are so friendly,' she went on, 'they will do anything to help.'

This was something I was about to find out. She was right about them being eager to help, perhaps a little too eager at times.

'Do you speak Spanish?' she asked.

'Well yes, some. But I haven't spoken it for over two years.'

I hadn't even had time to brush up on it because the trip had come up so fast and I had been too busy with work, Christmas and the Millennium. It was now three days into the year 2000 and quite frankly it didn't feel any different. I had seen it in with the usual family party just like any other year. While most other people were watching spectacular firework displays worth thousands of pounds, I was stood in my uncle's garden in a small town in Hampshire, trying my best to gain visual excitement from a box of Tesco Value rockets.

But none of that mattered now. This was the part I had been waiting for, my journey to the end of the world.

For years I had often stared in fascination at the world map on my wall, and wondered just what the tiny island that forms the far southern tip of South America looks like? Who lives there? And more to the point, how difficult would it be to get there? Okay so the easiest way would be to take an internal flight from Buenos Aires. But that would be too easy. Besides I try to make it a rule never to fly within countries. It detracts from the whole experience. How can you really get a feel for a country, its size and the people who live there, if you fly over most of it? That's my theory anyway. And that was the reason for my decision to get off at Buenos Aires and make my way down overland. After all, it's only a 3000 kilometres journey.

I had brought one of my Spanish books along with me in the hope that I could brush up as I travelled.

'In Argentina they have a very strange accent,' the old lady told me, 'for the ll and y they say sh.'

These letters are usually pronounced as a y, like in yellow. It seemed this could only be found in Argentina, and nowhere else in the Spanish speaking world. Therefore I would have to make a point not to adopt it.

We arrived in Buenos Aires the next morning. I stood up and put on my pack ready to go. On the other side of the plane I noticed her in the queue. She looked my way. I smiled. She didn't respond. Not a good start.

I assumed her to be Argentinean; after all she had the Latin looks. This posed another problem: my Spanish was extremely rusty. It hadn't been exactly brilliant in the first place, but I had always been able to clumsily barge my way through a conversation. Now however, it was all locked away in the foggy recess of my brain, and I figured it might take some time to retrieve. Time was something I didn't have.

First impressions count, and I had to gain her interest before she left that airport and got lost forever in the swirling metropolis of Buenos Aires. I lost her again on the way to immigration. But she still had to collect her baggage.

I kept one beady eye on the conveyor belt and the other on her. I then wrestled with how I was going to spark up a conversation. The best option it seemed, considering my lack of fluency in Spanish, would be to play the lost tourist in the hope that she would take pity on me and personally take me to my hostel. Yes that was definitely my best option.

I noticed her wave to someone across the room and looked over to see a podgy middle-aged man waving back. Must be her father, I thought. It was a little early to meet the family, but I was willing; after all, I had to respect the culture. He sauntered across and they embraced. She kissed him tenderly on the mouth as his hand went down her back and caressed her backside. My jaw hit the ground and I just managed to catch my backpack as it came into view. I grabbed it quickly and then turned to see them both walking off hand in hand.

'But what about my personal tour!' I shouted after her, but was met with silence.

As my Latin beauty walked off with a man twice her age, I slouched along behind with a dead weight on my back. I entered the arrivals lounge and was immediately accosted by a short man asking if I wanted a taxi. It was tempting. It would have been so much easier. But I couldn't. I planned to take the No 86 local bus. In order to fully understand a place you have to travel like the everyday people, then you get to see more of the local life and can listen in on conversations; or even get talking to someone yourself. A backpacker getting on a local bus often incites curiosity. Take a taxi and you invariably get involved in a conversation that you and the driver have had a thousand times. They will tell you about good hotels and the sights that all the tourists should see. Also the local bus stops many times during the trip and different people get on and off throughout, making it a much more interesting trip. And it's a lot cheaper.

'I'm looking for the bus,' I said to him.

He motioned me over to a ticket office.

'How much is the bus to the centre?' I asked the girl at the window.

What followed next was an unstoppable flow of unintelligible sounds.

'¿Cómo?' I replied, dumbly.

She repeated the words.

This time I just managed to catch the price. It appeared that my Spanish was far rustier that I had realised. Later I was to discover that it wasn't only that, but because the people in this city have a dialect all of their own. Their everyday conversation consists mostly of slang. This would be explained to me by a couple in a bar on the Bolivian side of Lake Titicaca. They were from here, but had kindly spoken to me in normal Spanish. The reason for this complex dialect is largely due to the city's cultural diversity. Starting in the 1860s emigrants, mostly from Spain and Italy, poured into Buenos Aires. The result today is that the city now has a large population with Italian heritage. The Spanish of the Porteños (the name given to residents of Buenos Aires) now comprises of many Italian words and expressions.

Judging by the price she gave me it wasn't the local bus, but I was too tired and lacking in the language to try and figure out how to get it. So I shoved her 14 pesos. The Argentinean peso is linked to the US dollar making it exactly the same value. Made it easier to work things out.

One bus and subway ride later and I was in the general vicinity of the International Hostel. I got off the Subte, as it's called, and emerged in the middle of a huge bus terminal. The road was crawling with people, and local buses pumping thick smoke into the atmosphere.

'Where is Brasil Street?' I shouted to a newspaper vendor.

'This is it!' he shouted back.

'I'm looking for number 675!'

He kindly pointed me in the right direction and I soon found it. I pushed open the extremely big and heavy door and ascended the steps to find myself in a huge building with wide corridors and high ceilings. The inside resembled an old stately mansion. To my right was a giant open flight of stairs. During my stay there I would often feel like a lord as I came down these stairs. 'Who's at the door, Jeeves?'

I checked in and for 15 pesos was given a bed in a dorm upstairs. The room fronted onto the road, and outside a large set of French windows was a nice spacious balcony. I intended to make good use of that.

Within half an hour I had made a couple of friends and headed out to see the city with them. Oscar was from Spain and Anna from California. Anna sounded spookily like Loyd Grossman. She also spoke fluent Spanish. When I had met Oscar in the room I had spoken in Spanish with him. He had exercised patience as I fumbled to retrieve the words from the depths of my jumbled mind. However as the day progressed it became more difficult. Jetlag was setting in.

I went with them to Plaza de Mayo. This literally signifies the city centre, as the city was built around this exact point. Surrounding it is the Casa Rosada (the presidential palace), Metropolitan Cathedral and Museo del Cabildo (also known as the Town Hall). The plaza is also famed for *Las Madres de la Plaza de Mayo*. These are the women who showed up at the plaza demanding information on the *Desaparecidos*. During the dictatorship of 1976-1983 thousands of men, women and children vanished at the hands of the military during a period called the Dirty War. These days the mothers of the disappeared hold an annual day of remembrance in the plaza, and still voice their demands for the truth.

Oscar and Anna had both been here for the Millennium celebrations. Judging by the state of the place everyone had had a good time. Empty bottles, paper and streamers lay strewn around the streets and parks. It was now the third day of the Millennium and it seemed that no one was going to clear it up.

'Perhaps they are hoping it will clean itself,' suggested Oscar.

Later that afternoon I collapsed on my bed. I awoke after nine that night, ventured downstairs and joined a group of people in the common room. Amongst them was a Swiss girl who was riding her bike around Argentina. Anita had no plan and would head in a direction and see where it took her. Accommodation wasn't a problem. She would just camp by the side of the road. I always admire girls like this. Yes you might say it's dangerous for a girl to travel that way, especially alone. But why should she let fear rule her life and stop her from doing the things she wants to do?

The truth is that it's a dangerous world we live in, and

that we are possibly just as likely to run into trouble at home. In fact more so because at home we have the mistaken belief that we are safe. We create this safe, secure little world for ourselves and think that as long as we don't step out of it then nothing bad will happen. Therefore when trouble comes, it's unexpected. Danger is everywhere. When you travel like this then you are aware of possible dangers and in most cases can take steps to avoid them. In other words you become streetwise.

Rick was from London and it appeared that he had been on the same flight as me, sat behind me in fact. He had managed to find the number 86 bus. It took him two hours to get here. When hearing of Anita's plan he was impressed and wanted to join her. Rick was over here for a couple of weeks. He had flown over on a cheap ticket by acting as a courier. Although when he presented himself at the desk in order to collect the parcel, he was told there weren't any to go. So he got on the plane empty-handed. The next morning he went out and bought himself a bike and rode off northward with Anita. There's nothing like spontaneity.

That same morning I roused myself from slumberland just as Oscar finished packing.

'Where are you going?' I asked.

'I don't know. I will just go to the bus station and take the next bus to wherever it goes.'

Now that's the way to travel, I thought. No rushing to catch your bus, no pondering over guidebooks and maps trying to decide where to go, just go to the station and get on the next bus out.

I had woken up too late for the hostel breakfast. So I trotted down the street to the supermarket. Inside I came across the most amusing sight. The aisles were filled with little old ladies pushing tiny shopping trolleys. They were half their normal size - the shopping trolleys that is. Personally I grabbed a basket. I would rather have been seen struggling along with all my shopping cradled in my tee shirt, and kicking a loaf of bread along the aisles. I bought a few items, had breakfast and then headed out to see the city.

It seems love is alive and well and living in Buenos Aires. The parks were full of lovers cooing and openly displaying affection. It was sickening, and I was jealous. If you have ever seen the women of Buenos Aires, then I'm sure you would agree with me wholeheartedly. You could spend hours just watching the girls. In fact some people, I was to discover, would look forward to their visits to Buenos Aires solely for this reason. Some say that this city has the best looking women of any city in the world. Until now Bilbao, Spain had held that title in my mind. But walking through the pedestrianised shopping centre, this title was in serious jeopardy. Now I know how a fox in a chicken cage must feel. They were everywhere, and my head nearly spun off my shoulders as the rest of me tried in vain to avoid dangerous obstacles in my path, like lampposts and other shoppers. These girls had the most seductive brown eyes and wonderfully feminine walk. The European features blended with the Indian dark skin made an attractive combination for many. It seemed that there were many more women as gorgeous as the one who had occupied my thoughts since boarding that plane.

Aside from all the beautiful women, there were other things to hold my interest - possibly less hazardous to my health. Street entertainers were prolific. I stood and watched Los Guererros, a four-piece band consisting of a man playing guitar and his wife and two children singing their hearts out. They sung with a passion that came straight from that heart, and put their all into it. Even the two girls, aged around ten, were holding nothing back.

'They are good, no?' said a little old man stood next to me.

I thoroughly agreed with him. The girls took it in turn to walk around with the money pot, thanking everyone with a heart-warming smile. During a break the old man helped me to get talking to them. When I explained that I was heading southward into Patagonia, the father informed me: 'Patagonia is the most beautiful place in all of Argentina. After that you don't need to see anything else.' In time I was to agree with him, although my body wouldn't be so quick to.

Buenos Aires has a distinctly European flair. It is often described as the most European in Latin America. I walked down the pedestrianised section of Lavalle street. This is the city's main shopping centre. It's extremely modern and con- tains trendy cafés and all the latest designer shops, of which all bore the sign *Liquidación*. It seemed that even Buenos Aires has January sales. As I wandered down the street, I stumbled across a most amusing sight. In the middle of the tiled street, amongst all the shoppers, sat a little girl of about four years old. She was sat on a tiny plastic seat, exactly her size. A paper Coca Cola cup was placed on the floor in front of her. On her lap was a child's accordion, which she played with quite a passion. As I pulled out my camera she turned and gave me a very stern look.

'You have to pay me for a picture!' she ordered.

'Don't worry,' I said, 'I'll pay you when I've taken the picture.'

She then continued to play, her face a delightful picture of determination that I was going to pay for this privilege. I didn't dare disobey her.

Buenos Aires has the oldest subway system in the world. It opened in 1913 and only has five lines. Despite that it is pretty efficient. You can get to a lot of places using it - you might have to walk a bit, but you can invariably get to a station near to your destination. Each trip cost 60 centavos. Fortunately where I wanted to go there was a station.

Near to the main train and bus station are a series of four plazas. Plaza Fuerza Aérea Argentina contains El Torre de los Ingleses (the English tower). So-called because it's reputed to be a clone of Big Ben. Well it seemed to me that the architect was quite obviously misled as to what Big Ben looks like. Either that or someone had a good laugh at his expense when he came to London to photograph it.

'Yea guvnor, that's Big Ben over there! For a few quid I'll tell ya all about it.'

It was by no means ugly. On the contrary it was quite attractive: intricately carved on the top and bottom and situated in the park, soaring high above everything else. It just looked nothing like Big Ben.

A short walk from there is the memorial for all the men who died in the Falklands War. I didn't know much about the Falklands; just that it's a chain of small islands 300 miles off the coast of Argentina. Argentina has consistently claimed the ownership of the Falklands. Before coming away I had read a book about three guys who cycled from Tierra del Fuego to Lake Titicaca. They had been involved in many conversations about these islands with Argentinean people. It seemed that the Argentines felt these islands were close to their hearts and that they wanted them to be a part of Argentina. I wondered how many of these people had ever even been to the Falklands? They claim love for a land they've probably never seen. It's the same for me. When I think of the United Kingdom the Falklands doesn't even come to mind. The main reason most people know the name is because of the war there in the eighties.

I was no different. But here I was standing in front of the result of this war: a large concrete monument containing the names of the soldiers killed in action. As the two armed guards stood either side, I hoped nothing I was wearing would give away my nationality.

This is the reality of it all. Forget all this bickering about who should own these islands, but remember the poor innocent men who were sent out to fight for islands they themselves had probably never been to before.

The decision should really be left to the people who actually live there. They are the ones to best decide which country they want to belong to. Mind you, as we put the British there they would more than likely vote for the UK. But much the same could be said for Argentina. The Spanish took this land from the Indians. I don't see anyone fighting for its return to them; the sad fact being that there are very few indigenous peoples left. They have been virtually wiped out. Their culture all but destroyed. The principle indigenous peoples remaining are the Quechua of the Northwest and the Mapuche in Patagonia. I'm sure that if these Indians laid claim to Argentina, then these claims would be rejected.

The sad truth is that every country in the world is guilty of these atrocities in some form or another. They have all been involved in the squabble over land for centuries. And the root of all this is money. I expect the real reason behind this squabbling is the offshore petroleum. Both countries want the wealth.

The unfortunate result of this all was standing in front of me right now. And all around Argentina were the children who had to grow up without their fathers because of this. Thousands of miles away from me were also families who had to suffer losing their loved ones. And let's not forget the ones who did make it home, but scarred for life. So instead of all this arguing, why not let the Islanders decide.

But of course I could never express this opinion to any Argentines who challenged me on the subject, I didn't know enough Spanish.

Feeling the need to chill out I took the Subte to Plaza Italia. As I emerged from underground I was greeted by a marvellous sight. The plaza was surrounded by the botanical gardens and the city zoo. Traffic and shops were in abundance. Dog walkers strolled along the paved streets in a contest to see who could walk the most dogs at one time. The area was clean and quite attractive. The only eyesores were the burnt out wrecks of cars that lined the side of the road. It was such a strange sight.

As I stared at these I was vaguely aware of someone calling my name. I looked up to see Tom and Donna from the hostel approaching. I had met them when I ventured bleary-eyed downstairs the first night. Tom and Donna had been travelling for near on three years now. They were both from the UK. They had worked as English teachers in Japan. This allowed them to save up a good wedge of money. They saved one wage packet and lived on the other. And they lived quite well too.

Their plan was to stop here in Buenos Aires for a while and look for work. After dropping off their CVs they now had some spare time on their hands and wanted to visit the zoo. I was invited along. I don't like zoos. I hate to see animals caged like that. Taking animals out of their natural habitat and putting them in a tiny confined area for people to gawk at, is to me quite disconcerting. How would you like it if someone took you away from your home and family and put you in a cage to be photographed and gawked at by tourists? It is one of the most degrading pastimes imaginable, and I wanted no part of it. And anyway there was an eight-peso entrance fee. So instead we passed the rest of the day relaxing in the gardens.

That night I got my first glimpse of Argentina's most famous export, the tango. The hostel was holding lessons in the large courtyard out back. Beautiful young Argentinean girls were being whisked around by their teachers. I must confess that this is an extremely graceful dance. Much self-control is needed. The moves are extremely intricate and well-timed. The women held a certain graceful poise and the most serious look on their faces, throwing themselves into poses that did wonders to complement their slender figures. As I looked on in admiration, I wondered what they thought of their artistic appreciation society being a group of leering backpackers almost falling off their chairs to get a closer look.

My intention had been to spend a few days in Buenos Aires and then start heading south. However Tom came up with a good excuse to stay.

'You can't go, tomorrow is Friday and you have to come for a beer with us.'

So that was settled.

It wasn't such a bad thing having to stay. I was living quite well. I was getting dormitory accommodation in a stately mansion. I had made a good bunch of friends. And I was getting fed each day for two pesos. Around the corner from the hostel was Ugi's. For two pesos you got a large cheese and tomato pizza. The takeaway box came with the motto:

No to drugs, yes to pizza.

I imagined the conversation:

'Hey dude, you wanna go get stoned tonight?'

'Nah man, I'd rather have a pizza!'

The irony of it is that after smoking dope then you could quite easily devour a whole pizza each. So perhaps it's a very clever marketing ploy?

On Friday I set out for the city again. The contrasts of city life reared their head. The day before I'd had a fantastic time, wandering through the centre. Today I hated it. All the people getting in my way was trying my patience. So I headed for the tranquillity of the park.

Parque 3 de Febrero is a beautiful area surrounding a large lake. It's a great place to chill out and soak up the sun. I wandered idly through its lovely gardens and along the lake, as others paddled leisurely along in hired boats, and spent the rest of the day doing nothing, in preparation for the upcoming evening's drinking session.

Beer around here was served in litre bottles. You could buy them at the nearby shop for around a couple of pesos, one of them being the returnable deposit on the empty bottle. One of the hostel guests, John from Liverpool, must have had a fortune's worth by the side of his dorm bed. John was a highly amusing character and a dead ringer for one of

Harry Enfield's Scousers. He sported thick, black curly hair, a moustache and a beer belly. And he tucked his tee shirt into his football shorts.

John joined us all for a drink at a bar down the road from the hostel. The litre bottles were slightly more expensive in the bars, but were still cheaper than in the UK. Many were downed by the large group around our table. I got talking to Peter from Australia.

'Did you see the tango last night?' he asked, a gleam appearing in his eyes.

'Sure did!' I replied.

He then proceeded to tell me all about Brazil.

'Brazil is the most amazing country!' he said, 'and the women are so friendly. They will come and talk to you in the street.'

'That's all well and good if you can speak Portuguese,' I replied.

However that didn't appear to have stopped him having his wicked way. He had spent many nights with a girl who spoke absolutely no English, and he spoke no Portuguese. Body language was apparently all that was needed.

The night progressed and much alcohol was consumed. Suddenly remembering something, I turned to another Peter in our group.

'What time is it?' I asked.

'2 o'clock,' he replied.

'I'm *thirty!*' I declared out loud, to many cheers and a request for another round of drinks.

However the bar was closing, so a Peruvian guy took us to another place in a nearby plaza.

It was hard to believe that I had left the middle of winter a few days before and was now in mid-summer. I was now sitting outside at two in the morning sipping cold beer and congratulating myself on reaching the age of thirty; even if I was celebrating it on the morning of my birthday instead of the night. But what the hell it's not everyday that you get to celebrate your thirtieth in Buenos Aires with a group of people from all over the world. And it's not everyday you reach thirty. Some say it's all downhill from now on. But I just say that if you think that then you are not living the kind of life you want to live. For me things were getting better and better with each passing year. I was pursuing my dreams. And they were getting closer everyday. Also with age comes wisdom brought about by the accumulation of knowledge over the years - even if the onset of senility means that you sometimes forget you have that knowledge. Even so I couldn't have been happier to reach thirty, and was looking forward to the next ten. Plus I now get cheaper motor insurance!

The one thing that was going downhill with age was my tolerance to alcohol. My body doesn't seem to be able to handle the hangovers as well as they used to. There was a time when I would go out every night from Thursday through to Monday and get up for work no problem. But not anymore.

I eventually got to bed at five that morning. I crawled out of bed at three in the afternoon feeling like someone had used my head and body as a trampoline throughout the night. I staggered downstairs and joined John in the courtyard. He was trying to figure out the cheapest way to get to Santiago, or 'Santiaygo' as he pronounced it. He also pronounced Buenos Aires, 'Bonus Airees'.

John spoke absolutely no Spanish whatsoever. As we sat and discussed the possible ways he had of getting to Santiyago, a guy came and sat down next to us. He asked John, in Spanish, if he would mind answering a few questions for a census he was compiling. John looked him straight in the eyes, pointed at himself and stated, quite simply: '*English!*' The guy then spoke in English, but with a very strong accent. John turned to me with a look that can only be described as a cross between sheer confusion and sheer terror. I repeated his words. He agreed to answer the questions. Each question was provided in English with me having to translate into English that John could understand. Each time he asked a question John would shoot me one of those looks, as a cue for me to translate.

After that I went to pay. The day before I had told them I would be leaving on Saturday.

'When are you leaving?' asked the receptionist, as I paid him for another night.

'Tomorrow,' I said.

As I did this, Peter, the Australian, came in looking very pissed off. He had just been a victim of the infamous Buenos Aires pickpocket trick. An elderly lady had squirted some liquid over his tee shirt, apologised profusely and tried to clean it off for him. Then in the ensuing confusion had somehow lifted his wallet. He had known instantly it was a scam and immediately put his hand on his wallet to make sure it was still there, then fought to get the woman off him. Once away and around the corner he noticed that she had somehow got it.

'I'll never trust an old lady again!' he ranted, 'I'm genna go home and punch me nan for making me believe all old ladies were sweet and kind!'

He was a bit angry.

I passed the rest of the day with my arse plonked on a seat on the balcony attached to my dorm, and my feet up on the railings. I was becoming quite attached to this balcony.

After another night celebrating my birthday I emerged to pay for one more night.

'I'm leaving tomorrow,' I told the receptionist.

'Hmm!' was his reply.

My reason for not leaving this day was the tango show in the plaza. Once again Tom had talked me into staying and going with them to watch this. So yet again I was to spend another night in the city I was finding so difficult to get out of.

_____2_____

No Direct Buses

I awoke to the sound of heavy rain and cracks of thunder. I love storms, especially tropical ones, and normally would have jumped out of bed to watch. However this night I was so tired that I simply thought, great a storm! And fell instantly back to sleep.

When I awoke again in the morning it was still raining. I ventured downstairs and, over breakfast, wrestled with my need to leave that day. I had been in Buenos Aires for a week now and really had to get going. Normally I don't have a time restriction, but I had to get down south while it was still summer.

The island of Tierra del Fuego is situated at the far southern tip of the continent, 58 degrees south of the equator; which is roughly the same as the UK is north. However, Tierra del Fuego doesn't have the Gulf Stream to warm its climate. Also there is nothing between the island and Antarctica, and the Antarctic current flows up to it and continues northward along the West Coast of the continent. All the ingredients for a very cold place.

This was the reason why I had to come at this time of year, and why I had to hurry. Now it was the southern summer, but the summer in Tierra del Fuego isn't very long, and possibly not that warm. I had to get down there before the really bad weather returned. I wasn't equipped for that.

As we ate breakfast Tom once again tried his best to convince me to stay.

'Leave it until tomorrow when the weather has improved.'

I had to agree that it wasn't a good day to make a move. Also I had a bit of a stomach-ache and could quite easily have just crawled back to bed. However after much deliberation I decided that it was now or never. When the sun comes back out I'll just want to sit on my balcony again. So I rushed off upstairs, packed and said a sad farewell to Tom, Donna and Anna.

I put on my raincoat, waved goodbye to the surprised receptionist and then dashed through the driving rain to the Subte. Once inside I burst out into an instant sweat. Away from the rain and wind the humidity was intense. I handed over the 60 centavos and the woman behind the counter threw my token into the tray with total indifference. Once through the turnstile I headed for a stream of cold air being produced by a large overhead fan.

As I stood there, temporarily relieved of my discomfort, I noticed the train next to me was empty. Now there is nothing worse than having to remove your backpack in a train full of people, so I kept a sharp eye on this train in order to be the first on when the doors opened. After about five minutes the train left empty. I turned to see everyone boarding the adjacent train. I barged my way in, to the stares of the other people, and removed my pack. I then spent the journey trying to stop it falling onto the legs of the woman sitting nearby.

I got off at Plaza San Martin. It was still raining. After changing a traveller's cheque I then made my way to the bus station. Walking through crowds of people with a large backpack is a bit like towing a caravan in a city during rush hour. You cannot just walk; you have to manoeuvre your way through carefully, occasionally having to back yourself out of a situation.

At the entrance to the bus station I boarded a conveyor belt and was whisked along the very long corridor. As I rounded the corner I was astounded by the size of this terminal. A row of kiosks stretched nearly 200 metres long. There were so many different companies. It was more like entering an airport terminal. I had absolutely no idea where to start.

I wanted to go to a place called *Sierra de la Ventana*. The guidebook had painted a pretty picture of it and also there was a free camping area next to the river. I liked the idea of camping for free. Also the surrounding mountain range provided good hiking.

The town was around 500 kilometres south of Buenos Aires. It was now midday and the only buses going that way went overnight. I didn't fancy the idea of waiting around this bus station all day. And I certainly had no intention of lugging my backpack all around the city. While I decided what to do, I removed my raincoat to find that the condensation inside had completely soaked my tee shirt. I would have been better off without it. In the end I decided to take the 1.30 pm bus to Pinamar.

After six hours of unrelentingly flat landscape known as the Pampas I arrived in Pinamar only to discover that the hostel was in Ostende, a neighbouring village. I noticed a kiosk bearing the sign *Tourist Information*. A girl wearing a light blue summer dress was beckoning me over with a smile. She arranged a taxi at the cost of three pesos and soon I was checked in at the hostel. I had the dorm to myself. The cost was the same as the one in Buenos Aires.

It was already quite late and I was in desperate need of fresh clothes. I was down to my last pair of socks. There is always someone in your family who buys you something hideous for Christmas; mine was a pair of socks from my aunt. Actually they weren't that bad: black but with a bright red and blue stripe at the top. I had brought them with me because they were the only pair of thick socks I owned, and would be good for hiking. They were the only clean pair left and I figured no one would see them under my jeans, so I put them on. After all it was only for one night. I then threw everything together in a bag and dumped it with the lady at the nearby laundrette, then proceeded to spend the evening relaxing.

Pinamar was nothing more than a coastal resort. However it was very peaceful and extremely attractive. Further south was the town of Mar del Plata, a not so peaceful coastal resort frequented by holidaymakers escaping Buenos Aires. I had absolutely no interest in it. However Pinamar had no direct bus service to Sierra de la Ventana, so I had to go there in order to get one. Therefore the next morning I headed off to the bus station. I didn't want to pay another three pesos for a taxi and instead decided to take the local bus, slightly cheaper at 90 centavos.

When it pulled up only one of the double doors opened. This usually presented a problem for me because my tent would get stuck. However in a flash of inspiration I had removed the poles and put them inside the pack, then rolled up the tent to a much smaller size and strapped it to the bottom of my pack, thus avoiding this kind of problem in future. So when the door opened I confidently strolled on, and was immediately brought to an abrupt stop, much to the amusement of two old men sat up front. An immediate inspection revealed the problem. I had neglected to take into consideration that I now had a sleeping mat strapped to the top.

The hostel owner back in Pinamar had told me that I could get a direct bus from Mar del Plata. This was not to be the case, though. Upon arrival in Mar del Plata's bus station I set off to buy a ticket. The old man behind the desk said I would have to go to Bahía Blanca and change there. Bahía Blanca was 125 kilometres south of where I wanted to go. It would be incredibly stupid to go there, travel north again, only to have to come back the same way when I left Sierra de la Ventana.

I consulted the map.

'What about if I go to Tres Arroyos, can I change there?' I asked him.

'I expect so,' was his reply.

The next bus was at six the following morning, so I was forced to spend the rest of the day in this tacky tourist resort.

It was just after three in the afternoon so I made my way to the Hotel Pergamino, which was affiliated with the International Hostelling Association. Dormitory-style accommodation was provided in some of the rooms. It was a very friendly place.

'Your roommate is German,' the receptionist kindly

informed me.

I wasn't sure if that was meant as a warning. Perhaps she thought we still held grudges against each other.

Once checked in I was shown to my room and asked if I wanted a towel or some soap. It's not very often you get this kind of treatment in a hostel. The room had two bunks squeezed into a tiny space. On the upside though, it did have an en-suite bathroom. I took the top bunk by the window. Normally I hate top bunks, but these were low and I wanted to look out the window. My German roommate was out. I changed out of my jeans, threw on a pair of shorts and headed for the beach.

I couldn't see the sand for sizzling bodies. I wandered along the beachfront market in the hope of finding something interesting. But found only tourist crap. Mar del Plata was reminiscent of any holiday resort: arcades, ice cream parlours and souvenir shops. I didn't like it one bit. I wandered for hours in the hope of finding something remotely interesting to do.

As I crossed the road I noticed the girl in front turn and look at my feet, then say to her friend:

'Maybe they were a present!'

I looked down and discovered, to my horror, that I was still wearing the socks my aunt had bought me for Christmas. This caused a major fashion clash with my army green shorts. In my haste to go out I had forgotten I was wearing them.

I stood there for a moment, pondering my next move. It seemed to me that I had two choices: either trek all the way back to the hostel and change them. Or give everyone else in this town a good laugh. There was no contest really. Besides I would never see these people ever again. I certainly had no intention of ever returning, so why bother. So with that I continued to stroll along the streets of Mar del Plata taking a fashion risk.

To add even more misery to my day it rained. I waited it out at the entrance to a large building. When the rain finally stopped I made my way back to the hotel and passed the rest of the evening on my bunk. I was munching biscuits and reading an incredibly boring book I had acquired back in Buenos Aires, when the door opened and in walked a tall blond-haired guy. We greeted each other in Spanish and he introduced himself:

'Soy Joe.'

I returned the courtesy.

Upon establishing that I was English he began speaking in English.

'You're from Germany, are you?' I asked.

'No I'm from the States,' he replied.

'Oh Sorry, the woman at reception said you were German.'

'Huh, this is fucking South America, man!' he raved, 'if you've got blond hair then they think you're German. They never think you can be from the United States.'

It seemed I had a live one here.

He was certainly very outspoken and highly opinionated, a bit of lad also; swigging wine from the bottle. Or at least he obviously thought he was. Once the initial shock wore off he didn't seem quite so bad and we actually had a good conversation. However I was glad he wasn't planning to leave the same time as me. Somehow I don't think we would have made good travel partners.

The next morning I rolled up at the bus station bleary-eyed and got on the bus. Four hours later I arrived in Tres

Arroyos. I queued patiently at the ticket office and asked if there were any services to Sierra de la Ventana.

'No!' replied a man whose face just ached to be punched. Why the hell do people employ these miserable gits and put them in positions where they can do nothing other than totally piss people off?

'Where can I get one?' I inquired.

'Bahía Blanca!' came an even frostier response.

I was getting pissed off now. I had come to this little town in the knowledge that I could get to Sierra de la Ventana from here. Now it appeared that wasn't so, and this dickhead in front of me wasn't helping much.

However, my temper was calmed somewhat by the lovely Susanna, who was stood behind the adjacent counter. She beckoned me over with a smile and an offer of help. I explained my predicament and she pulled out a map and we looked at possible ways of getting there.

Shortly after Marcelo, her boss, joined us. Between the three of us we deduced that my best option was to get the next bus to Coronel Pringles. From there Sierra de la Ventana was just 50 kilometres away. Marcelo felt sure there would be a bus from there. I agreed. I thanked them both for their help and returned to the other counter and bought a ticket to Coronel Pringles.

I had over five hours to wait. I drank a cup of coffee in the station café and did some writing. Then I sat myself down on a bench and prepared for a long and boring wait. The station was quiet. Git-face was doing some paperwork. Marcelo and Susanna had disappeared into their office. And a toothless old gypsy woman was wandering around looking lost. She approached me and started waffling something about wanting money and that she would find me a beautiful woman. I told her I could find my own beautiful women for free. And almost to prove that fact to her, Susanna came wandering over and sat next to me.

Susanna's face turned to complete shock when I told her I was thirty. She couldn't believe it.

'You look about twenty,' she said.

Nice girl.

She then proceeded to ask me where I was going and if I would be returning to Tres Arroyos anytime soon. The sparkle in her lovely blue eyes made me suspect that I might have good reason to. However, my trip was to take me a long way from here. She then invited me over to their office and introduced me to maté, the herbal tea that is drunk by nearly all Argentineans. It consists of the maté herb poured into a small pot. Water is then added periodically. The tea is sieved through a metal pipe called a bombilla. The idea of this is that the pot is passed around to each person in turn, thus creating a social atmosphere.

I took a sip and then shuddered from head to toe.

'It's strong, no?' grinned Susanna.

It certainly was. However I soon acquired a taste for it. Marcelo rejoined us and the three of us drank maté and discussed the world. The two of them helped make my time in Tres Arroyos much more interesting.

When the maté was finished they decided to go for lunch. I was feeling quite hungry myself. Marcelo suggested I check my bag at the front desk. Or at least that's what I thought he meant at the time. After a brief conversation with git-face, Marcelo told me to give him my pack. I did that and he shoved a ticket in my hand. I fixed him with an icy stare and said:

'Don't lose it! That's my home!'

It was true; a traveller's backpack is his castle. I dreaded to think what I'd do if I ever lost it.

I followed Marcelo and Susanna outside to a beat-up old silver Cortina. It wasn't a Cortina really; it was the Latin American equivalent. It was pretty much the same thing though. As we chugged and banged down the street Marcelo proudly informed me that the car ran on gas. I wouldn't have been surprised if it ran on coal, looking at it. They dropped me off outside a garage where I could get a cheap meal. All the garages in Argentina, I was to find, contained a relatively cheap café. I sat down to eat just as the rain started. After eating and relieving myself of the previous meal, I ventured into town, just as the sun was beginning to show itself again.

I passed some time in the plaza before heading back. I sat on a bench under the shade of some tall trees. At the centre of the plaza I noticed a tiny section of grass had been neatly trimmed. A beautifully arranged group of flowers had been planted in the middle. Around it sat a couple of people on benches. The sign on a pole stuck in the grass read:

Patio del 2000

Tres Arroyos's contribution to the Millennium, it seemed. And I'm sure they were proud of it too.

Back at the bus station I gave Susanna my e-mail address and in return she offered me a kiss on the cheek. If only I wasn't passing through, I thought to myself. I got on the bus, hoping my bag was going to follow. When I had travelled in Australia I had to check my bag all the time when travelling by bus. I never lost it then, so perhaps I was being a bit too paranoid. But I didn't trust that miserable sod behind the counter to give enough of a shit to make sure it went on. In the end I decided that I was just being stupid and that I should relax. So I sat back and enjoyed the beautiful scenery for the next couple of hours.

At Coronel Pringles I got off and patiently waited for the baggage attendant.

The first luggage door was opened.

No pack.

The second door was opened.

No pack.

'Do you have any bags?' she asked me.

'Yes, I have a backpack,' I replied, my fear growing.

I followed her around to the other side where she flung open all the doors.

No pack!

A lump went to my throat, and I started to shake with fury. My worst fear had come true. I wanted to throttle that ignorant git back at Tres Arroyos.

The baggage attendant, obviously sensing my inner pain, informed the driver that my bag was missing. I fumbled to explain what I'd done with it in Spanish, emphasising the fact that git-face was supposed to have put it on the bus. He instantly got on the phone to Tres Arroyos and waffled to someone there.

'Is it a backpack?' he asked me.

'Yes.'

He waffled some more and then turned to me again.

'They were only looking after the backpack for you. You were supposed to collect it and put in on yourself.'

'Oh!'

It was the only articulate sound that would come from my mouth. It seemed that I'd been a bit of an idiot. How was I supposed to know? They didn't tell me.

Panic was starting to set in now. I felt like I had lost a

limb.

'Is there a bus back?' I asked, in a slightly irrational manner.

'You want to go back?' asked the driver, obviously thrown by this strange request.

'I need my backpack!' I continued.

My eyes were wide and displayed the look of a man about to have a breakdown. He calmed me down and explained that the company will put it on the next bus. This was by far the more sensible solution.

'Be here at four o'clock in the morning to collect it,' he stipulated.

I shook his hand and thanked him profusely for his help, nearly taking his hand off in the process. Then I wandered off into the station. It looked like I would be spending the night here in Coronel Pringles. There was nothing in the guidebook about this town, so I asked a taxi driver at the entrance for directions to the centre. He pointed left to a turn off and told me to walk down it several blocks.

As I ambled on into town in just my jeans, tee shirt and carrying my daypack, I hoped to god that my bag would arrive on that bus in the morning. I wouldn't get very far with a camera, personal stereo, guidebook, travel clock, box of artificial sweeteners and an inhaler (the contents of my daypack).

Coronel Pringles was quite a charming little place. It was obvious they didn't see many foreigners here, judging by the curious looks from passers-by. I passed the interestingly named *Farmacia Bastard* and found a hotel around the corner. The hotel San Carlos looked extremely inviting and, I rather suspected, quite expensive. However there didn't seem to be much choice. The only other hotel I had seen was definitely out of my price range.

I entered the reception area and was greeted by a very friendly middle-aged lady. María's grandmother had come over from England and settled here many years ago. María and her mother had both been born here in Argentina. She gave me a private room with shared bathroom for 15 pesos, exactly what I had paid for the hostel accommodation back in Mar del Plata. I explained my predicament to her and she said she would make sure someone was here to let me out and back in during the night. She also offered to arrange a wake up call for me.

Once settled in I took a brief walk around town, the hunger pains directing me in search of a place to eat. Eventually I came across a pub on the corner that advertised food. I took a seat at the bar and ordered a toasted sandwich, then washed it down with a well-needed cold lager. The guys behind the bar found my story highly amusing. I couldn't blame them; it was quite funny when you thought about it. In fact I was beginning to laugh about it myself. Once my pack arrived, no doubt I would laugh a lot more.

The pub was having live traditional music that night. I would have liked to see it, but as I explained to the barman, if I got drunk then I might not get up for the bus.

'Go straight there,' he suggested.

'But if I get drunk then I'll more than likely lose track of time,' I replied.

'Drink sodas.'

Hmm!

It was a tempting offer. However it had been an extremely long day, starting at five, and I needed sleep.

'Can I come once I have my backpack?' I enquired.

'Yes, but you will have to knock on the door because the

police are out in the streets at night.'
I decided I would be better off doing that.

At half three the next morning I presented myself at the station, just in case the bus arrived early. I was taking no chances. To my immense relief my pack was there when the driver opened the luggage compartment. As I trotted off back to the hotel, I had never felt so grateful for that weight on my back. I hadn't slept very well due to a fear of not hearing the alarm, so therefore I felt too tired to go back to that pub. And I certainly didn't have the energy to try talking in Spanish.

Back in the room I opened up the pack and pulled out my towel. A sort of radioactive green mould glowed where it had once been wet. This is one of the biggest downsides to travelling this way. You invariably have to travel with a wet towel in your pack, especially when you take an early bus. Normally you can remove the towel soon after and dry it out. However this one had been in there for near on 24 hours. I stood it up against the wall and fell back into bed, planning to wash it in the sink when I awoke.

Later that day I checked out and wandered off to get some money. None of the banks would change my traveller's cheques, so I was forced to use my visa card. I had most of my money in traveller's cheques and only a small sum on the card, figuring that it would be a lot more difficult to use the card in the more remote parts, like Patagonia (I wasn't even in Patagonia yet and already I was having trouble). However it was the opposite. Each bank had a machine that accepted visa, but wouldn't change the cheques. It had been a similar story back in Buenos Aires. The only place I could change them there was in the American Express office. However there was no American Express office here in Coronel

Pringles, so I had to use my visa card.

With my wallet replenished I headed off to the bus station.

'Are there any direct buses to Sierra de la Ventana?'

'No! You have to go to Bahía Blanca.'

This was getting ridiculous. I was 50 kilometres away from my destination and still being told I couldn't get there. I consulted a recently purchased map and saw that the quickest route was by dirt road through a couple of small villages. A taxi driver offered to take me there for 20 pesos. A bit too extravagant for my meagre budget. He said there were no local buses. However I suspected he might be just telling me that in order to get my business. So instead I decided to try and hitch.

The day was extremely hot and it was a long walk to the main road. Once there I removed my pack to allow the sweat patches to dry and assumed the position. There wasn't a lot of traffic on the road. I asked a passing youngster on a bike which way it was to Sierra de la Ventana; there had been no sign at the junction to indicate that I was hitching in the right direction. He paused for a minute to think and said that I was going the right way, but that I should walk up to the petrol station ahead, as that indicated the start of the road to Sierra de la Ventana. I thanked him and began walking.

Shortly after he came zooming back on his bike, apologised and explained that he had made a mistake. The other way was better because it was a main road and there would be more traffic. Nice of him to have done that, I thought. Most youngsters not would have bothered. However after much difficult discussion I decided that as the way I was heading would take me to the start of the dirt road, that would be a better place to go. The other way was longer.

The sweat was pouring off of me as I trudged my way along the road with two packs: one on the front and one on the back. I should have emptied the contents of my daypack into the big one, but couldn't be bothered to sort it all out. The road ahead rippled with the heat, the occasional vehicle or truck emerging from the haze. The heat of the midday sun was slowly boiling the water in my daypack. It did nothing to quench my thirst.

In the distant haze I saw an Esso sign appear, and idly wondered if that was my destination. Unfortunately it wasn't. There was no junction. However I desperately needed a cold drink, so I wandered up to the door and poked my head in. Three guys in greasy overalls looked up from what they were doing.

'Oh sorry!' I said, 'I was looking for somewhere to buy a drink.'

It seemed I had entered a workshop. They told me that the petrol station was further down the road.

'Where are you going?' asked one of them.

I explained what I was trying to do, and they proceeded to give me directions, and even drew a map.

'It's a bit late to try and hitch,' said one guy, 'the only traffic that goes that way is work traffic, and they will all be at lunch now.'

'Are there any local buses?' I asked.

'No, there are none,' he replied, confirming this with his colleagues.

I thanked them for their help and headed back out into the heat of the sun.

Out on the road I sat down, sipped the warm water from my bottle and pondered my situation. The junction was another two kilometres away. I was so hot you could have cooked a fry-up on my stomach. It wasn't looking all that promising. My destination was just a short leap away and I couldn't get to it.

Sod it! I thought. And decided to go take that taxi.

Trudging back through the dusty streets, the children eyed me with curiosity. I suppose seeing a sweaty man walking through their street with a dead weight on his back and a defeated look in his eyes, wasn't an everyday occurrence.

I arrived to find the bus station deserted. The caretaker, a toothless old man, was the only person there.

'Where is everybody?' I asked him.

'Lunchtime.'

Of course it was! Argentina, like Spain, still respected the tradition of the siesta. Therefore everything ground to a halt for a few hours in the afternoon.

I dumped my pack down and slumped into a chair. I was at the end of my tether. I was so close and yet so far. A sign on the office window advertised the next bus to Bahía Blanca at 3.30 pm. Two hours time. Oh what the hell! I thought. I'll just get on that bus to Bahía Blanca and forget all about Sierra de la Ventana. From there I'll just continue southward. All this hassle just because I couldn't be bothered to wait around that bus station all day in Buenos Aires. If I'd have just exercised patience then I would have been there yesterday. But would it have been so much fun? In the last two days I had been to places that I wouldn't have otherwise seen, and met some extremely nice people in the process. María had said that they never see people like me in this town. The only people that stopped off here were locals driving to Sierra de la Ventana. I had also experienced nothing but extreme kindness from the people of this little town. That in itself more than made up for the fact that I wasn't going to get to where I wanted. So I decided to get on that bus.

I left my backpack in the care of the old man; something I would not normally have done. But I felt that I could totally trust him along with all the other people of this wonderful town. In fact I was sorely tempted to stay another night. But I had to start heading south. I had failed in my attempt to get to Sierra de la Ventana, but in the process had quite an adventure. As for the mountains, I figured there would be plenty more down south.

Although if I'd known then just how I was going to spend my nights I might not have been so hasty.

___3___

From One Extreme to the Other

Bahía Blanca is South America's largest naval base. The port is used to export grain from Buenos Aires province, along with produce from the nearby Río Negro valley. But most importantly it is the gateway to Patagonia. This was my main reason for coming here.

Patagonia is an enormous region stretching from the southern edge of Buenos Aires province and covering the rest of the continent right down to Tierra del Fuego. It has a total area of 260,000 square miles. I was going to head down the eastern edge of this region. Bahía Blanca itself really didn't have all that much appeal to me. So upon the discovery that buses ran south overnight, I decided to take one. I selected a town called Trelew, for no other reason than it represented the exact halfway point from here to Tierra del Fuego.

After obtaining prices from the many different companies serving the area I chose Don Otto, as it was the cheapest at 26.50 pesos.

'¿A qué hora llega (what time does it arrive)?' I asked

the girl behind the counter.

She fixed me with a very confused stare, so I repeated the question. The confused look remained. Then, almost as though someone in the back had thoughtfully just switched on her brain, a look of comprehension slowly started to appear on her face.

'¡Ah! ¿A qué hora shega?' she repeated, only with the Argentinean accent.

Yes, that is what I have been saying.

'Sorry,' I said, 'it's my accent.'

'Oh that's okay!' she replied, with a smile.

I don't know why I was apologising. It wasn't my fault the Argentines have this strange dialect. The way I spoke that sentence was correct, and therefore she should be the one apologising to me for her total ignorance of her own language. Mind you, I'm sure any non-English speakers who go to Liverpool have exactly the same problem.

When departure time arrived I frantically looked around me for a bus with *Don Otto* on the side. I couldn't see one anywhere. I was beginning to worry. At half eight I watched a bus pull up with Chubut - the region I was in now - and Coche Cama written on the side. I wandered up and noticed the display read *Trelew*. Pulling out my ticket I questioned the driver as to whether this was my bus. It was. The seats were luxurious: large with plenty of legroom. So I settled in for a comfortable night.

We arrived at seven in the morning. I retrieved my backpack and headed out of the bus station. The guidebook advertised a very cheap hostel in Mitre Street for five pesos per night. I asked an old man for directions and he sent me the wrong way. After obtaining the correct directions from a shop, surprisingly open that time of the morning, I found the street but couldn't find the hostel. I was tired. Even though the bus had been comfortable I didn't sleep all that well. I never do when I'm in transit. In the adjacent street was Residencia Rivadavia. I got a room there for twenty pesos - so much for my cheap accommodation. However I did have my own room with private shower and breakfast included.

Refreshed after a short sleep I headed out. At the entrance I handed my key to a different woman.

'Are you staying another night?' she inquired.

'I've just arrived,' I explained.

I don't suppose many people arrive this early normally. Still at least you get value for money this way.

110 kilometres south of Trelew is *Reserva Provincial Punta Tombo*. From September to April half a million Magallanic penguins breed there. My intention was to see if I could get there by local bus. I didn't fancy paying 45 pesos for a tour. First thing though, I had to change a traveller's cheque. Shouldn't be a problem. Or at least that's what I thought.

Following the advice of the guidebook, I went to Sur Turismo. They in turn directed me to a bank across the road. The bank then directed me to another bank. And so on. I trudged from bank to bank, from travel agency to travel agency with no luck whatsoever. Hope was sparked in one bank when the assistant took pity on my look of despair at having traipsed around for the past two hours, and got on the phone to see if there was any way they would accept one. But to no avail. He then directed me to a Casa de Cambio (Money Exchange).

Finally, I thought. There was no doubt in my mind that they would change a traveller's cheque. This was their business. I queued patiently and arrived at the counter only to be told *no* once again. They only changed cash. My blood started to boil.

'Sorry,' said the guy behind the counter, his hand moving slowly towards the alarm button under his desk.

I stomped off and kicked open the front door in a manner that had the security officers poised for a confrontation, and stormed off down the street muttering to myself.

As the other people on the street moved out of the path of a ranting madman cursing everything in his sight, I spotted another travel agent. I entered and waited, pacing back and forth as the girl dealt with another customer.

'Can I help you?' she asked.

'Can you change me a traveller's cheque please?' I begged.

'Of course, take a seat and someone will be with you shortly.'

I wasn't quite sure I'd heard right.

'It's for 200 dollars,' I explained, still waiting for the bubble to burst.

'No problem. Please sit down.'

I heaved the biggest sigh of relief ever, and gratefully took that seat.

It was now past midday as I trotted off to the bus station weighed down with money. Normally I wouldn't change so much, but considering all the trouble I'd just had, I thought it would be a wise idea. At the bus station I discovered that there was no way to Punta Tombo other than taking a tour or renting a car. I couldn't afford to rent a car on my own, and it was too late to take a tour. So I headed back into town.

I passed an Internet place and went in. They told me to come back at half three. A rainstorm swept in, forcing me to take shelter. There really wasn't a whole lot to do in this town. I could have taken a local bus out to the neighbouring Welsh villages of Gaiman and Dolavon - remnants of the heavy Welsh settlement in the mid-eighteen hundreds - but quite frankly couldn't be bothered. Why fly halfway around the world to visit Welsh villages when there are plenty in Wales? That's my theory anyway. Instead I returned to the hotel and relaxed for a bit.

Next thing I knew it was nearly four o'clock. I had fallen asleep. Groggily I made my way back to the Internet place and then had to wait ages for them to sort out a working computer. When I finally logged on the system responded slower than a tortoise on marijuana. I shouldn't complain really. After all, I was on the edge of Patagonia. I was lucky to even have Internet access.

I checked my e-mail and discovered that I had a job offer. A company back home was offering me a few months work. That's the beauty of the Internet. Here I was in a little town on the edge of a remote part of the world, and I could easily be contacted and offered work halfway across the globe. It's ironic to think that I couldn't change a traveller's cheque, but could instantly send a message back to England turning down three months work.

After that I decided to compose a long letter to everyone, telling them of my experiences so far. It took me ages and was quite a fine piece of work. I clicked the send button and waited... and waited. The system crashed. This was not turning out to be my day. All was lost. I certainly wasn't going to write it again.

My mood blackened once more, I headed out into the street as it started to rain again. Across the road rave music was blaring from large speakers set up on a podium in the centre of the plaza. I absolutely hate rave music, and at this moment it was especially annoying. I can fully understand why people have to take mind-bending drugs when they listen to it. Now you could call me an old man, and possibly I'm sounding like my father here, but it's so monotonous. There is absolutely no rhythm to it whatsoever, just a constant *thump, thump, thump* followed by sounds that remind you of that Yamaha home keyboard you always wanted for Christmas as a child. You know the sort, the one where you press a button and various pre-programmed tunes come out that, when different keys are pressed, delude you into thinking that you are actually quite good at playing.

As I stood on the corner waiting to cross the road, the contents of a large puddle were sent flying all over me. I grimaced as the offending car sped on. Stomping off across the plaza I had a mild understanding of why certain people flip and start attacking others with a gun or knife. You really don't know the circumstances that have led up to that fatal point. I'm not making excuses mind, but it's a plausible explanation. It might seem like a simple thing that started it off, someone knocking into him possibly, but that could just have been the straw that broke the camel's back.

Walking through that plaza, soaking wet, sounds were starting to mix in my head: rave music, people talking and teenagers shouting. My nerves were teetering on the brink. My temper was growing by the second. My head was positively throbbing with anger. All it would have taken was someone bumping into me.

Suddenly though, through all the noises in my head I made out a girl's voice saying, 'Excuse me.'

I turned to see two attractive teenage girls sat on a bench.

'Do you have the time?' asked one of them.

I pulled out my travel clock.

'Seven o'clock,' I replied.

'Gracias,' said the girl, and they both flashed me big smiles.

My rage simmered. My ego soared. If only I was fifteen years younger, I thought to myself.

The citizens of Trelew had been saved by this selfless act of friendliness. And I had been saved from spending the night in an Argentine jail. Good thing really, as it could have been quite embarrassing anyway. I didn't have a gun or knife, and would have looked rather foolish running through the streets attacking everyone with my *backpack*.

The rage gone, all that remained was depression. I wanted to find a bar, drink copious amounts of beer and tell my problems to the bartender. However I wasn't proficient enough in Spanish to express myself in such a way that would have the other drinkers putting guns to their heads and the bartender throwing me out on the street. So I consoled myself with a bar of chocolate from a nearby shop.

I returned to my room and took a shower. What is it about cheap hotels? A space of about one and a half by one metre contained the shower, toilet, bidet and sink. The shower was not contained and therefore the entire floor got wet, along with the contents of the bin, the toilet roll and any other personal hygiene products that happened to be lying around. The water was supposed to drain off through a small drain in the middle. This took a while. On top of that when I flushed the toilet I had to put up with ten minutes of strange gurgling noises as the system refilled.

As I put on some fresh clothes I decided that after the day I'd had I deserved a treat. So I headed out in search of a slap-up meal. As I passed the plaza the rave music had been replaced with a rock band. I continued on to a nearby restaurant that offered a *Tenedor Libre* (all you can eat). For five pesos I stuffed myself to bursting point then headed off to catch the end of the performance. There weren't that many people watching so there was enough room for me and my protruding belly. Once back at the hotel I removed that excess food and then slowly drifted off to sleep as the gurgling toilet system ran in sync with my gurgling stomach.

In the morning my breakfast consisted of three small croissants and a cup of coffee. I had hoped for a fry-up. I checked out, ventured off to the bus station and bought a ticket to Comodoro Rivadavia. When my bus pulled in ready to load, a group of roly-poly men in matching blue uniforms and sunglasses came waddling single file out of a small office and began unloading and loading the bus. Between them they must have had more rollovers than the National Lottery. I wasn't given a seat number so I took one at the front. The passenger compartment was above the driver's section and therefore seating went right to the front of the bus, affording a panoramic view of the landscape ahead. I decided all buses should be like this.

I spent the journey sat next to a five-year-old boy and his slightly older sister. They were on their first ever journey to see the sea, and to visit their aunt. They were very excited. For the next five hours the bus rolled on through mile upon mile of rolling desert hills, and was being constantly battered by the infamous Patagonian winds. Upon arrival in Comodoro Rivadavia I went off in search of Residencia Atlantico. The guidebook said it had hostel-style accommodation. So I hauled on my backpack, got directions from the tourist office and headed off. It didn't look that far on the map. However after climbing steep streets and negotiating stony side streets I finally arrived at the hotel a mile or so on the outskirts of town. Once again the guidebook had mis-informed me. There was no hostel-style accommodation. A room was only 15 pesos, though. And as I had walked so far to get there, I decided to stay.

Comodoro Rivadavia was a very dry, hot and windy place. Walking through its streets I realised that it was also very dull. Other than a few shops and a tiny pebble beach, there was nothing but dry sand and an intense heat. Buses to my next destination left at night. It was already quite late in the afternoon and the idea of having to spend an entire day in this town wasn't looking all that appealing. What the hell would I do? But I had already taken a hotel room, so I was stuck here. Or was I? I could quite easily just pack up and leave, forfeiting the 15 pesos. But that would be quite unfit-ting behaviour for a budget traveller. There was no way I would get my money back, that was for sure. So I would be wasting 15 pesos. On the other hand I would also be wast-ing my time if I stayed here. And I was getting fed up of my own company. I was beginning to realise that I didn't like myself all that much, especially when I'm bored. I hadn't spoken English for days and was sick of having to speak Spanish. I was starting to have conversations in my head.

I seemed to recall that there was an International Hostel at Río Gallegos. Back in Buenos Aires there had been a map on the wall of the hostel showing the locations of all the International Hostels in Argentina. I felt sure I had seen one in Río Gallegos. So I returned to the hotel, grabbed my bag and, handing my keys to a very surprised receptionist, head-ed off to the bus station.

The next bus was due to leave at 9.40. However, that

cost 32 pesos. The cheapest option was Don Otto at 24 pesos, but that didn't leave until half twelve. But seeing as I'd just wasted fifteen I felt that I ought to save that eight.

I bought my ticket. It was late afternoon so I had a long wait. I ventured outside and bought a sandwich and drink from the nearby garage. Then I found a spot by the waterfront, dumped down my pack and perched myself on a rock. As I scoffed my sandwich I gazed idly at the distant mountainous coastline. The temperature was somewhat cooler now. The ocean was sparkling blue. The tide was far out and a handful of people wandered about the rock pools. The ebbing tide had left behind a flat terrain sparsely covered in green seaweed. It was possibly the only green that was to be seen for a hundred miles. The surrounding hills were dusty brown and so was the landscape I had passed through on the way here. Most of this part of Patagonia is just miles and miles of rocky, treeless terrain. However, it's not without its rewards. This town was founded in 1901 and a few years later well-diggers made a huge petroleum strike, fuelling (if you'll pardon the pun) the town's economic boom. Argentina is completely self-sufficient in petroleum, and around one-third of it comes from this area. Considering the vast distances to any other form of civilisation, I figured it would be needed.

Despite the intense heat and dry hostile landscape, it was a very beautiful and strangely alluring place; now heightened by the sun setting over those distant mountains. At any other time I might have been quite happy to stay. It was just the type of place to spend a few days alone, doing nothing but think and reflect on life. However I wasn't in the mood for that right now. Sometimes you can think too much. Right now I wanted to interact with others again, in English preferably.

Once darkness fell I headed back to the station and passed the time upstairs in the café; paying an extortionate three pesos for a cup of coffee, and forcing myself to read my boring book. I had to stay awake or else I would miss that bus.

Once on that Coche Cama bus I settled into my comfortable seat. When the bus departed I was fortunate enough to have both seats to myself. I removed my boots and stretched out across them both. Before I knew it I was cradled in that warm delirium of dreamland. It was all quite nice, until for some strange reason I started to shake uncontrollably in the middle of my dream. I awoke with a start to realise that it was just the bus vibrating. Soon after we came to a stop. It was early in the morning but we hadn't arrived at our destination. This was just a break. A very long break with the door open. Unfortunately my seats were right at the top of the stairs by that open door. The relentless Patagonian wind was howling across the open plateau and whistling past the bus, resulting in a chilling breeze right up my back. Further sleep was inhibited until the doors closed and the bus finally started moving again.

That breeze escalated into a very strong wind that whipped through the streets of Río Gallegos. The temperature had dropped quite considerably with it. It was hard to believe that overnight I had gone from intense desert heat to a chilling cold. Inquiries in the bus station's tourist information had proved that I had been wrong about there being a hostel here. The cheapest accommodation was in Residencia Rivadavia, on the street of the same name.

I made my way through the empty streets, fighting a

constant battle with the wind. It always seemed to be against me, sending litter and dry leaves flying with it. All I needed next was to see some tumbleweeds come rolling past. Where is everybody? I wondered. The occasional person working in their garden would shoot a curious look my way. They each had a strange disconnected look in their eyes. For a town with a population of 65,000 there weren't many of them around. It was a bit like walking into a Hitchcock movie. Then I realised that not only was it Sunday, but it was also midday; siesta time. So that explained it. But where did they go?

I found Residencia Rivadavia in a small yellow-fronted building with a battered and rotting front door. My knock was answered by a short, dumpy woman with a big smile. Accommodation was available in a two-bed shared room. So far I was the only occupant. Looking at the register this was obviously a popular place with other backpackers. It wasn't the Ritz, but it would do for a night, I figured.

I showered, put on some fresh clothes and headed out in search of some life. A few blocks down I hit the main street. Except for a few cafés and bars everything was closed. I popped in to one of those cafés for a bite to eat and a cup of coffee. I sat myself down at the window and watched the street as I waited for my food to be delivered. The occasional car drove past. A few backpackers wandered aimlessly past looking totally lost; possibly searching for the International Hostel.

My coffee arrived along with three sachets of sugar. This had been a regular occurrence. It seemed as though Argentineans put a lot of sugar in their tea and coffee. As a result of this their teeth must be very sensitive because my toasted sandwich arrived with the crusts neatly trimmed off.

*

Río Gallegos is a major port town that ships coal and refines oil. It also services the area's massive wool industry. Although most of Patagonia seems hostile to life, its other major economic institution is sheep farming. This vast area is sprawling with sheep estancias. The dry Patagonian hills form the backdrop of this town. It's actually quite striking when the sun comes out, which was quite often as the strong winds were whisking the broken cloud along at a phenomenal rate. The town sits beside the outlet of the Río Gallegos river. I wandered down to it through a street lined with leaning trees. This town is obviously no stranger to fierce winds.

I reached the riverbank and took a stroll along the very long and quite attractive promenade. A metal railing ran the length of the riverbank. It was painted bright red; obviously the act of some locals desperate for colour in their otherwise dull and grey town. The mystery of where the people went unfolded as I walked along. They were all doing Sunday things: sitting on benches, hanging out in the nearby parks, painting fences or cutting grass. A rickety old food trailer stood on the other side of the road. The proprietor's bored expression suggested that he wasn't getting much business.

At the end of the promenade was a small section of wasteland with a small scattering of abandoned, rotting wooden boats. At the back of this were some apparently deserted buildings. In front of these stood a little stray dog with shaggy fur and a lost look on his face. The fierce wind was sending his fur flapping in all directions. As I knelt down and stroked him he instantly rolled onto his side and nuzzled into my leg.

I petted him for a while and then got up to leave. He

fixed me with those sad eyes. My heart sank.

Just turn around and walk away, I thought to myself.

I did.

Don't look back!

But I did.

He was still sat there watching me.

'I'd take you with me if I could,' I shouted, 'but I have to cross an international border tomorrow!'

Christ, I thought, I'm starting to talk to dogs. I really need to find someone to speak English to.

I continued to walk, looking back every now and then. Each time he was still sat there watching me, a forlorn little figure lost in the emptiness that surrounded him. As he shrunk off into the distance I couldn't help but feel bad. Perhaps I had filled him with the hope of actually being wanted by someone, only to cruelly dash that hope when I'd had enough. On the other hand I could have added a moment's joy to his otherwise dull life. I decided to stick with the latter theory, as it helped ease my conscience.

My prayer was answered as I returned to the hotel. A new arrival had been put in my room. Although Sten was from Belgium he spoke excellent English.

Sten had a slight dilemma. He had hitch hiked down here and arrived with only two pesos in his pocket. As it was Sunday he couldn't change a traveller's cheque. Judging by my experience I wasn't sure if he would be able to change one anyway. The woman had allowed him to stay on the proviso that he pays her in the morning. Apart from a half-hour break to go out for something to eat, we stayed in the room and talked for the rest of the day. Well after all, there wasn't much else to do. Plus it was getting colder outside.

Sten told me all about the bad roads in Bolivia. It seemed

that taking a bus in that country wasn't the most pleasant experience. The majority of the roads were unpaved and twisted along perilous mountain ridges. One particularly bad spot was the road between La Paz and Coroico.

The road drops 3000 metres in 80 kilometres. Again it is unpaved and notorious for vehicles sliding over the edge and plunging to certain destruction below. The chances of survival are zero. Buses are the most common vehicles to go down. At least forty a year, so I was informed. Only recently a group of Dutch girls had been on one that had fallen into the depths of the canyon. However, this hadn't deterred Sten from going, although he wasn't too proud to admit that he spent the entire journey shitting himself. It seemed that it was a backpacker must, the reason being the incredible scenery, and possibly the peer pressure involved. It's one of those things on the backpacker trail that you can be sure everyone will ask, 'Did you go on the bus to Coroico?' You wouldn't want to be the odd one out, would you? After all you have an image to uphold. But is it worth the risk? This was something I would have to give much thought.

The other topic of conversation was the perils of travelling alone. If you were murdered and the culprit stole your bag and all forms of identification, how would anyone know who you are? Similarly how would your family ever know what happened to you? The same applies to the other backpackers you meet. You could keep in touch via e-mail, but what if they suddenly stopped writing. How do you know something bad hasn't happened to them? Something like that happened to me once. I met an Irish girl whilst travelling Australia. We wrote to each other and even made arrangements to meet again in England. One day I wrote to her and said that a friend and I were planning to come to Bath, where she was studying, on a certain date and would she be there? I never heard from her again. Now to all intents and purposes she more than likely changed her mind and didn't want to see me again after all. But I was actually a bit worried. For all I knew she could have been hurt or even killed. I wrote again. No reply. So I sent a letter to her parents' house in Dublin. Still no answer. To this day I still wonder what happened to her?

The following morning the winds were even more ferocious. I had spent a warm and cosy night in my new sleeping bag. As this was the first cold place on my trip, I had decided to try it out. My old sleeping bag was in actuality a lot warmer, being rated at -15 degrees centigrade. But it was also quite big and I wanted to conserve space and weight in my pack. So before I came away I went off in search of one to this effect. The dopey youngster who sold me it couldn't find an actual temperature rating in amongst his tiny pea-like brain. Instead he informed me that it was suitable for two to three seasons.

'I'll be using it in summer, but in Tierra del Fuego,' I told him.

His expression suggested that his cerebral system was about to go into overload at the mere mention of this totally alien place, and so I said I'd take it to avoid having to wipe pieces of exploded brain from my face and clothing.

I set off for the bus station. Again the wind was against me as I struggled through the once again empty streets. I realised now why they were so empty. This cold and bitter wind was enough to keep anyone indoors by the fire. I wished Sten luck for electing to stay here for another day. At the bus station I bought a ticket for the midday bus to Punta Arenas, Chile. I was about to enter a new country, only to leave again shortly after. To get to Tierra del Fuego I would have to take a boat from Punta Arenas. The island is unequally divided between Chile and Argentina, one of the many arguments over land between these two countries.

'Is it always so windy here?' I asked the girl behind the counter.

'Yes,' she replied, 'cold also!'

The tone of her voice suggested that she longed to be elsewhere, preferably tropical.

She then presented me with a customs form to fill in, which informs you of the various things you are not allowed to take into Chile like: animals, vegetables, fruit and semen. *Semen!* How was I supposed to help that? Perhaps I would be asked to remove it before entry. I imagined arriving at the border and being directed to join a long line of men, eventually leading to a door where a nurse would be handing out magazines.

I got on the bus and took a seat next to a Japanese guy who was throwing out the zeds a bit too noisily for my liking. The bus pulled out of the station and headed to the border. We disembarked at a building in the middle of nowhere and formed a line at immigration. We were officially leaving Argentina and got a stamp to prove it. However we weren't entering Chile yet. We then had to drive another mile to the Chilean border and be stamped in. (Thankfully I wasn't asked to surrender my semen.) I wondered to whom the section in-between belonged. No-man's land I presume. But as it's just barren desert I doubted anyone was all that bothered. It certainly wasn't the most secure of borders. There was no fencing, or patrols. The officers quite sensibly remained inside out of the wind and cold. It would have been quite easy to sneak across, had you so desired. But for me there was no need, this had been the easiest border crossing ever.

Once in Chile we were welcomed in with a sandwich and glass of coffee, served on the bus by a short man dressed in a shirt and tie. The road to the border had been unpaved, but once in Chile we were back on concrete. We now glided through more parched landscape along the coastline. The sun was out and the clouds cast patchy shadows across the neighbouring mountains. We arrived in Punta Arenas four and half hours after leaving Río Gallegos. The colourful bungalow-type houses made a refreshing change from the dull windswept streets of Río Gallegos.

Once off the bus I made my way to a hostel called Backpacker's Paradise. The owner took me on a guided tour through the huge open-plan section containing most of the beds, and then to the only actual room. Fortunately there was a spare bed in there, so I took that.

I had two new things to get used to here in Chile: a new currency, and the laid back attitude towards payment for your bed. The owner of the hostel was quite unworried when I told him that I had to change money first.

'No problem, pay when you want,' he said with a nonchalant wave of the hand, and then directed me to a Casa de Cambio.

Chilean money is also in pesos, but there were 500 to the US dollar. This, I figured, could cause confusion. Much to my relief I was able to change my traveller's cheques here with welcome ease. Once done I immediately returned to the hostel to pay. The guy almost seemed reluctant to accept the money. I paid him 2500 pesos. I was relieved to find that things were a bit cheaper here in Chile. Argentina had been quite expensive, from a traveller's point of view. Once I left Tierra del Fuego I would have to make a point of keeping out of Argentina.

____4____

The End of the World

'The ferry has been cancelled,' said a German couple as I approached.

It was seven-thirty in the morning and I wasn't the happiest of people at having to get up that early. I dumped my pack down in disbelief and allowed my own bulk to fall upon it. It seemed that high winds in the channel were creating conditions unsuitable for the small ferry.

I had bought a bus ticket to Ushuaia, a city at the southern end of Tierra del Fuego, on the Argentine side. The ticket would take me from outside the travel agent here in Punta Arenas right through to Ushuaia, including the ferry crossing. I'd already had to wait two days to get a place on this bus, now it looked like I would have to wait longer.

I didn't have a clue what was going on. The German couple had been told to come back at three that afternoon. As the trip was over twelve hours in total, this meant arriving in the middle of the night. I didn't like the idea of that. I wanted to go back to bed, but decided to wait around as no one else seemed to be leaving.

I entered the building and found a guy shouting at the man behind the desk. He was complaining about missing the connection in Río Grande, and subsequently having to pay for a night in a hotel. Others were queuing to have their tickets amended. At least that's what I thought. I joined the queue. When the girl in front of me reached the counter she seemed to be having trouble with her Spanish. I jumped in to help her and we both ended up confused.

'What are you trying to say?' I asked her.

'I want to know when we leave,' she replied.

I translated this for the girl behind the counter.

'When the bus arrives,' she stated.

I was confused.

'But the ferry is cancelled, isn't it?'

'Oh no!' she replied, looking at me as if I was quite mad, 'it's going.'

I scratched my head.

'Give me you ticket,' she said.

So I handed it over and watched as she prepared a boarding card for me and handed it back. I wasn't about to argue.

Dana was from Israel. She was one of many Israelis travelling South America. She had split from her group, and was now alone. Upon arrival in Ushuaia I would be meeting up with Nick and Kirsten, friends I'd met in Punta Arenas. They had managed to get on a bus the day before. I had been invited to go hiking and camping with them in the Tierra del Fuego National Park. In turn I invited Dana to come along with us. She happily agreed.

A very cold wind cut right through us as we shuffled on to the boat that would take us across the Strait of Magellan. This is what separates Tierra del Fuego from mainland

South America. The channel is 560 kilometres long and between 3 and 24 wide. It was discovered by the Portuguese explorer Ferdinand Magellan in 1520, and subsequently named after him. We passed the two-hour crossing in the shelter of the cabin compartment. Another smaller bus met us at the other end. When the tiny compartments underneath were full luggage was loaded along the back seats, forcing three people to stand in the aisle. The driver thoughtfully stopped at a nearby house and managed to obtain three stools for them. With that we headed out of town and bounced our way south along the gravel road.

Once through immigration we soon arrived in Río Grande. It's not much of a town and I was glad to be just changing buses. Río Grande and Ushuaia are the principle towns in Argentinean Tierra del Fuego. Ushuaia is the largest with a population of 42,000. It also holds the title of south-ernmost city in the world (in case you're interested). While we waited to change buses Dana and I went for a bite to eat in the service station across the road.

The wind was blowing a gale outside and it was cold. I couldn't believe I was really here. I had journeyed to the end of the world. I'd dreamed of this place for years. I first read about it in a book. A James A. Michener book if my memo-ry serves me correct. Considering the remoteness of the island and its situation in one of the world's roughest seas, getting here had been considerably easier than anticipated. As for what it looked like, well so far just like the rest of Patagonia. I guess time would tell what the people were like.

One thing for sure, they were a lot more emphatic on the Falklands belonging to Argentina. As the bus had pulled into town I had noticed large signs bearing the words:

Las Malvinas son Argentinas

(The Falklands are Argentinean)

Up until now I had managed to avoid conversations on that topic. The only time I came close was when I stumbled home at three in the morning after a late night drinking session at the aptly named *Lunaticos* bar in Punta Arenas. A group of Argentinean guys decided that they wanted to discuss British rock music and the Falklands with me. I was far too drunk and tired, and politely excused myself.

So anyway here I was at the first focal point of my trip. It certainly had all the ingredients for the end of the world: bad weather, bleak, barren landscape, a wind-beaten town by a grey sea with an apparently small population. And Leo Sayer's *When I Need You* playing on the radio; the latter adding a sense of nostalgia to the moment.

As we ventured further south the landscape became more verdant. We passed along the very big and awesomely beautiful Lago Escondido (hidden lake) and pulled into Ushuaia at ten o'clock at night. We collected our luggage and shivered our way past the steamy windows of bars and restaurants, from which emanated much warmth and laughter, to the hostel where I'd arranged to meet Nick and Kirsten.

We entered the welcoming warmth of the St Christopher hostel and were happy to find there was space. We got beds for 11 pesos each. Once settled in we joined Nick and Kirsten for a drink in the common room.

Nick was originally from Australia but now lived in Munich with Kirsten. They had met a few years before on the Inca Trail in Peru; on a section called *El Paseo de las Mujeres* (women's pass) to be exact. They kept in contact and Nick went to see her in Munich, staying for a couple of weeks. Shortly after they arranged to meet again in New

Zealand where they travelled together for five weeks. It was during this trip that they both realised they wanted to be together. So Nick, who had been living in the States, upped sticks and went to live in Munich. He got a good job and learned to speak German. For two years they lived together in Munich before coming on this trip, after which they would return. Now isn't that the most romantic story you've ever heard?

I got up around nine the next morning. The air outside was brisk and clean. I left Dana talking to a group of Israelis and went for a walk. Although Ushuaia was the largest city on the island, it still contained all the charm of a small town. Its situation on the coast, surrounded by large snow-capped mountains certainly helped add to that charm. It was almost like an Alpine village - not that I've ever been to one you understand, but I've seen pictures. Two decades ago this was just a tiny village. Now it's a thriving town that is a key naval base for Argentina. It's main industries are fishing, tourism, forestry and, oddly enough, electronics assembly. I figured I could quite like it here.

Ushuaia was also the embarkation point for trips to Antarctica. The German ship *The Bremen* ran 14-day tours to the Antarctic peninsula, along with the Falklands and many other islands. Everything was provided for the trip, at a price of $6000 US. However, we had discovered, on the backpacker grapevine, that if you showed up last minute that price could be slashed to $2000. One woman had got on for $1500. The best option, it seemed, was to turn up at the ship one or two hours before it was due to sail. If there was a space, the price was very negotiable. I was tempted. So were Nick and Kirsten. But in the end we had unanimously decided to leave it until another day.

After a trip to the local supermarket in order to stock up on supplies for four days of camping, we slumped off to meet the bus that would take us the short distance to the national park. Much of our stuff had been left back at the hostel. In the minibus were a couple of American guys, and a very lovely Argentinean girl. She told me that she didn't care about the Falklands and had no problem with English people. Nice girl.

The bus dropped the four of us at the pier where boats left for Isla Redonda. We had each bought a ticket that would take us to the island and then on to the campsite at Laguna Verde. Unfortunately the boat wasn't running and we were taken out to the island by Zodiac, but it wasn't big enough for the journey to the campsite, and therefore would be taking us back to the pier.

Isla Redonda contains the southernmost post office in the world. In fact that's just about all it contains, other than an abundance of wildlife. No one lived on this tiny island, so I failed to see the logic in having a post office. The only apparent reason for its being here was to provide visiting tourists with a stamp in their passport to prove they had been to the southernmost post office in the world. And of course to send a postcard.

'Can you send post from here then?' I asked the old man who had just filled two pages of everyone's passport with stamps - except mine because I had left it in my bag on the mainland. It seemed he didn't get to use these stamps much, and was therefore taking advantage of the opportunity.

'Of course,' he replied, 'it's a post office!'

This confirmed in my mind that we really were in the company of a madman.

We each selected a card, wrote our messages and put them in brown envelopes, which the old man ceremoniously covered in stamps.

'¡Hay mas (there's more)!' he exclaimed proudly after each stamping.

We then headed back outside.

The island lies just off the coast in what is known as the Beagle Channel. Surrounding Tierra del Fuego is a huge archipelago. Many of the neighbouring islands belong to Chile. It felt strange to be stood on a hilltop in Argentina and be looking at Chile. I expect it would be difficult to ascertain which islands belonged to whom, had it not been for the many Argentinean flags dotted around the pier. The two neighbouring countries are not the best of friends. The fact that General Pinochet allowed the British to use Chile as a base during the Falklands War probably didn't help matters much. They are also locked in a battle for land. The island of Tierra del Fuego is unequally divided between the two, giving Chile the largest chunk. However it seemed to me that Argentina has the most beautiful section. The main island is 76,000 square kilometres in size, and two thirds is owned by Chile. However, the southern half is abundant with scenic lakes, glaciers, rivers and mountains, while the north is dry, flat and wind-beaten. And anyway, don't they have enough land? I mean look at the size of it compared to Chile or the UK. Honestly, some people are just so greedy!

Back ashore we were given a lift to an area called Lapataia. The national park contains one official campsite called Camping Lago Roca. However there are many other free camping areas, which were described in the guidebook as 'disgracefully filthy'. We found a nice secluded spot near Laguna Verde that was by far that. It was beautiful and very clean. The area was peaceful with a gentle breeze that occasionally turned into the odd blast of cold wind from over the mountains. Over the hill was a placid bay with one of the most magnificent views I'd ever seen. Behind us were snow-capped mountains. All in all it was a totally idyllic spot, and far from being 'disgracefully filthy'. We pitched camp, built a fire and proceeded to burn the potatoes and corn on the cob before settling down for the night.

We rose bright and early the next morning - well nine o'clock anyway, but it was early for me - to the discovery that Nick and Kirsten had been the victims of a cunning fox. Before going to sleep we had tied our bags of food to the branches of a nearby tree. Unfortunately Nick and Kirsten had chosen a branch close to another that came up from the ground at an angle, thus allowing the fox to walk up and rip a hole in the bottom of their bag. He then proceeded to munch his way through anything that didn't require cooking, namely the bread and biscuits.

Over at the organised campsite you could use the showers for a small charge. I wanted to take one. The others argued that as we were going hiking that day then I should leave it until afterwards. The campsite was a good half-hour walk away and my argument was that after a whole day of hiking, I certainly wasn't going to do any more. So, forfeiting breakfast so we could leave on time, I trotted off with a towel to take my shower.

The walk was well over half an hour and I arrived to discover that showers were only permitted from five until eight in the evening. *Bastards!* I returned to the campsite with the news. They had news for me too. Our planned hike was to take us past that campsite. So I had to walk all the way back.

This was not a good start to my day.

Once past the campsite we started uphill. The trail took us along a twisty, rugged path that led through dense forest. After much puffing and wheezing we stopped for a break.

Nick had an altimeter on his watch.

'We're at 200 metres,' he announced.

'Great!' I exclaimed, 'how high is the peak?'

'940 metres.'

That wasn't so great.

'You don't have to go all the way,' said Nick.

Unfortunately I did. I had taken a Millennium vow to finish the things I start. To go after the things I want and not be held back by anything or anyone. So therefore I had to complete this hike, at whatever cost.

Plus I didn't want Nick and Kirsten to think I was wimping out.

Dana on the other hand didn't share my determination and went back to the campsite. Her reason being that she had recently spent five days hiking in the Torres del Paine National Park. She didn't see why she should put herself through all that pain again.

A fair point.

I soldiered on, alternating last place with Kirsten. At 300 metres we broke into the open to a breathtaking view. Aqua blue lakes shimmered in the sun far below. From this altitude they looked like large puddles. We were surrounded by the glacial peaks from the nearby mountain range whose highest rose to 1500 metres. Not really that high when you think about it, but that didn't detract from its dazzling beauty.

We were climbing the section named Cerro Guanaco. Continuing on again, we made our way through more forest and emerged at 600 metres to find ourselves standing on a vast, green plateau. Tiny pools of water were scattered across the field. Also strange squashy green lumps protruded from the ground like bubbles. I had absolutely no idea what they were, but they did help add a spring to my step. Another strange aspect was that no matter how hard I tried, I just couldn't leave an imprint. I would jump up and down and even ram my fist in and then watch helplessly as it slowly puffed back out into its original shape, leaving absolutely no trace that I had ever been there.

At the other end of the field we started uphill again. The grass and trees disappeared and the last 340 metres led up through a mountain of loose slate and stones. I was beginning to develop a certain disinclination towards hills. I expressed this aloud to Nick and Kirsten, who were already quite far ahead, and to other passing hikers. I wondered if they had seen something bad at the top because they all ran back down. Maybe other hikers had warned them that a mad Englishman was pigeon-stepping his way up and muttering to himself in a slightly psychotic manner.

The muscles in my legs were slowly shutting down one by one. My chest felt like it was going to explode as my lungs desperately fought for more oxygen than they were able to contain. The muttering turned into articulate sentences convincing myself that I could make it to the top. I started swinging my arms in a vain attempt to gain more momentum.

It was no good, I had to try and take my mind off things. I started singing to myself; a trick I'd picked up from a Swiss girl on a hike in Ireland. Through the sweat in my eyes I could see Kirsten waving at me from the top. I definitely had to make it now. The top came into sight. I sped up my steps and came to an abrupt halt at the brow of the hill, just before plunging over the other side into a very steep valley. I wasn't quite there yet though, Nick and Kirsten were perched on a rock slightly further up. I took a deep breath, summoned up a last burst of energy and hauled myself up the final hill. Once at the top I punched the air in triumph and collapsed in a heap next to them.

Our efforts were well rewarded. There we sat on the top of the end of the world. We had a panoramic view of a totally wild and untouched landscape. There were no towns, no noisy traffic, no electricity pylons and not a single manmade thing to be seen. It felt like we were the only human beings for a thousand miles. All the other hikers had gone and we were left to soak up this atmosphere alone.

From behind the mountain came a bitterly cold wind that appeared to be blowing thunderous-looking black clouds our way. There was no shelter on this barren mountaintop, and so reluctantly we were forced to start making our way back down after ten minutes. Off to my right I could see a large, deep hole, about one metre in diameter, filled with snow. It was the only snow I had come across and, acting on a sudden impulse, I sprinted over and launched myself off the ground. I made a perfect touchdown right in the middle.

Nick and Kirsten watched in dismay as my whole body slid through that tiny hole of snow and into the icy depths of the mountain. Actually that didn't really happen, but it could well have done. So let that be a lesson to you all. It was an incredibly dumb thing to do, and I never want to hear about any of you attempting such a stunt.

It *was* fun though.

Nick and Kirsten, scoffing at the crazy antics of a snow-deprived Englishman, continued on down. Well we don't get much snow where I'm from. I clambered back out, shook off my boots and continued after them. Nick was way ahead and running.

'What's his rush?' I asked Kirsten.

'If you run down it's easier on your knees,' she explained, before trotting off herself.

I joined in also, and the three of us trotted down that mountain as the oncoming rain sprayed the backs of our necks.

Fortunately the worst of the rain held off until we got back to the campsite. At the bottom of the mountain we sneaked into the showers at Camping Lago Roca. We each took a very refreshing shower, unnoticed by the owners. I also took a roll of toilet tissue; I felt it was the least they owed me for the inconvenience caused that morning. Then we casually strolled off in to the campsite as if we were staying there, and rejoined the road once out of sight; our consciences coming in the form of a very worried Kirsten.

'We really should pay them, it's not right you know!'

Yeah, yeah!

We returned to the campsite to discover my tent being severely battered by the strong winds that now came howling over that mountain. I had a very thin dome tent that really wasn't adequate for this climate. The strong wind was bending the poles right over and threatening to rip the tent from the ground. Had it not been for Dana sitting inside I might have returned to find it floating in the Beagle Channel. My attempts at securing it were met with failure. So I had no choice but to move it into the shelter of the trees. As the rain finally swept in we all dived into our respective tents and spent the rest of the night there.

In the morning the rain had subsided, leaving behind a grey

and gloomy sky. Dana left that day to catch a flight to Buenos Aires. The three of us remained. We spent the morning eating breakfast by the fire and trying our best to get motivated for another hike.

At around one we got going and hiked a trail leading along the coast and ending at the departure point for Isla Redonda. As the boat was now running again, we managed to convince the owner to give us a free ride back to Laguna Verde, as compensation for missing out yesterday. The only drawback was that we had to go to the island first and wait.

We sat outside the post office and waited. Down by the water's edge a group of men were preparing to go diving.

'What is the temperature of the water?' asked Kirsten.

'Around six degrees,' replied one of them.

'You are all mad!' I exclaimed.

'We dive using dry suits with all our clothes underneath,' he explained.

Kirsten was fascinated by this, and peppered them with questions as to what they were doing and what there was to see down there. She had never dived in anything other than tropical seas.

'¿Quieres bajar (you want to go down)?' asked one of them.

This was unexpected.

'Do you have your diving permit on you?' he continued.

Kirsten produced this. He looked it over and confirmed that she was quite welcome to come along. It seemed that one of the guys was too hungover to make the second dive, so they had a spare set of equipment.

The boat back wouldn't wait for Kirsten, so Nick and I left without her. We didn't fancy waiting around. The guys said they would take her back to the pier and she could walk or hitch the rest of the way. We were dropped off at another much larger pier further along at Bahia Lapataia.

We wandered off into a small car park. A sign by the side of the road explained that this was the end of Ruta Nacional 3. This was as far south as roads go. I was now 3242 kilometres from Buenos Aires. It seemed hard to believe that I only left there a couple of weeks ago. But here I was in a totally different landscape and climate. In Buenos Aires I had been wandering around in minimal clothing. Now I had on every available item, and had even been forced to buy a woolly hat, which was now pulled down over my ears to protect them from that wind chill factor.

We walked four kilometres along the dirt road to where we were camped. The first order of business, naturally, was to get that fire going. Once sufficiently roaring we settled down to cook.

Tim, who was camped nearby, came wandering around the corner carrying more firewood than was humanely possible.

'Hey, you mind if I join you?' he asked.

Anyone with that amount of firewood was more than welcome in our camp, so we welcomed him in. Tim was from Maine, and travelling around in-between his studies.

An hour or so later Kirsten returned with some very bad news. She'd had her first diving accident. As this was the first time she had ever dived in a dry suit, she was unfamiliar with its workings. Her dive buddy had given her a full rundown and she knew what to do. All had been going well and they'd both been underwater for quite a while. However when Kirsten tried to adjust her buoyancy compensator it all went wrong and she floated rapidly to the surface, pulling her buddy with her. She was so flustered that she wasn't sure at what depth she was, and therefore risked the bends; a diver's worst nightmare.

She was returned to dry land and, shivering from the cold, was whisked into the warmth of the only building, the post office. The old man wrapped her in a blanket and poured her two very large shots of rum followed by a coffee laced with more rum. Her buddy then proceeded to explain the effects of the bends, so she could monitor herself for possible symptoms.

'Do the symptoms include feeling slightly drunk?' she asked.

'No, that will be the rum,' he chuckled.

He gave her the phone number for a place in Ushuaia that had a decompression tank, along with his own phone number. He didn't think there would be a problem, but wasn't taking any chances. He also said that they would come by the campsite a bit later to check on her.

True to their word they turned up about an hour later, putting poor Kirsten's mind at rest. The danger time had passed and if she hadn't felt any symptoms by now, then she would be all right. We celebrated by cracking open the bottle of wine given to her by the old man in the post office.

Edwardo and Marcelo both lived in Ushuaia. Edwardo invited us to an asado (barbecue) at his house on Tuesday night.

'When you get back to Ushuaia you phone me,' he insisted.

We looked forward to it, mainly for the chance of eating decent food for a change.

Away from the fire I realised just how bitterly cold the night had become. This was by far the coldest yet. We said goodbye to the others and settled down for the night. Not only did I have an inadequate tent, but now I was deprived of the extra warmth generated by sharing the tent with someone else. I threw on my thermals, jeans and two fleeces and climbed into the welcome warmth of my sleeping bag. Much to my disgust the cold started to creep in after me, uninvited I might add. My sleeping bag was proving to be entirely unsuitable for this climate. I regretted not bringing the other. For the sake of a few pounds less weight I was now freezing my nuts off in sub-Antarctic conditions. It took me a very long time to get to sleep.

We returned to Ushuaia the next day. The cold grey day decided that for us. The welcoming warmth of the hostel was just the tonic I needed after that awful night. I longed for a nice warm shower, and so did the others. Being a gentleman I allowed Kirsten to go first, then eagerly stepped in myself. It was heavenly! I allowed the warm spray to massage my aching frozen joints, then stepped out a moment to soap up. Stepping back in I discovered, to my immense shock, that the water had turned unbearably cold. My screams echoed through the hostel. I swore and cursed until I was blue in the face. I was cursing myself really for being so bloody nice and letting Kirsten go first and steal all the hot water.

I rinsed my body bit-by-bit and returned shivering to the welcome warmth of the dorm.

'How was it?' asked Kirsten.

'Bloody freezing!' I grunted, 'you must have used all the hot water!'

They both found this highly amusing.

I didn't.

'Did you run the tap in the sink?' she asked.

I frowned at her, confused by this strange question.

It seemed that there were signs plastered all over the walls explaining that due to a problem with the water pressure, in order to have hot water it was necessary to leave the tap in the sink running whilst showering. However I still clung to my theory that Kirsten had stolen all the hot water; that is until Nick emerged feeling refreshed and cleansed after his lovely hot shower.

Bastard!

As promised we phoned Edwardo on Tuesday and went to his asado. He came to collect us in his pickup. Tim had left earlier that day to begin hitch hiking northward. Edwardo lived in a beautiful house made mostly from wood. It was in a secluded part of Ushuaia, right up on the hill behind the town. The area contained a small scattering of houses partially surrounded by woods and affording a great view of the ocean. Out the back was a huge clearing that was, to all intents and purposes, his back garden. He had to share it with the other residents mind, but there was plenty to go around.

'If you don't mind me asking, how much did you pay for your house?' I asked Edwardo.

'This is the most expensive area in all of Ushuaia,' he replied, 'because of the space, the location and the tranquilli-ty.'

'Yes, yes, but how much?'

'$25,000.'

I gulped. '$25,000!' I exclaimed.

'I know, it's a lot eh?' commented Edwardo.

'That's not expensive,' I informed him, 'a small flat in England would cost you $75,000.'

It was Edwardo's turn to gulp.

All our efforts to help him set up were shrugged off with

a casual wave of the hand. Our only contribution was to collect some firewood from the nearby woods. We were the
first there and Edwardo proceeded to teach us all about an
authentic Argentinean asado. He pulled out an entire lamb
from the back of his truck, already skinned and gutted of
course, and fitted it to a special frame. The firewood was
loaded on and the fire stoked up. He then skewered the
frame into the ground and positioned the lamb over the
open fire. For the next three hours we sat and drank wine
while occasionally turning the lamb.

As darkness fell the other guests arrived. One of them
was getting married in the morning. He had been with his
girlfriend for ten years and they already had four children. I
guess he wanted to be sure first. No women turned up.
Kirsten was the only one. Now I'm not sure if this is normal
practice for an asado here or whether it was just because
there was a group of lads on a stag night, but the whole pro-
cedure was quite neanderthal. The ingredients for the asado
were: meat, bread, beer and wine.

'Nothing more!' explained Edwardo.

At the stroke of three hours each person was handed a
small carving knife and encouraged to cut off large chunks
of meat and eat with their bare fingers. No plates were needed. The meat, I have to say, was gorgeous. My knife just
sliced through as if I was cutting air. It was so tender and
juicy. Rarely have I ever tasted such a succulent lamb, and
I offered my compliments to the chef unreservedly.

Kirsten was feeling guilty for not being able to help out
or bring anything. But Edwardo had insisted that he didn't
need anything. Still she felt bad.

'But they have been so kind to us!' she said.

She was right of course, so I suggested that she return

the favour by inviting them to Munich. She could take them skiing in the Alps, get them into an accident and cook a barbecue for them the following day. It was only fair! She agreed and that helped put her mind at rest.

In all seriousness though, it seemed that their hospitality knew no bounds. There was no reason for them to do this. In fact they didn't even know us that well. Yet Edwardo had invited all three of us into his home and been a most gracious host. And he had shown remarkable patience with us regarding our Spanish. We exchanged e-mails and extended invitations to them to come and visit us in our own countries. The chances are that we will never see each other again, but you never know.

This total act of selfless friendship from a relative stranger will never be forgotten by any of us. Edwardo even insisted on giving us a lift back to the hostel. It's moments like this that restore your faith in the goodness of people.

__5__

The Pendulum

I had been on the bus since six in the morning and now found myself squashed against the window by a woman with the biggest arse in living history. I had just managed to remove my cake from the seat before she squashed it. She was now sat there smiling benignly at me. When the bus started moving once again she got up and walked to the back. I later discovered her sat somewhere else. Was I that obvious?

We were at the exchange point in Río Grande, on our way back to Punta Arenas. I was quite disappointed to be leaving Tierra del Fuego. I wanted to explore it more in-depth. Unfortunately as this was the Argentinean part, it was expensive. I couldn't afford to stay longer. Also I only had three months in all and many more miles to cover. One of those months was almost up. So I now had to begin my trip northward through Chile to Lake Titicaca. Chile is another country that has held a certain fascination with me. The country is 4270 kilometres long, but only 180 at its widest point. On a map it almost looks like it's been squashed against the edge of the continent by Argentina. I was curious to see what it looks like. One thing for sure, Chile would be a little less demanding on my traveller's cheques. I hoped.

With room to turn around now I resumed the conversation I'd started with Andrew as we were getting back on the bus. Andrew was from the States and had just completed five and a half months in Paraguay on some sort of exchange program. With him were three Canadian girls who had also been on the program. They were now travelling a while before going back home. He had coupled up with Ewa (pronounced Eva), one of the three girls. Susie and Sheila were her friends.

We arrived in Punta Arenas at seven that evening. Nick and Kirsten wanted the privacy of a guesthouse as opposed to the dormitories of the hostel, so they went off in search of one. I trotted off back to Backpacker's Paradise, closely followed by the Canadians. Once settled in I met up with Nick and Kirsten for a bite to eat and to discuss our next move.

I was well and truly on the backpacker trail now, and it seemed the next stop was the Torres del Paine National Park. This 180,000-hectare national park spreads around three giant granite pillars soaring high above everything else and forming the centrepiece of the park. The area contains an abundance of shimmering turquoise lakes, rivers, glaciers, dense forests and cascading waterfalls. It also contains a huge network of walking trails.

The two most famous trails are known as the W and the Circuit, their names naturally denoting their shape. Whether you were heading to or from the park, you could guarantee that a discussion with another backpacker on the subject would always include one of these questions: 'So did you do

82

the Circuit or the W?' or 'Are you going to do the Circuit or the W?' The difference being that the W can be done in four to five days, where the Circuit takes at least seven or eight. In time I was about to radically alter this way of thinking.

And so it was I found myself on the way to catch a bus to Puerto Natales, equipped with a brand new sleeping mat and cooking set, and loaded down with food. As I would be hiking and camping for seven days or more, I'd need the food. I hoped the new mat would give me warmer nights than those of Tierra del Fuego. What I really needed was a better sleeping bag, but I couldn't afford that.

The plan for the next few days was simple. I had been invited to share the hire of a car with the Canadians. They planned to cross the border into Argentina and visit the Moreno Glacier and Cerro Fitzroy. After that we would all hike the Circuit in Torres del Paine, and finally take a four-day boat trip to Puerto Montt. I had left the Canadians in the middle of sorting out their food, and rushed off to buy my ticket to Puerto Natales before they sold out. As I trotted along the road I realised that I'd left my towel hanging on the line back at the hostel, and trudged all the way back to retrieve it.

Upon arrival in Puerto Natales Nick and Kirsten once again opted for the privacy of a guesthouse, while I followed the Canadians to a hostel they had been recommended back in Punta Arenas. Hostel Magallanes was a small and homely place run by two brothers.

Once settled in I took a walk into town. Puerto Natales contained all the makings of a frontier town. It wasn't very big and the supermarkets were seriously lacking in stocks. The town is situated 250 kilometres north of Punta Arenas.

There is no road north from here, except into Argentina. From here on the Chilean Fjords stretch right up to Puerto Montt, at least 800 kilometres away. Supplies were delivered once a week to this town, so the only thing in real abundance here was local produce. So if you wanted packaged goods that would last, then you didn't have much choice. We were fortunate enough to have bought our food back in Punta Arenas on the advice that it would be more expensive here.

I bumped into Nick and Kirsten in one of the streets.

'We saw the Canadians at the bus station,' said Nick, 'they said to tell you that they couldn't get the car until next week and are now going to Torres del Paine tomorrow.'

Great, I thought.

'I'd better go see them and find out what time they plan to go,' I said.

We arranged to meet for a meal in about an hour or so.

Back at the hostel I found the others in total chaos. They had all bought tickets for the 8.00 am bus to the park, but the girls were now considering going later. They said that they still didn't have enough food. I eyed the eight shopping bags piled in the corner and wondered what else they needed. Susie was also having trouble with her visa card. They were such a disorganised bunch. The problem is that too many heads cause so much confusion. It's a problem I've seen many times amongst large groups travelling together. There are too many conflicting opinions and ideas about what to do. This was happening here. Andrew was sat with a concerned look upon his face at the realisation that he would probably have to carry all this food. The other problem was that he wanted to get going early in the morning. So in the end it was decided that he would leave and meet up with them later. The girls seemed more interested in meeting up with some friends for a drink that night, than getting ready for a major hike.

I bought a ticket for eight the next morning then, after getting some last minute supplies, met up with Nick and Kirsten for that meal in a nice little restaurant called *El Rincon Tata*. The plan was to get some good food inside us before the hike. We ordered some beers and discussed our situation. I had serious doubts as to whether Andrew would be leaving the same time as me. I had also read that it is forbidden for people to hike in the park alone, and that I could be refused entry if I didn't enter with someone. Therefore I decided to change my ticket and go in with Nick and Kirsten. They were leaving at seven the next morning. Nick also pointed out that I ought to get myself a camping stove. He suggested I rent the one we had seen nearby.

So whilst Nick and Kirsten decided what they wanted to eat I nipped out and changed my ticket, then popped in that rental shop. I was too late. The owner directed me to the International Hostel around the corner. There I managed to rent a stove for one dollar a day. All I had to do was give them a ten-dollar deposit and pay when I return it.

'Do you have your passport?' asked the man behind the desk.

'No I don't I'm afraid,' I replied.

He just shrugged and took my name, put the ten dollars in an envelope and wished me a good trip.

Back at the restaurant I told Nick how easy it had been to get that cooker. 'They don't have any details about me, just my name and ten dollars,' I told him, 'I might as well keep it. It's well worth ten dollars.'

He agreed. However Kirsten wasn't having any of this. 'You cannot be so dishonest,' she warned me, 'you are going to take that back!'

Nick and I both chuckled, but Kirsten, it seemed, was deadly serious. We then tucked into our food in the hope of fuelling those muscles for their upcoming strenuous activity.

That night I was woken up at god-knows what time in the morning by the sound of the doorbell ringing. Andrew got up and answered it.

'Hey dude! I'm totally wasted and can't find my hotel. Can I crash on the floor or something?' came a very loud American voice.

He took the spare bunk in our room. Shortly after the bell rang again and two more people came in. They climbed onto the bunk above me. After much shuffling they eventually settled down. I was beginning to drop off again when the bed creaked.

No! I prayed.

But alas it was.

What followed next was a constant gentle rocking and loud squeaking of the bunk. I spent the next half hour with my head buried under my pillow in a vain attempt to drown this out. Finally it stopped. Peace at last, I thought. But no, they started talking! Eventually it all quietened down and I began to drop off once again, just as the alarm went off. It was *6.00 am*.

It took two hours to get to the park entrance. We got off the bus and headed for the queue to the entrance. The entrance fee cost 3000 pesos for Chileans, 6500 for foreigners. Isn't that slightly prejudice? I bought my ticket and was directed to another counter.

'Are you doing the Circuit or the W?' asked the park ranger as I showed him my ticket.

'The Circuit,' I proudly announced.

'Please write your passport number here,' he replied, unimpressed.

We all then got on a minibus, which would take us to the first campsite. As we bounced along the narrow dirt track no one had asked me for the fare money. Also I had left the hostel in Puerto Natales without paying. It had been so early that no one was up and I hadn't thought to pay the night before, and the owner hadn't asked. Is it my fault they are so laid back about payment here? I was becoming a regular criminal, as Nick and Kirsten were telling the Canadian couple sat next to us. Mind you I had left some stuff back at the hostel so I would no doubt pay them when I returned.

'Has everyone paid?' asked a voice from the front, directed right at me.

I paid him.

All that remained now was for me to remember to take back that cooker, and all my sins would be absolved. I had the feeling Kirsten would help me with that one.

We pitched camp and started our first hike, 940 metres up to view the Torres. Now I'm not sure if it was the steak I ate the day before or if my hikes in Tierra del Fuego had improved my fitness level, but I was moving a lot quicker up that mountain. On the way up we met Tim and his friend jogging back down. It seemed he had done well to hitch this far so quickly. He and his friend had started up the mountain at 7.30 am and were now on the way back down to start the circuit today.

'Well they are twenty years old,' I told myself in consolation.

Rain moved in after a while and we took shelter in the refugio halfway. These refugios are dotted around the walking trails and most have dormitory-style accommodation, albeit somewhat overpriced at $16 US per night. We had lunch there and continued on when the rain abated.

Once above the tree line we were once again faced with a climb over loose rocks and slate; only this mountain contained monster boulders that didn't look that stable.

'I thought I had found someone who hiked as slow as me,' said Kirsten as she puffed her way up behind me.

I don't know what had got into me today, but the further up I got the faster I seemed to move. I broke over the brow of the hill to a sight that instantly took my breath away.

'*Holy fuck!*' I blurted, somewhat impetuously.

Three huge granite towers rose before me, soaring into the icy cold mist. Below them floated small icebergs in a motionless grey lake. It was magnificent! The weather was in our favour also. The rain had stopped and the sun was starting to burn through the mist. We took a few victory photographs and then wandered off in different directions, me to the lake. I was curious to see just how cold it was.

Let me tell you I have never in my life felt water so cold. I dipped in my fingers and then wondered where they had gone. I retrieved my hand to find they were still attached but that all feeling had disappeared.

I sat down by the lake rubbing my fingers and marvelling at this superb piece of natural beauty. On the other side of the lake a giant glacier clung to the side of one of the granite pillars. It looked so cold and threatening, yet strangely alluring. All of a sudden the sun broke through the clouds and the lake, glacier and cliffs underwent an amazing transformation. No longer was it cold and threatening, but startlingly beautiful and almost inviting. I wanted to swim across that lake, climb up and touch the glacier. I wanted to climb this soaring rock before me and see how it felt to be on top of the world. Fortunately for me I kept my head and remained where I was. I wouldn't have lasted more than a few minutes in that icy water.

After about an hour the weather took a turn for the worse once again. So we headed back down. As we passed the refugio I wondered how they got their supplies. The answer came trotting around the corner. A group of horses, recently relieved of their load, were being ridden by a group of children. They looked to be in their mid-teens.

Once back down off the mountain we showered, prepared our food and then started the fire. No camp is complete without a campfire. Okay so your clothes stink of smoke in the morning, your throat is as dry as a bone from breathing it in and no matter how hard you try, you simply cannot escape from the line of smoke that comes your way. When you move, a few minutes later it engulfs you once again. There is no winning. Even so we cannot keep away. There is something strangely mesmerising about a campfire at night. Aside from the fact that it keeps you warm, it also adds to that outdoor feel and provides a great social ambience.

We were joined by a couple from Concepcion, in central Chile. They were down this way on a short holiday and planned to hike the Circuit also, starting tomorrow. However they weren't keen on our idea for an early start, and politely refused our offer to join us.

I didn't blame them really. Getting up at 6.30 and having to pack the tent away required much self-discipline. I didn't have any, so I relied on Nick and Kirsten to kick the tent until I got up. Today was going to be the real killer. We had an eight-hour hike to undertake with the full weight of our backpacks. The plan was to make it to the second campsite along the trail, which was free.

The outlook was good, scattered cloud and not too cold, yet not too hot. We made our way past the hostel and up into the mountains. The Torres form the centrepiece of the park and the Circuit runs around them. It had snowed heavily during the night but only up on the mountain. It hadn't touched us in the campsite. In fact it hadn't felt that cold, which meant that I had got a good night's sleep. The result was that once I got going I felt fresh and invigorated. There was a renewed spring in my step as we trudged single file up the hill and into the forest that climbed the edge of this mountain range.

As time rolled on, the clouds began to roll in. A light snow started to fall. This didn't bother me. In fact I quite liked it. I almost wished it was Christmas again. Being here in the forest as the snow gently fell made it feel more like Christmas to me.

We threw on our raincoats and continued onwards. Today I was to learn a valuable lesson when it comes to hiking: *Don't wear boxer shorts!* As you hike your way up that mountain, they hike their way up your arse. Most of your time is spent pulling them back out again. Many a time Nick and Kirsten would stop and wait for me as I waved at them from below with one hand, and fumbled under my backpack with the other to retrieve my boxers.

After a couple of hours we decided to take a break. I gratefully allowed my pack to fall to the ground. As I did I noticed, to my dismay, that the bag for my tent had come undone. I looked inside to see that the little bag containing my tent pegs and ropes had vanished. They must have fallen out somewhere along the trail. But where?

'Shit, they could be anywhere!' I exclaimed.

'Don't worry I can spare a few pegs,' offered Nick.

But that was no good. I had to have mine. My tent wasn't the most secure as it was, but without all the pegs and ropes it could be disastrous in the mountains. There was no other choice, I had to try and find them.

Feeling it would be quicker and easier without the weight of my pack, I left it at the rest spot. Nick and Kirsten agreed that if I hadn't returned after fifteen minutes they would continue on without me and we'd meet up at the campsite. We selected a tree in which to hide my pack behind and Nick said that he would mark the spot with a stick. They wished me luck and I marched off.

I had been walking for five or so minutes when all of a sudden that light snow that had so lifted my spirits earlier, now turned into a blizzard of thick wet snow, engulfing me in the process. It smothered my eyes and drenched my jeans and feet. My waterproof trousers were in my backpack. I stood there shivering and silently cursing the mountain weather, as the water rapidly seeped into my boots and formed patchy puddles under my feet.

I figured as I was already soaked I might as well carry on, so I squelched my way onwards trying my best to scan the ground through the snow in my eyes.

It was a hopeless nightmare. Although there was only one trail, it broke off into side trails that ran parallel for a while or formed little detours, then rejoined at some point further along. I couldn't remember, or tell, which ones I had taken. It all looked different from the other way. Also I hadn't really taken a lot of notice of the trail. I had been too busy talking or looking at the scenery.

After about twenty minutes I gave up. It was no good.

They could have fallen out anywhere between here and the campsite. What were the chances of me finding them again? I had no choice but to head back. With a bit of luck I might bump into the Canadians, or at worst I could book into that hostel for the night. But first I had to retrieve my backpack. So I turned around and started the long and weary trudge back.

The snow had stopped and turned into a light drizzle. I was cold and soaked to the skin. My nose never seemed to stop running. I decided to try Nick's technique, which he called the Bushman's Flick. This consisted of blocking one nasal passage with one finger and propelling the contents of the other with a short, sharp snort. I took a deep breath, pressed the side of my nose and blew with all the force I could conjure up. A large volume of stringy mucus came hurtling out, and was blown back into my face by an uncannily timed gust of wind. I stood there in a state of shock as the pieces of snot hung from my nose and chin. This was definitely not my day.

My spirits were low. I had come so far and all had gone so well. What had I done to deserve such bad fortune? I had paid for the bus here in the end. And I was going to pay the owner of the hostel when I returned, honest! I didn't really intend to keep that cooker either. It was just a joke! It wasn't fair to punish me like this.

Such was the state of my weary mind as I traipsed along the now muddy trail with sunken eyes and a heavy heart.

'It just isn't fair!' I kept saying to myself.

Then purely by chance, something blue flashed into the corner of my eye. I looked down to see a blue bag lying on the side of the trail. My heart stopped. It couldn't be, I thought. I stooped down and picked up the item. It *was!*

I stood there feverishly clutching my tent pegs and yelled at the top of my voice: 'There is a god!' Then clinging on to them like a long-lost friend, I strolled on with renewed vigour. My fear now was that I wouldn't be able to find where I'd left my backpack, and would be stranded on this lonely mountain with no shelter and nothing to eat. There really had been no need to hide it. We hadn't seen a single soul on the entire walk so far. I guess the weather had deterred them. What a surprise they would have in the morning if they stumbled upon a frozen corpse on the side of the trail, with nothing but a bag of tent pegs firmly clutched between his hands.

However there was no fear of that, as Nick had made sure I wouldn't miss the spot by building an intricate wall of sticks right in the middle of the path. I found my pack behind the tree. They had thoughtfully concealed it using branches. However the snow had soaked into the wood and made a complete mess of the pack. Guess I should have told them about the waterproof cover that came with it. There was no point in putting on the waterproof trousers, I was already wet. So I cleaned off the pack as best I could, threw over the cover - which didn't fit all that well on account of the tent and sleeping mat being strapped to the outside - and started after the others.

I figured that if I sped up my pace, then I could catch up with them at the campsite. I assumed they would have lunch there. The first campsite along the trail was *Camping Seron*. The main reason we had chosen not to stop there was because of the cost. We wanted to camp wild for the night and have a fire. I had been told that other than the site at the start of the trail, no campfires were allowed. At least in the free campsites there would be no one to enforce that law.

With things the way they were, a fire would be just the thing I'd need at the end of this day.

The rain had remained and showed no sign of clearing. The temperature had dropped somewhat with it. Surprisingly I managed to catch up with Nick and Kirsten before the campsite. They hadn't expected to see me again. There was still a fair way to go before reaching the campsite, though. As we walked along Nick monitored the temperature variation with the thermometer on his superwatch. In the space of ten minutes we went from 1 degree centigrade to 6. This was mountain weather, unpredictable and fluctuating. We came back down to ground level and, after crossing a stream - fast flowing out of the mountains - by means of a rudimentary footbridge, made our way across a meadow of daisies that sat alongside a large river. It would have made a lovely spot for lunch, had the sun been out. In the middle of the field we had to negotiate a flood plain. The rangers had scattered driftwood through the area in order for hikers to cross. Once across that we walked for another half an hour until we came to a gate. A sign read:

Campamento Seron 500m.

Our relief was obvious.

Kirsten had heard about a woman who lives at the campsite who, if you arrive early enough, sells you freshly baked empanadas (pies). Saliva gushed uncontrollably from the sides of my mouth at the thought of a hot empanada. I increased my pace, leaving the others behind.

'Must get there!' I repeated to myself.

Then I spied a small wooden house by the river. Smoke emanated from the chimney. I started to run. The front window was steamed up and the curtains were drawn halfway, revealing the warm, soft flickering light of the fire inside. I reached the front door and just managed to knock before collapsing in a heap on the steps. The door slowly opened and I looked up. There she stood with a tray of piping hot empanadas, her soft black hair flowing in the wind and her big brown eyes looking warmly down at me. She was beautiful! As she knelt down I reached up and touched the side of her face, feeling the warmth of her dark skin.

'Right now, 500 metres at our pace, we should be there in about three minutes!' she mouthed.

What!

'Come on,' said Nick, 'we're nearly there. Only a few more minutes.'

Suddenly I realised I was still stood in the freezing rain, staring at the dreary field ahead.

I hate it when people interrupt my dreams.

Reluctantly I continued on. Nick was in front strolling along with his hands in his pockets, as if he was taking a walk in the park on a warm sunny day.

'Two more minutes!' he shouted back.

I grunted.

Nick always made hiking look so easy. Even on the mountains as I puffed and climbed my way upwards, he would be ahead carrying a large backpack, hands in his pockets and whistling.

'One more minute!' he shouted.

Right that's it! I thought, I'm going to kill him. I don't care if he is my friend, he deserves to die. I tried to increase my pace, but my legs wouldn't respond.

'Move faster, damn it!' I commanded.

But they wouldn't listen.

'Thirty seconds!' he said, grinning.

I tried to scream, but my voice wouldn't respond. My

blood was boiling. The sound of my squelching feet irritated me with every step. Then all of a sudden we rounded some trees to see a tiny stream with camping spots on the other side. We were there, finally.

We crossed a small footbridge and read the sign on the other side. An arrow pointing left indicating the office. It also stated that fires were prohibited. So we definitely weren't staying here. Besides, the campsite was deserted. We squelched our way along a path to a small wooden house by the river with smoke pouring out of the chimney. It was just like in my dream, but there was no beautiful woman with a tray of empanadas. Instead, framed by the window was the blurred figure of a man sipping maté. He beckoned us in. We dumped our packs down in the hallway, removed our raincoats and entered the house.

Huddled around an antique stove powered by a log fire were other unfortunate hikers. So we weren't alone on the trail after all. There was a gorgeous Chilean woman, but she was Christian's wife. Running around the room was their little boy, also named Christian. They welcomed us in and made space for us around the stove.

As the heat soared back into our bones and the colour returned to our cheeks, we chatted with our hosts. Christian and his wife lived in that little house all year round, and ran the campsite. The place was very basic, with just two rooms: the one we were now standing in, and a tiny bedroom. My jeans were drenched, so I changed into a pair of shorts and hung them over the stove to dry, finding a space amongst the abundance of socks.

'You have another pair?' asked Christian.

'No,' I answered, 'I left them back in Puerto Natales.'

He went to a cupboard in the corner and pulled out an old

pair of lightweight black trousers.

'Here you can borrow these,' he said, handing them to me, 'They are very good for walking.'

'But I might not be coming back this way,' I replied.

'Don't worry. Just leave them at the front gate and tell the rangers to send them back to me here.'

It's times like this that make you realise what kind and wonderful people there are in the world. I thanked him wholeheartedly.

'¡Ah, por nada (for nothing)!' he replied, nonchalantly.

It was amazing to think that this guy had done me the biggest favour, and quite possibly saved me from contracting hypothermia, yet he considered it nothing more than a simple matter of me needing dry trousers and him having a pair. To him it was only natural that I should take them. Even though he would more than likely never see me again, the thought probably never entered his head that I would run off with them.

The weather outside was starting to clear. Things were beginning to look up. We had lunch there and then prepared for the next stage of the hike. It had taken us around five hours to get this far. The next part was estimated at another three. My jeans had dried and so I put them into my pack and took out my waterproof trousers. I wasn't about to be caught by surprise again. They were cheap, but would do at least for now. I put them on and bent down to put on my boots. They tore straight up the middle. Just my bloody luck! I thought. Still I'd just have to put up with it.

We bade farewell to Christian and his family and left the warmth of their home just as the rain returned. The weather got progressively worse as time went by, and so did my tear. After a couple of hours we had to climb a very steep hill.

We weren't alone now. The groups of hikers from Christian's house were alternating places with us.

At the top of the hill the cold grey water of Lago Paine came into view. A chilling wind blew from it, instantly freezing the beads of sweat on my forehead. I shivered as it cut through me. I looked and felt totally pathetic. The tear in my waterproofs was making its way down one leg, the battering wind causing it to flap uncontrollably. I had no choice but to finish the job. Nick and Kirsten couldn't help but laugh at the sight of me strolling down the mountain sporting my new look: one black leg and one white; the protected leg to my windward side.

The trail now took us along the hillside that ran down to the lake. We traversed a series of trickling streams and passed trees full of green parrots, and headed for the outlet of another river, which was where the campsite was situated. After what seemed like an eternity we reached our destination. I threw down my backpack in triumph and looked around me as the other campers flicked through their nature guides in the hope of identifying this strange, wild creature that had just entered their campsite.

We pitched our tents by the stream and built a big fire. It was still raining. I climbed into my tent and was immediately engulfed in steam as my clothes started to dry.

'Jeez, it's like a sauna in here!' exclaimed Nick as he stuck his head in to make sure I was still alive.

They had both expressed their concern that I was cooking inside my tent. Yes I know it's dangerous and shouldn't be done, but I had no choice. I needed the warmth. Everything was wet, including my sleeping bag and mat. However Nick provided me with an ingenious solution.

'Once your soup is boiled, put on the lid and use the pan

as an iron to dry things.'

So for the next ten minutes more steam was produced as I slowly but effectively dried my sleeping bag.

I spent the rest of the evening attempting to dry other clothes over the fire. The rain continued on into the night. It was hopeless. My tent was leaking, condensation was soaking the insides and I had burnt a hole in my mat trying to dry it by the fire in the dark. I lay in my sleeping bag clutching a small mineral water bottle filled with hot water, and passed a very restless night, as the top and bottom of my sleeping bag soaked up the condensation from the sides of the tent. It felt like I didn't sleep at all.

In the morning the sun was out and the air much warmer. I sat by the fire - a row of hot water bottles lying next to me, each with a pair of socks rolled over - and contemplated my next move. Today was nice, but that's how yesterday started. I consulted my map. The next part of the trail took us past a glacier, then over a 1000-metre pass and along a giant ice field. I had to face facts, I just wasn't equipped for this: a thin leaking tent, an inadequate sleeping bag, the tattered remains of waterproof trousers and, worse still, a supply of wet clothes. To go on would be suicide, or at the very least, stupid. Therefore I decided to go back to the very first campsite, sort myself out and then maybe tackle the trail from another direction.

And so I embarked on another eight-hour hike back. Nick and Kirsten continued on and I said that maybe I would see them at the other end. My lack of a good night's sleep made the walk back quite arduous. However the sound of Andrea Corr's sweet voice singing in my head helped take my mind off things. I made it to Camping Seron in three hours. A good time, considering. On the way I had met a group of Israelis: two guys and three girls. Two of the girls were having a hard time. They offered to let me join them, as they had three tents. But I had just made it over that high pass and didn't fancy tackling it again.

Just past the campsite I bumped into the Canadians, two at a time. They had eventually arrived the day after me. Again I got the offer to join them and share a tent. It was tempting, but I just couldn't retrace my steps a third time. So I continued with my plan. The mountains were covered with snow from the night before. However the weather had so far remained good. The sun was beating down and I was stripped down to my tee shirt. A far cry from the day before.

It took me six hours to hike the second part of the trail. The flood plains and rivers were higher today and harder to negotiate, due to all that snow melting on the hills. I arrived at eight in the evening. I considered staying in the hostel. I could have done with a good night's rest. But it cost $16, and I was short of cash. So I pitched my tent in the campsite and spent the evening by the fire, bursting and drying my blisters over it, and then managed to get a good night's sleep.

I awoke the next morning to rain. I took a nice warm shower and then walked to the nearby hotel. As the cheapest room there cost $100 US per night, I figured they would be able to change a traveller's cheque for me. They could, but I had to go back at 1.30 pm. So I passed the time by the fire, sipping coffee and drying clothes in the rain once again. Once my money had been changed, I dismantled my tent and spent the night in the hostel for $16. I was shocked to find that for $16 they provided a bunk with no bedding, pillow or even a bottom sheet. Still, it was warm and comfortable.

I awoke the next morning feeling refreshed and ready to

embark on a new hike. I wanted to see Glacier Grey, which is part of the 14,000 square metre ice field; the third largest in the world, next to Antarctica and Greenland. After a few inquires I discovered that I could take a bus and then a boat across Lago Pehoe. From there it was a three-hour walk to Camping Grey, which was situated below the start of the glacier. I could pitch camp there and take a day hike up to the glacier. Two buses left from the hostel, one at eight and the other at nine-thirty. I had planned to take the eight o'clock one, but was talked into having breakfast with Siobhan from Ireland. Her pot of Dulce de Leche clinched the deal. This was something to which I was becoming rapidly addicted. Basically it was sweet condensed milk boiled for three hours to produce a sort of caramel. And blooming tasty it was too!

As the bus trundled up the road I realised that I had left my woolly hat back in the hostel. Not a good thing to lose, considering the changeable weather. But it was too late now.

The day was nice once again, fortunately. At the embarkation point for the boat I spotted two familiar faces getting off a large catamaran. It was the Canadian couple from the bus that first day in the park. I told them my story so far and they found this highly amusing. They thoughtfully gave me some black bin liners in which I could wrap my stuff. I thanked them, stuffed them into my pack and got on the boat.

The boat across the lake took half an hour and cost an extortionate 7500 pesos. The Canadian couple had told me that Camping Pehoe, our arrival point, was extremely windy. And how right they were. I made my way through La Quebrada de los Vientos (the valley of the winds) - an apt name - and up into the mountains that ran along the shore of Lago Grey. The first breathtaking view was of floating blue icebergs in the lake. The second was coming over the crest of a hill to the sight of the glacier in all its glory. It was like something out of a dream. Stretching off into the horizon was a giant field of jagged ice peaks. I wanted a closer look.

It took me four hours to hike to the campsite; after all it was a nice day and there was no rush. It was located on a sandy beach by the lake. Pieces of ice broken off from the larger bergs bobbed around in the shallows of the shoreline. It was surprisingly warm and sheltered here. The site was backed by tall trees that ran through a small valley and back up into the mountains. I pitched my tent and headed off for a closer look at the ice field - with a smaller pack this time.

I made my way along a rough unmarked trail that led along the lake edge and up over some rocks. The glacier was so close, yet getting to it was a lot more difficult than I had anticipated. Another couple had apparently had the same idea as me. They were stood debating whether to continue when I caught up with them.

'Well, I didn't come this far to turn back now,' I announced, and stumbled on over the sloping pebble beach.

They followed shortly after.

It took well over an hour but I made it to the rocks lining the edge of the glacier. All I had to do was climb over them. Or so I thought. I spent the next hour scrambling over rocks, through narrow crevasses and following rough trails, but each one emerged at a point where water separated me from the glacier. Finally I came to a point where I could make a very steep descent to the edge of the ice.

However it was now eight-thirty and the sun was beginning to disappear behind the distant mountains. I sat on the mountaintop and pondered my next move. I could make it down, but it would be tough. Also once the sun went down, climbing back up would be risky, and I still had to find my way down off the mountain and back to the campsite. It had taken me a good few hours to get here. With that reasoning I took the decision to return in the morning and try again. I stared down at my goal; so close. As the mist rolled in on the distant horizon I could almost believe I was in Antarctica. I had to come back.

And so the next morning I awoke early and got dressed, eager to get going. I stepped out of the tent only to discover that it had rained in the night. I hoped it wouldn't return. I had decided to hike the trail to the next campsite and make my way down from there, figuring it would be a lot easier. Halfway there I bumped into Nick and Kirsten coming the other way.

'Told you you'd never get rid of me!' I shouted, as they approached.

They were glad to see that I was all right. They had been worried, bless them. I told them of my grand plan to touch the glacier. They had just spent the night at that campsite and were now on their way to Camping Pehoe. I warned them about the winds. I intended to hike back down to Pehoe that day, depending on what time I got back from this hike. We said goodbye and agreed to meet up in Puerto Natales if I didn't get to Pehoe today. With that I continued on.

When I reached the campsite I followed a rough trail that broke out of the forest and on to a cliff overlooking the glacier. It was quite high but I felt sure that I could make it down. I set off along the rocks, and slipped up and landed straight on my arse. The rain had made the surface very slippery. I'll just have to be more cautious, I thought to myself. However twice more I slipped up; one could have been quite fatal, had it not been for a tenacious grip on my part. This was no good. If I wasn't careful I would end up a permanent fixture on that glacier. A bloodstained backpacker impaled on the jagged ice below wouldn't have been a pleasant sight to other hikers, I'm sure. I didn't fancy the idea much either. So I abandoned my mission and headed back to camp, disappointed. It was still early so I scoffed a packet of biscuits, packed my stuff and hiked back down to Pehoe to join Nick and Kirsten.

What I want to know is, what stupid idiot thought it would be a good idea to put a campsite in an area well known for its constant battering by strong winds from the adjacent valley? It was even named *Valley of the Winds*, as if that wasn't a huge enough hint. All the tents were pitched behind any form of shelter that could be found; bushes mostly. The bushes I found didn't help all that much. Although it did stop my tent from flying away, the cold air was still blown in. I spent the evening in Nick's four-season tent. It was so warm. I was very reluctant to return to mine come bedtime.

I was woken in the morning by the sound of someone walking around my tent. I opened my eyes to see the shadow of Nick pulling out my tent pegs.

'Oye,' I shouted, 'I'm awake now!'

'Good,' he replied, 'want some breakfast?'

I decided I'd had enough of freezing my nuts off in a tent and wanted the comfort of a bed. Kirsten felt the same. She had foolishly washed her hair the night before and was now suffering from a cold. Nick would have carried on forever, given the chance. But he was also quite happy to leave. He loved hiking. Stick him in the mountains with a backpack and he could walk for days. I loved it too, but I wasn't properly equipped for these conditions. Next time I would be better prepared, I hoped.

From Pehoe we took a five-hour hike over some small mountains and then over flatland. As we headed away the snow-capped Torres formed a picture perfect backdrop. The walk was quite easy in comparison to the last few days. The weather was in our favour too. Kirsten was suffering with her cold. Although she showed admirable restraint and never once complained. We had lunch in the free campsite halfway along the trail. A sign in both languages warned hikers to take care of the area. It read:

Irresponsibility is a destructive disease.
Don't let it infect you.

It had to be American. It was too perfect. On all the other signs we'd seen the English translations had been literal, and quite bad. This time it was the Spanish translation that was bad. Plus only in America could they come up with such bollocks.

The campsite was situated by a large river. The sun was shining and the day was warm. We were all stripped down to our tee-shirts. Behind us was the picture perfect backdrop of the park centrepiece: a vast array of beautiful snow-covered, glacial-peaked mountains stretching wide around the three towering granite pillars. The sky above was deep blue and the landscape stretching before us was lush and verdant. The tranquility was broken only by the gentle rush of water from the adjacent river. This was the kind of place that made you glad to be alive. I gazed over at the mountains.

From this distance they looked so serene, just shimmering there in the midday sun. You would never have believed that such a place could be so unpredictable. My heart swelled with a love for this place; this place that had put me through hell, yet given me a renewed appreciation for life and the wonders of the world.

This moment also made me realise just what a formidable force Mother Nature is. She has complete control over your life. To think she can destroy you in an instant with flash floods and raging hurricanes, but at the same time create something that can only hold you in complete awe. She has the power to make your life total hell one minute, then calm and soothe you the next. She controls the weather. On a nice, warm sunny day she can make you totally happy, or fill your life with total misery when she decides to turn bad. To view this marvellous creation of hers she had made me pay with blood, sweat and tears. I'd had to climb steep hills, battle fierce winds, rain and snow, risk my life on surfaces that threatened to slide away beneath my feet or send huge boulders crashing down on top of me. All in all, she had made me work damn hard for this reward. But to be able to stand here now, after all I'd gone through, and feel so grateful to be alive and living on this beautiful planet, made it all worthwhile. No matter how far we evolve as a race, we will always be under her control.

Isn't that just like a woman?

For the last two hours we were chased by an approaching storm. The gusts of wind were upsetting my balance and pissing me off slightly. We arrived at the main road and made our way to the visitor's centre, just as the storm hit. An hour and a half later we were on a bus heading back to Puerto

Natales. It seemed that our ticket in to the park had been a return. I had thrown mine away, thinking it was a one-way. However when I informed the ticket collector of this, he either believed me or thought it was a good excuse, and didn't charge me again. At the front gate I gave Christian's trousers to the rangers, along with a can of lager as a small thank you, and instructions for where to send them.

We arrived in Puerto Natales at ten that night. The hostel was full, but the owner offered to put a mattress on the floor by the heater.

'It is the best I can offer,' he said, apologetically.

After the past seven days, it was heaven for me. Nick and Kirsten and I had decided it would be a good way to round off our week by eating in El Rincon Tata again. I liked it. It was a quaint little place with wood décor and low lighting. Plus the food was great and the waiter bore a striking resemblance to Odd Job from Goldfinger. So I threw my bag down and headed straight out again.

Our combined smell after days without a shower meant that we had no problem getting a table. We had made a collective decision not to take one before eating because it was already late, even though we so desperately wanted to. Also if we showered then the chances were that we would not want to go out in the cold again. Besides, after seven days of living like this, you kind of become immune to it.

The waiter threw the menu over to us and we ordered a nice cold beer each, followed by a main meal, then reminisced on our adventure. I had certainly learnt some valuable lessons: always be prepared for bad weather possibly being the most beneficial. But more importantly I had pioneered the way for a new generation of hikers. I had invented my own trail. Most people hiked the Circuit, which basically circumnavigates the Torres. Others hiked the W, which starts at the first campsite, goes up to the Torres and down again, along to Pehoe and up and down a trail there, then finally up to the Glacier Grey; thus forming the W shape. My hike had led me around part of the Circuit and back again, then onto the other side and up to Glacier Grey, and back again. Therefore I decided to name it *The Pendulum*. In future when anyone asked me:

'Did you do the Circuit or the W?'

I could reply:

'Neither, I did *The Pendulum*.'

Maybe it would start a new trend.

With a belly full of good food and a few beers inside us, we said goodbye and headed to bed. Sleep was delayed for me by Willie, the hostel owner, offering me some wine. It would have been rude to refuse. Once the bottle was empty I crawled into the warmth of my sleeping bag by the heater, and slowly drifted off into blissful sleep, Kirsten's last words echoing in my head:

'Don't forget to return that cooker!'

__6__

A Patagonian Journey

Before I had left for the national park I had discovered that my notebook was missing. The realisation soon dawned on me that I had left it by the hostel computer in Ushuaia. It contained all my e-mail addresses. But worse still it contained two of the codes for my Internet banking. Instantly I e-mailed my dad to ask him to send them. Now I was back in Puerto Natales I could retrieve that mail. However when I tried to log on to my account the pass number was rejected. I tried it a couple more times, but with no luck. So I mailed my dad back and asked him to send them again. I hoped that he had just got the number wrong. I was fairly confident that no one could penetrate my account because there was a third number needed. That one was in my head, and no one dare go in there. All the same I wanted to be sure.

The Canadians had arranged the hire car for the 8th. So I had a few days to kill. Judging by their recent show of disorganisation, I wasn't very confident in that arrangement. However I was far too exhausted after the past seven days and just wanted to relax. So I figured I'd chill out in Puerto Natales until then, and if they didn't show I'd make my own arrangements. The ferry had been booked for the 10th. So whatever I did, I had to be sure I was back here by then.

Partly to ease a bad conscience brought on by Kirsten, but also because it fitted awkwardly into my backpack, I returned the cooker. Then I spent the day doing nothing much. The majority of my clothes were being washed, including both fleeces. Therefore I did that nothing much in the warmth of the hostel. The common room was warmed by an old stove much like the one at Christian's house. The reason the hostel had been full the night before was due to a large booking by a group of families. Now they were gone, along with their noisy children, and the hostel was peaceful once again. As I sat by the warmth of the stove two women from Santiago introduced me to a Chilean tradition. Fanschop is a mixture of lager and fanta orange. A disgusting thought, to say the least. But it didn't taste quite as bad as it sounds.

Two girls had arrived earlier in the day. Doris was from Germany and over here to travel and work. Claire was from Australia and had met Doris along the way. As I sat talking to Doris two of the Israeli girls I had met on the trail checked in and came immediately to the warmth of the common room. They had broken away from the others at the first opportunity. It seemed that friction had built up amongst them. Their biggest gripe being that the others showed no consideration for the fact that these poor girls were struggling to keep up with them. But now they were safely back in civilisation and all they wanted was a shower.

When they had gone Claire poked her head around the corner and said to Doris, 'Those Israeli girls aren't in our dorm, are they?'

Doris shook her head.

'Good,' she replied, and disappeared.

'What's that all about?' I asked.

'Oh, she doesn't like Israelis because one upset her in the national park.'

'In what way?'

'Well, when we arrived at Camping Pehoe we pitched our tent next to some Israelis and one of the girls went mad and started hurling abuse at us, telling us to keep quiet and that we hadn't been invited to camp next to them.'

'Right, so because of that she hates all Israelis.'

'I know,' said Doris, shrugging.

Doris had the kind of face that rarely showed emotion. She often seemed indifferent to anything you said to her. However this couldn't have been further from the truth. In actuality she had a fantastic dry sense of humour, and was quite passionate about things. She just didn't show it in her face. She was also adamant that when the drinks came and we said the customary cheers, that I look her in the eyes. She explained this when we went out one night.

'In Germany we always look each other in the eyes when doing this,' she explained. 'It is very bad if you don't.'

She never did tell me why, but further along the way I was to find out for myself.

By the end of the next day Claire accepted that she was wrong about the Israelis. She had spent all day with them and now found them both to be two of the nicest girls she had ever met. That same evening I went for a last meal with Nick and Kirsten. They were leaving in the morning for El Calafate. As they were taking the boat the week after me, the chances were that we wouldn't see each other again. I was quite sad to be leaving these two. Usually it can be quite awkward for one bloke to hang around with a couple. You often feel a bit of a gooseberry. But I had felt equally comfortable in the company of either of these two. Over the past couple of weeks we had become good friends, and had quite an adventure together too. Also I had provided them with much hilarity over my string of disasters. Kirsten had joked that I was creating these disasters for myself, in order to obtain good material for my book. I wish that was so, but there was no way I would have put myself through some of the things that had happened in the last seven days, solely for the purpose of literary gain.

We decided to try a seafood restaurant down by the waterfront. The food was excellent, although the restaurant was bare and quite lacking in character; in comparison to the last place. After the meal Kirsten returned to the hotel to pack and get an early night. Their bus left at six. Nick, ever the die hard drinker, came with me for a beer. We stopped off at the hostel to get the others, but it was just Doris who came. The others had eaten too much and were now lying on the floor by the stove, making strange gurgling and burping sounds.

We went to a nearby bar called *Ruperto*, and over a few beers Doris told us all about her job here in Chile. She would be working at a refuge in the Lake District further north from here. The refuge is run by a nun and was set up to house teenage Mapuche Indian girls who are thrown out by their families when they become pregnant. The Mapuche are indigenous to that area of Chile. Several hundred thousand Mapuche still live there today. The sad fact is that most of these girls have no idea why they are having babies. Their families do not educate them in such matters. Also their pregnancies are often a result of being raped by the older men. When the pregnancy is discovered the girls are thrown out because the family cannot afford to look after them. The girls are then taken in by the refuge and given the education they need.

The Canadians had returned the night before and after a day's convalescence we picked up that hire car. We didn't actually get around to doing that until eleven that particular morning - two hours after we had arranged. The woman in the office seemed unconcerned by this though, and even gave us a couple of hours extra on the return time. At a cost of $40 US each we got the car for two days, including insurance for driving in Argentina.

Once all the relevant paperwork had been filled out, she led us to our car. It was evident that with five people it would be a tight squeeze. I also wondered why the front headlamps were protected with a thick perspex shield. Three of us were allowed to drive the car: myself, Ewa and Susie. The girls unanimously voted for me to take the first shift. I felt it only fair to warn them that firstly I was used to driving on the left, and secondly that it had been a while since I had driven a vehicle of the four-wheeled kind.

I got in the car and then spent the next five minutes familiarising myself with the controls. That done I pulled away and drove off down the road, and then proceeded to smash my hand against the door. Having to change the gears with my right hand was going to take a bit of getting used to.

We had left a lot of our stuff at the hostel, due to the lack of room.

'Keep right!' I thought to myself out loud, as I pulled out of a junction.

I was then ordered not to voice my fears out loud by Ewa. Once on the outskirts of town the paved road ended and from then on we glided across the gravel road. I felt like I was in the Dukes of Hazzard as the car fishtailed and spewed dust from the back wheels. The reason for the headlight protectors soon became evident. The underneath of the car was being bashed by flying stones and gravel. I managed to average 80-100kph for the next hour until we reached the border crossing. Another tiny hut in the middle of nowhere. I pulled up outside and switched off the engine.

'Shit guys! I don't have my passport,' came a little voice from the back seat.

'I hope you're taking the piss,' I told Andrew.

But he wasn't. The dozy idiot had left it in his backpack at the hostel. There was no choice but to return. So while he and Ewa drove back the rest of us waited in the nearby café.

They were back in an hour. I thought it best not to ask how fast he drove. We then proceeded to have ourselves stamped out of the country, only to find that the rental company hadn't included the forms that would allow us permission to take the car into Argentina. So we had to drive into the nearby village and use the phone in the tourist office to arrange for it to be faxed through to here. Another hour wasted. However it did leave me alone in the car with Susie, who not only had the most beautiful piercing blue eyes I'd ever seen, but was also someone I was finding increasingly more interesting each time we spoke.

'Hey, do you realise that we arrive in Puerto Montt on Valentine's Day?' she announced, as she leafed through my cassettes. She then looked me straight in the eyes and smiled.

'Is that right,' I replied, meeting her gaze.

I had the sneaking suspicion that maybe she was finding

me as interesting. All of a sudden my head was filled with the romantic notion of spending four bliss-filled days sailing through the spectacular scenery of the Chilean Fjords with Susie. I could almost picture the scene: the ship sailing into the harbour at Puerto Montt on Valentine's Day, the sunlight reflecting off the placid sea water, Susie and I gliding in at the very bow of the ship - like the *Titanic* scene - her in my arms; okay maybe that bit was rather far-fetched. We would then head north together to Lake Titicaca. It was a nice dream. But would it come true?

We actually entered Argentina three hours after leaving Puerto Natales. We had filled up with petrol back in Puerto Natales, but as we approached the turn off for Cerro Fitzroy, after many hours of driving, the needle was wavering on the quarter mark. A brief look at the map told us there were no petrol stations anywhere near the park. You'd have thought that such a popular destination would have a petrol station, wouldn't you? The nearest was forty kilometres away in a little place called Tres Lagos. Therefore we had no choice but to go there. We just hoped we had enough to get us to that town.

Ewa took over the driving now. The roads were becoming worse. The gravel was piling higher and we had to zig zag around to avoid huge stones that threatened potentially serious damage to the underneath of the car. On the upside though, the scenery was incredible. A stark arid and mountainous landscape stretched out before us, changing contrast with the movement of the sun. There wasn't a single tree to be seen. Every hill and curve brought renewed gasps and exclamations of, 'wow!' from each of us. However as the sun dipped lower on the horizon, so did the needle on the petrol gauge. Yet there was still no sign of Tres Lagos.

We hadn't seen a vehicle for miles, just a desolate gravel road that never seemed to end. Every hill was driven over with the anticipation of seeing some kind of civilisation, but instead we saw only more dirt road. Things were looking extremely grim. Then hope was sparked by the sighting of a vehicle emerging over the distant horizon.

'Look here comes a car!' shouted Ewa.

Immediately everyone perked up.

As the jeep approached Ewa slowed down and we all started frantically waving for them to stop. They waved back as we slowed to a stop. All five heads twisted round as they sped past, and watched them shoot off into the distance, and disappear over the horizon once again.

'What are we going to do now?' asked Ewa.

'Just keep going, it can't be much further,' I replied, trying to sound encouraging.

Ewa crept forward again. At the brow of the very hill we were on, the glorious sight of a glowing YBF sign down below brought huge sighs of relief. This is Argentina's principal petrol company. It also triggered the realisation that we could have found ourselves in a very embarrassing situation had that jeep stopped and allowed us to relay our fears to the people inside.

We pulled up by one of the pumps, then suddenly realised that none of us had thought to change any money. All we had in our possesion were Chilean pesos. With a bit of luck they might be accepted. When questioned as to what forms of payment he would accept, the attendant stated quite firmly:

'Only cash, Argentinean pesos. Nothing else.'

Further enquiries proved that Tres Lagos had no bank. We were really up the creek. There was nothing around us for miles, and we had no petrol. What were we going to do?

'What's the problem?' asked a guy who had just pulled up with his family.

Andrew explained the situation to him. To our delight he very kindly offered to change up some of our Chilean pesos. Andrew managed to get $30 worth. We thanked him wholeheartedly and proceeded to fill up the tank. The guy was from Ushuaia and travelling through Patagonia with his family. Unlike us he was well aware of the need for cold hard cash in these parts, and had come well prepared.

It was really late now and we were advised not to try and make it to Cerro Fitzroy today. These roads were extremely dangerous to drive on at night. The sun was already setting. There was no choice but to find somewhere to pitch camp. So we filled up our water bottles and drove into town.

Tres Lagos really was a one-horse town. As we made our way up the dimly lit main street it bore no sign of life at all. It wasn't long before we were at the other side of town and back in the desert. We stopped the car and contemplated our next move. To our right was a mountain range, behind which the sun had already set. The sky was already dark blue and a few stars were beginning to show. A small dirt track seemed to lead off to the mountains. We took the decision to try and head down it and see if it led to a good spot in which we could make a wild camp. We had plenty of food and water, so why pay for one when there was miles of wild and free landscape surrounding us? So off we went. Susie was driving now; in fact it was the one and only time she drove throughout the entire trip.

The track was rough and strewn with rocks. The surrounding landscape was littered with rubbish that had obviously been blown about by the strong winds. Now I firmly believe that the odd piece of rubbish, beer can or burnt out wreck of a car lends a certain character to the desert, but this was going too far. Obviously no effort had been made to combat the effects that the ferocious Patagonian winds were bound to make on the town dump. It's a well known fact that the wind in these parts is extremely strong, and the openness means there is no shelter from it, so why had no effort been made to see that the rubbish is well contained? Equally why had no effort been made to clear up this scattered rubbish? Okay so it's easy to say, 'Why bother? It's in the middle of the desert.' But surely that should make no difference. It's near a town and therefore should be a concern for the inhabitants. The most alluring thing about the desert is its wild and natural rugged beauty. I hated to see it treated with such disrespect.

The road led on, turning off into a pass that opened out to a startling deep red horizon. We drove over and on to another dirt track that led behind the mountains. Here we pitched camp in the softness of the waning twilight, our back garden being an undulating sea of brown rocky hills. Surprisingly there was no wind and the night air was relatively cool. I decided to sleep in the car, partly to make sure no one stole it in the night (as if they would in the middle of nowhere. But you never know) and also because I wanted to see the stars, and it was the closest I could get to sleeping outside. Unfortunately it wasn't quite warm enough for that.

Fed and watered, we all settled down for the night. As I lay there snug in my sleeping bag, staring out the back window at the clear starry sky, and listening to the occasional gentle breeze whistling past outside, I slowly drifted off into blissful sleep.

I awoke the next morning to the sound of Sheila banging on the window. The sun was already up. Sheila was the only one awake, but the others soon followed; Susie being last as usual. We packed everything up and drove to the petrol station where we washed the stuff from the previous night and made breakfast. After that we refilled our water bottles and drove to Cerro Fitzroy.

El Parque Nacional Los Glaciares is a 6000-square kilometre national park that is home to almost four dozen major glaciers. The northern part is characterised by its sharp jagged peaks, one of which is Cerro Fitzroy. It's a mecca for trekkers and mountaineers. The tiny town of El Chaltén serves as a starting point for climbers brave enough to attempt the climb. For the hikers there are two trails: one that leads to the base camp for climbing the spire of Cerro Torre (3128 metres), and the other which leads to back-country campsites, lagoons and on to the base camp for Cerro Fitzroy. Due to our tight time-schedule we decided to take a short hike along part of a trail - don't ask me which. Andrew had elected to remain behind, so we gave him the car keys. Upon return he was nowhere to be seen.

When Andrew finally returned we drove to El Calafate. It was already quite late when we arrived and the town's only two banks were shut. Their ATMs wouldn't accept any of our visa cards. So once again we were stuck for money. Andrew had a little leftover from the thirty pesos and he bought some ice creams and a bottle of orange. As the girls wandered out of the shop slurping on their ice creams, Andrew went to pay and discovered that he had lost ten pesos. He immediately retraced his steps in the hope of finding it, while we waited outside the shop to assure the owner that we weren't trying to pull a fast one.

The money was never found, so once again we were in deep shit. The shop owner was pacified with the offer to keep Sheila's driving licence until we returned in the morning with the money. As we headed back to the car Andrew decided to try another of his cards in the machine. To our surprise it worked. So once again Andrew saved the day. The shop-keeper was paid and Sheila's license returned. The nearby lakeside had been recommended as a good place to camp for free, so we found a good spot and set up camp for the night.

We rose early and drove to the Moreno Glacier, situated in the southern part of the park. The road took us past the magnificent Lago Argentino. It resembled a giant mirror, perfectly reflecting the broken cloud in the sky above. The road from El Calafate had been unpaved all the way, and so was the entire national park. I would have thought that one of Argentina's most popular tourist attractions would gener-ate enough money to help pave the roads. I can understand the majority of the roads in Patagonia not being paved; the huge lack of traffic over the past two days had testified to that. But surely here in a national park where thousands of visitors come every year, they could actually pave the roads? It's not too much to ask, and would have been a lot easier on my joints.

The Moreno Glacier is equally as awesome as Glacier Grey. Unfortunately that's where the comparison ends. Glacier Grey is wild and located in a more natural setting. Trying to get to it I had not felt like I was in a national park, or even anywhere remotely touristy. I had arrived there after hours of hiking through a wild and rugged landscape. There had been no traffic, hardly any other people and certainly no car park and manmade boardwalks like the one I was now walking across.

A series of walkways and lookout points had been specially built from which to view the glacier from a safe distance. The primary reason being that the glacier is advancing. This river of ice stands 60 metres high and is periodically damming the Brazo Rico (rich arm) of Lago Argentino. The water behind the glacier rises, resulting in an immense accumulation of pressure. Roughly every four years the ice can no longer support the weight of the rising water and the glacier breaks up. The resulting explosion is supposed to be quite a spectacular sight. Unfortunately this wasn't one of those years. However in-between those periods pieces of the glacier have been known to break apart and topple into the water below. This, and the fact that it's such a popular tourist attraction, is the reason for the walkways. It is now prohibited to view the glacier from anywhere other than these boardwalks.

I made my way down as far as possible in order to get away from the crowd of people slowly gathering on the main lookout point. The tranquil sound of the water running in front of the giant wall of ice at the front of the glacier was broken only by the occasional loud crack and thunderous boom of breaking ice from within the glacier itself. A giant field of jagged ice peaks soared up high into the misty mountains. I found a nice secluded spot and enjoyed the view, uninterrupted.

We were running extremely late. The car was due back at 2.00 pm today, so I figured we ought to get going. We drove back to El Calafate, fuelled up and bought some food, then started back. It was already 1.30 pm. The road was paved for about an hour and then we had to turn off onto the gravel roads once again. It had been raining, and a good part of the road was still wet. The resulting spray coated the entire car with mud. The inside was becoming quite hot too, so Sheila turned on the air conditioning. Two days of accumulated desert dust was blasted in our faces.

As I drove down the road, trying to maintain a relatively fast, yet safe, speed, passing cars would flash their lights at me. I thought it was a greeting, but the others seemed to think they were telling me to slow down when I passed them.

'Why?' I asked, 'They don't slow down for me.'

Cheeky gits, I thought.

Another flashed.

'You fucking slow down!' I yelled out the window, a case of road rage beginning to set in.

I think the others were becoming slightly worried that I was losing it. Especially when the car fishtailed.

Still we made it back to Puerto Natales safe and sound, albeit three hours late. The woman in the rental office didn't seem concerned by this, though. Nor was she bothered about the state of the car. She then quoted a price much cheaper than she had originally.

'But wasn't it supposed to be...' the outspoken person being immediately shushed by the others.

However her suspicion had been aroused by this obvious shushing. Soon she remembered the fax and the fact that we had taken the car into Argentina, and the price went up.

Back at the hostel we sorted out our stuff. We didn't have to get on the boat until ten that evening. We ate in the hostel and then relaxed. Suddenly I remembered I had to sort out my Internet banking. My dad should have sent through those codes by now. I had phoned him the day before we started our journey with the car because he hadn't replied. The twelve-minute call had cost $12, and most of it was spent waiting for the time delay. My dad had been answering my previous question after the current one. Despite this I had managed to explain the situation to him and he agreed to send them again, so I headed off to the Internet café around the corner. It was nine o'clock by this time.

The codes were there. It seemed the reason I couldn't get in was because he had inputted the last two digits wrong on one of the numbers. I sifted through my other mail and then logged on, with the correct numbers this time, to confirm that all was well. The system crashed and cut me off. I re-entered and tried again. My password was rejected each time, and the system kept crashing. I came very close to putting my fist through that screen. But instead I dashed off to a nearby restaurant that also had Internet access.

Time was ticking. I had to catch that boat. Impatiently I waited for the slow process of logging on, then proceeded to access the site. Just as my password was being processed the connection was lost. I reset the connection and waited. Once logged on I punched in my details once again. Still the system wouldn't allow me in. Up popped a cocky little dialogue box in the middle of the screen that read:

You have entered your details incorrectly.

'No I fucking haven't!' I yelled back.

Spoons were dropped in shock, and silence filled the room as the diners all stared at the deranged madman shouting obscenities at a computer screen. Realising I was making a spectacle of myself, and that I was getting nowhere slowly, I logged off, paid and rushed back to the hostel.

The others had already gone. New arrivals began questioning me about the Torres del Paine. This was all I needed.

'How was it?' asked one of them.

'Great, we spent seven days hiking,' I replied, whilst hurriedly stuffing the remaining things into my backpack.

'Is it difficult?'

'Very. And the weather is unpredictable. Four seasons in one week,' I answered, impatiently.

I hauled on my backpack.

'Did you do the Circuit or the W?'

'No, I did *The Pendulum*.'

I took one look at their confused faces and decided that there wasn't time for an explanation, and headed out the door. I thanked the owner for his kindness and dashed off down the road. I was in a very bad mood by this time.

I passed Andrew and Ewa and they directed me to wait in a large portakabin crammed full of people and baggage. The others were sat across the room. I couldn't get to them because of all the backpacks strewn across the floor. Susie turned and waved. I waved back, attempting a smile, but I was too wound up. I had to try and calm myself down, so I took my stuff and went back outside so I could smoke a cigarette and hopefully chill a bit.

It didn't work. A strong cold wind blasted in from the harbour and cut right through me. There was no shelter from it either. I finished my cigarette and re-entered the warmth of the cabin, found a space on the floor and sat cross-legged with my head hung low. I was seriously worried about my accounts now. What if someone had hacked in and changed the codes? For all I knew they could have been slowly emptying my savings account. Ten o'clock had come and gone and we still hadn't been allowed to get on the boat. I was tired and pissed off and just wanted to get on that boat, dump down this load I was carrying and drink a nice cold beer.

___7___

A Welcome Return to the Warmth

We hadn't got on the boat until midnight. Even then we'd had to queue for ages to get on a large platform that had taken us up to another level, only for us to go back down again to our cabins. We were in the economy section: cramped compartments containing a number of bunks in the depths of the ship. To get there we'd had to negotiate two flights of very steep and narrow stairs. The bunks however, were quite big and some even had a curtain to pull across for privacy. Mine only had half a curtain for some strange reason. I wanted to pull the curtain to the middle and sit back to back with someone, while watching through a small gap to see the reactions of passers-by as they saw two sets of legs emerging from either side.

Joe, my roommate from way back in Mar del Plata was on the boat. So was the Irish girl I had met back in Torres del Paine. Siobhan quite obviously possessed the gift of the gab because in the space of a few hours she had talked her way out of economy and into one of the upper cabins. Upon return to her cabin that night she discovered cockroaches clambering over her toothbrush, and by the next morning had been upgraded once again to a $300 cabin behind the bridge of the ship. I suspected that by the end of the voyage she would have the captain's quarters, while he slept out on deck.

We had remained in port during the night and set sail first thing in the morning. I was rudely awakened by the sound of winches clanging and whirring as they pulled in the mooring lines. The winch room must have been right next to our compartment. The entire dorm was vibrating and at first I thought we were sinking.

Fully awake now, I looked at my clock and realised that there was only five minutes left before breakfast ended. Throwing on some clothes I sluggishly made my way up to the top deck. I wandered into the main cafeteria and was informed that the animals in economy ate down below. This section was for the upper class cabins. So I made my way downstairs and stepped into a tiny room crowded with people. It was a bit like being in the brig. We queued up with a tray and had our meal scooped from a large pot by an overweight man in a dirty chef's outfit, who just grunted when you thanked him.

The weather outside was looking very grim. The ship was making its way through a narrow waterway riddled with tiny islands. The offshore mountains were enshrouded with mist, and it was far too cold to sit outside and enjoy the view. Our ship was clearly not designed to run as a passenger liner. It had quite obviously been modified for this purpose. Apart from the sleeping compartments, the only other place to go was the main cafeteria, which also contained a bar and a seating area in front of a television. The windows were too high to see out of from a sitting position, and therefore you had to stand. The ship's onboard entertainment's manager couldn't have arranged a blow job in a brothel. Over the next few days we had one game of bingo, a small selection of videos from his private collection - most of which were very bad copies - and a school disco.

Two sets of small disco lights were provided for this occasion, and the mirror ball above the reception area was turned on. The seating was adjusted to create a small dancefloor. The music was then provided by CDs or cassettes, with no apparent DJ. It was like a game of musical statues, everyone having to stop dancing and wait for the next song to start. Each of us had brought boxes of wine on board in anticipation of the bar being quite expensive; much of which was consumed this night.

Up until now my interest in Susie hadn't really been pursued. Mainly because of the close proximity of the others. In the few times we had been alone we seemed to get on well. She was quite funny. But she was very much a part of that group. I, however, had always felt like an outsider with them. Don't get me wrong, I got on very well with all of them and thought them great people. But we just didn't seem to have all that much in common. I think it was mostly to do with the age difference. They were all in their early twenties. Also they had been travelling together for so long and had fallen into the habit of doing everything together. I am very much a solo traveller and more often than not make my own decisions. I don't like travelling in a large group. I find it too restricting. Your every move has to be discussed with the others. I don't like having to discuss, or even plan, my next move with others. I prefer to just drift my way along, fluttering from place to place and joining up with various people who happen to be going the same way, and then parting when our journey takes us elsewhere.

However, the group was splitting up upon arrival at Puerto Montt. Both Andrew and Ewa were heading back to Paraguay and then home. Susie had already told me that she wanted to hitch northward, and Sheila didn't want to hitch. Therefore Susie would be going alone, or would she? We had already hypothetically discussed travelling northward together.

My main concern was with our age difference. She was twenty-three. However she often appeared much older than that. But the whole situation had been a bit strange. I couldn't quite make it out. Sometimes there had seemed to be a real spark between us, and other times real awkwardness. I figured it was time to find out whether or not this could actually go any further.

The music was pumping and I was sufficiently loaded with alcohol to combat any nerves. Susie was sitting by the dancefloor. It was now or never. So I strolled up and casually asked her to dance. She happily obliged and I led her out by the hand and we started to dance. The moment of realisation came like a punch in the mouth. Our moment had been lost way back there on the vast plains of Patagonia. In that relaxed atmosphere we had been able to talk freely about anything and begun to warm to each other. Yet here on the dancefloor, with loud music pumping in my ears, I could hardly hear a word she was saying, and just couldn't make conversation without having to shout and propel saliva into her ear. It was so undignified. The situation was very awkward and when the song ended we went our separate ways.

Thus I sought consolation in another carton of wine and soon found myself performing unusual dance moves underneath the mirror ball. Siobhan was there also, looking equally as drunk. Soon we were both slumped in the corner speaking a strange dialect of English that only others with as much alcohol coursing through their veins could possibly understand. I ended up staggering to Siobhan's room along with some others. A good thing really because it would have been suicide to try and climb down those stairs to my bed in the condition I was in.

Her room contained six bunks crammed three at a time into a tiny compartment. Our two other companions climbed into theirs with relative ease. Siobhan had the bottom bunk next to the bathroom. There was about a one-foot gap between the two. You had to be a contortionist to get into it. As we squeezed in and settled, a voice from the darkness ordered, 'Do it quietly!' in a Dutch accent. He had nothing to worry about, we were both far too drunk to do anything had we wanted to. I soon fell asleep but awoke during the night in desperate need for the toilet, and proceeded to fumble around in the darkness and climb into the cupboard before eventually finding the bathroom, which was right next to the bed.

I awoke to the feel of the ship rocking about quite vigorously. We were now out in open sea. People kept making surprise entrances in the hope of catching Siobhan and I up to something. But each time they found us just talking. Finally we emerged to another bleak day and a choppy grey ocean that matched our complexions. I left Siobhan talking to someone and headed off to get some warmer clothes.

I found Susie downstairs suffering from seasickness. Things would never be the same between us now, I realised that. I had got myself into a hell of a situation and was stuck for the next two days on a boat with nowhere to hide. Was there any hope of salvaging things with Susie, or do I pursue things with Siobhan now? I liked Siobhan, she was funny and great company, but I fancied Susie more. It was a hell of a dilemma and I just wanted to crawl into a corner and hide from it all.

The lack of people at dinner testified to the amount of sickness onboard. I wandered up to the main area and found everyone just sat around with bored expressions, drifting in and out of consciousness while their brains slowly decomposed. The weather was bad and the entertainment's manager had once again lived up to his reputation and done bugger all. Most people had nothing to do but wait for the next meal. Eventually a video was put on and everyone crowded around the television.

No party was laid on that night. Obviously the stress of arranging the one the night before was enough for our entertainment's manager. Instead he just put on the occasional video. When he went to bed we broke into his little cupboard, damaging the door in the process, and raided his video collection.

I tried my best to focus attention on Siobhan for the rest of the trip, but just wasn't comfortable with the situation. I felt guilty every time Susie was near. But there shouldn't have been any reason to. Nothing had happened between Susie and I. Or had it? Did we really make a connection back in Patagonia, only for me to screw it up whilst under the influence of too much wine? Did she like me, or was it just wishful thinking on my part? If so then she must have thought me a complete bastard for now being with someone else. But I preferred her! Such was my confused state of mind.

For the third day of the voyage we had glorious weather. The events of the past few days had drained me of all energy. I hadn't slept properly due to an overactive mind, and was feeling very lethargic. And on top of that the floor of our dorm had somehow been flooded and once again my pack and everything in it was soaking wet. I had no way of drying anything out. Was there any end to my bad luck?

I wandered up deck and found everyone scattered about the roof soaking up the sun. No sun loungers or deckchairs had been provided, so people just lay and sat wherever they could. Because of the good weather the captain had stayed out in the open ocean in order that we could get to Puerto Montt quicker. The route should have taken us through more of the Chilean Fjords. Instead we passed the large island of Chiloe and were docked in Puerto Montt by six.

The crew gave us the choice to get off now or spend the night on the boat. I wasn't happy about this at all. I had paid good money for a boat trip through the Chilean Fjords. The idea was to take a leisurely trip to Puerto Montt, not get there as quick as possible.

The thing was that this boat was also used by Chileans as a mode of transport. Families and truck drivers were onboard and, quite understandably, were happy to arrive early. But I was not. I had paid $200 in the belief that this would be a relaxing cruise, not to spend two nights in port. Quite frankly I felt ripped off.

Susie was going to Chiloe with Jen, who had joined us from the hostel back in Puerto Natales. Siobhan was going with them and wanted me to come too. That wasn't a good idea. Plus I'd had enough of being in a group and wanted to head off in a different direction. So I made the decision to head northward. I had no idea where though.

I sat at a table and discussed the options with Frank from Canada. He was going that way too. North of here lay the vast landscape known as Valle Central (central valley). It is littered with volcanoes, lakes and national parks. It's also known as the Lake District. I had pretty much decided to go to Villarrica and relax for a couple of days by the lake. We had left behind the cold climate of the south and were now back in the warm. After all those weeks of cold I was glad to be feeling the warmth of that sun again. All I wanted was to lie down on a beach and let the sun purge the cold back out of my bones.

However that plan was put on hold for a while when Frank mentioned a place called Temuco. This town is a centrepiece for Mapuche culture, and houses a huge market of arts and crafts. I had been in South America for six weeks now and had seen nothing of the indigenous people. One of the things that draw me to this part of the world is the Indian culture. I was sorely disappointed that there were none in Tierra del Fuego. Like many children of my generation I grew up watching westerns. My trip to Mexico had been like going back in time. I had visited dusty pueblos that were a scene right from the Wild West. Men in stetsons and barefoot Indians still wandered the streets wearing traditional clothing. Not so long ago the Indians were the masters of these vast plains. Ferdinand Magellan had first arrived at Tierra del Fuego to the sight of Indian campfires flickering across the landscape; hence his inspiration for the name, Land of Fire. That is how I imagine South America: wild and indigenous.

And so it was I found myself sat next to Frank on a bus to Temuco the next morning. Siobhan had tried her best to convince me to go to Chiloe, but I was determined to head northward. I had made such a cock-up of things on that boat and felt that it was best to make a clean break. Siobhan wanted to know my itinerary so we could meet up somewhere along the way. But I don't believe in itineraries, it takes the adventure away from it all. She was beginning to despair at her inability to get a straight answer from me.

'Do you have any plans?'

'I don't make plans.'

'Can we meet up sometime?'

'I don't know.'

'Well, when will you be in Santiago?'

'I've no idea.'

'Are you going there?'

'Not sure.'

And so it went on.

The bus pulled in for a break at one of the towns along the way. Frank and I ventured out for a bite to eat. It seems that the words *form an orderly queue* have no meaning in this country. I stood patiently while others before me placed their orders, then began to mouth my request.

'A packet of cigarettes please,' interrupted a little old lady.

Being a well brought up fellow, I allowed this old lady to go first.

'Right now, I'd like...'

'A bottle of coke,' interrupted a short, fat kid, already slurping on an ice cream.

In the interests of foreign relations I resisted the urge to accidentally knock his face into that ice cream with my elbow as I turned around.

'Right now, I'd like a pa...'

'A Magnum please.'

This was becoming infuriating.

'A packet of biscuits, please,' I shouted, forcing my way in front of the short guy in a suit who was about to interrupt me again.

And so it was I learnt how it's done in Chile. Now if I did that at home I'd soon find myself wrestling that person down the aisle. But here this is the way it's done, and therefore the other guy graciously accepted defeat and waited.

One thing Chile is, and that's enterprising. As I returned to the bus I found a guy stood by the door with a large coffee machine strapped to his chest.

'¿Café?' he asked.

'How much?' I replied.

'200 pesos.'

Well why not, I thought.

I got back on the bus with my steaming cup of coffee and we resumed our journey northward.

Frank and I discussed the boat trip. He wasn't happy at all with it. He had been one of the other occupants in Blaithin's room and had therefore paid $300 for his cramped bunk. The beds in economy had been roomier, as he had seen for himself. Even the showers down below were roomier than the private one they had. He felt ripped off too. Personally I hadn't expected a luxury cruise, but all the same didn't feel that it had been worth $200. I was just glad I hadn't opted for the so-called upper class compartments.

We arrived in Temuco five hours later and made our way to the hostel. Frank had been travelling around on a bicycle, but now had a problem with it. Fortunately he had been able to load it on the bus. He wheeled it along as we made our way through the crowded streets of Temuco. This definitely felt more like South America to me: people swarming around on whatever mode of transport they could find, and rickety old minibuses chugging and banging their way through the streets. The city had a certain roughness around the edges that gave it charm and character.

We passed a large Indian market loaded with fruit and veg and other local produce from the nearby rural communities, and made our way up Rodríguez Street in search of Residencial Temuco. I found the street number but no sign outside, just an old man sat on the doorstep. A local assured us this was it, so I rang the bell. The door miraculously opened of its own accord. We both hesitated for a moment, slightly spooked by this strange occurrence, and then cautiously poked our heads inside. At the top of the stairs stood a middle-aged lady beckoning us both up. As I turned and closed the door I discovered her very neat trick: a piece of string tied to the latch, which ran up the banisters.

María Eugenia, as she introduced herself, was a short, middle-aged lady who carried an air of grace and charm about her. She was the owner of Residencial Temuco, and couldn't have been more helpful. She had this amazing ability to know just when you needed something. I would be stood in the kitchen scratching my head as to where the cups were, and she would appear from nowhere and ask, '¿Qué necesitas joven (what do you need, young man)?' And soon my question would be answered.

Her place was actually a hotel affiliated with Hostelling International. Therefore we got a room with just two beds, and no large dorm full of loud snorers or couples having sex in the bunk above. All for the bargain price of ten dollars each. It was the ultimate in luxury, even down to the toilet having a cushioned seat. María allowed me to hang my wet clothes on her line and provided us with much information about the area. I was going to like it here.

Mercado Municipal was the town's main artisan market. It contained row upon row of stalls cluttered with Mapuche clothing, musical instruments and shelves full of wood-carved ornaments. Mapuche men stood around them blowing into horns and banging on tribal drums. I didn't buy anything. My trip would end in Bolivia, and things there would be far cheaper.

The market also contained an abundance of food stalls, outside each of which stood an eager woman trying her best to drag you in. We wandered around until we found the best deal. I decided to try the delicious looking *pastel de choclo*, which is a large pie filled with an assortment of red meat, chicken, onions and egg. However all that was surrounded by a sickly sweet pastry, which I ended up pushing onto another plate. The rest was washed down with a nice cold beer.

The next morning we took a bus out to the neighbouring Indian village of Chol Chol. It was nice to be able to get the shorts back on again. We were dropped off in a dusty life-less plaza in which stood a lone kiosk, the odd person sat on a bench and a couple of passing children. The children were intrigued by the two pale gringos who had just got off the bus and were now standing in the street looking totally lost. A couple of them whizzed shyly past on their bikes, shouting their only known word in English, 'Hello!' We questioned a passing policeman as to whether the village had a market or something. There was nothing. However he directed us to the Mapuche Cultural Centre. This turned out to be a small hut with three Mapuche women inside selling a small selection of artisans. They did give us a map of the area and directed us to a nearby town called Nueva Imperial. This didn't look like the sort of place to fill a day, so we caught the next bus there.

On the outskirts of town we crossed a wooden bridge that took us over a small valley. Children played by the shallow stream that meandered off into the surrounding countryside. It was beautiful. It seemed we had been a little hasty in our judgement of this place.

For some unusual reason we didn't have to pay the fare until we reached our destination. The old bus chugged and rolled on along the bumpy road, past fields full of local farmers. The produce was being taken into town on an old-fashioned two-wheeled cart pulled by two oxen and guided by Mapuche men fanning themselves with a large stetson.

Nueva Imperial was much livelier than Chol Chol, that was for sure. However, once again there was no market. But I was content to sit on a bench, have lunch and watch the local life.

After a while I left Frank and went for a wander around town, trying to capture some of the life on camera. I wandered past a group of youngsters, one of which greeted me in English. It turned out that Marcelo had lived for three years in Fiji and studied English there. He spoke it very well. They were all on holiday from Santiago, and had been staying with a couple of girls from here. The holiday was now over and they were waiting to catch a bus to Temuco and then a train to Santiago. Marcelo gave me his phone number and said that if I come to Santiago I should get in touch and we would all go out and drink Joté, the local drink of red wine and coke. I was intrigued to say the least.

On the bus to Temuco they were sat at the back playing guitar and singing. It was almost like being in the sixties.

Since Pinochet's two-decade reign of terror most Chilean people have experienced a renewed sense of freedom. One of the results was that more people were travelling. Many young Chileans were actually backpacking around their own country, something we never think of doing. We all want to go elsewhere. But although they are curious about other countries, they are also curious about their own. And rightly so, for they live in a beautiful country with much diversity. I actually wished I had more time to explore it more in-depth, but I had plans to fulfil elsewhere in the world. One thing for certain, I would definitely be returning someday.

Back in Temuco I decided to buy a new notebook to replace the one I'd lost in Ushuaia. I wandered into a stationary shop for a look around. Everything was stacked on shelves along the walls. In front was a long counter obstructing any access to the items. I was therefore forced to stand at the counter and view from a distance. A smiling young girl soon blocked that view.

'Can I help you?' she asked.

I explained what I was looking for and after many different items had been plucked off the shelf, I found what I wanted. She tore off a scrap piece of paper and wrote something totally illegible on it, then handed it to me and, keeping hold of the item I wanted to buy, directed me to a nearby kiosk. At the kiosk I was asked to pay and then given a receipt. As I stood there, receipt in hand and looking confused as to what to do next, the guy pointed to the adjacent kiosk where another smiling assistant waited. I handed my ticket to him just as the young girl arrived with the notebook I was purchasing. She handed it to the guy behind the

139

counter, who in turn handed it to me. I thanked him and walked out of the shop.

'And just what the fuck was all that about?' I said, to no one in particular.

From here on in this was to be a common custom in Chile when trying to buy anything. Frank pointed out that it created more work for people. But at what cost? For the mere price of a tiny item like a notebook, three people were employed to help me make that purchase, when the whole thing could have been done by the first girl in a lot less time and would no doubt have cost less than the book. It was all quite mind boggling. The other thing I had noticed here was their love for paperwork, the one thing everybody hates back home. In most supermarkets you were given a full computer printout for a receipt. Many times I had attempted to sneak off without it, but was immediately called back by the girl at the till waving it in her hand shouting, 'Don't forget your receipt, sir.' The most amusing thing so far was when I received a receipt for an ice lolly, which had cost me a measly 100 pesos.

All said and done though, at least things were a bit cheaper here. I intended to remain in Chile for the duration of my trip to Bolivia, and stay out of Argentina. Not because I didn't like it mind, I loved it, but money was getting tight. Bus journeys here were cheaper. The five-hour trip from Puerto Montt had cost a mere $6. A similar journey in Argentina had cost double that. Also accommodation was less. My other concern was that hopping back and forth across the border was filling up the pages of my passport. Each time I crossed a border I would obtain two new stamps, one for leaving the country and another for entering. So far four pages of my passport had been used for this purpose.

We spent the evening in the Plaza de Armas. Another smaller market surrounded this. I wandered around and was surprised to find a stall selling pots made from a cow's udder. The teats had been used as the legs while the surrounding skin had been dried and hardened to make the outer shell of the pot. It's quite possibly the most bizarre thing I have ever seen. And not something I was keen to purchase. The rest of the stalls were selling more sensible things like stationery, jewellery etc.

That night Frank left on an overnight bus to Santiago. His place was taken by Richard from Canada. Richard had just come from Villarrica where he had taken a hiking tour to the summit of its currently active volcano. He told me that it was forbidden to hike the trail without a guide, due to the amount of ice and snow at the peak. A tour cost $40. I wasn't about to pay that, especially as I'd already hiked an active volcano in Hawaii. I was interested, but not enough to part with $40 at this moment in time. Besides, as Richard pointed out, you were lucky if you got a good view inside the crater due to the amount of steam and cloud. But the upshot of it all was that you get to slide back down the ice on your back, using a pickaxe as a brake. Now that sounds like fun.

Richard had started his trip with a friend from back home. They had travelled through Brazil together and had the most fantastic time.

'Ah man, the girls are so friendly there,' he said with a revealing smile.

A similar story I had heard from many a sexually satisfied male on this trip so far.

By the time they had arrived in Villarrica Richard was fed up of travelling with the same person all the time. He expressed his desire to go off on his own for a while, much to his friend's dismay. Richard explained that he had tried his best to convince his friend that he would soon meet others and have a great time again. Travelling alone is a lot more fun than people realise. It's a lot easier to make friends when you are alone. Richard said that his friend had reluctantly accepted his decision. Even so, Richard was feeling a bit guilty about it.

'Don't worry,' I reassured him, 'he'll soon meet others and wonder what all the worry had been about.'

Richard agreed.

8

A Bloody Big Volcano

A huge snow-capped volcano rose high in the air and dominated the landscape ahead of me. I was now sat in a bus heading back southward. In my haste to go to Temuco I had unwittingly shot past Villarrica. It was right there on the map, as big as day, and it just didn't click that maybe I should have gone there first. However the trip was only an hour and a half, so I felt sure I'd get over it.

Upon arrival I hauled on my backpack and headed for La Torre Suiza, a hostel recommended by Frank. I was in a much happier mood now, as my bank had informed me that my accounts hadn't been tampered with. It seemed that as I'd entered my pin number incorrectly three times in a row, this had disabled it. I now had to set up a new account.

As I approached the front gate, so did a tall, thin starched-looking man with glasses and a moustache. He opened the gate for me and I thanked him. He said nothing, just stared at me with a wry smile. I walked on and he followed. I turned to look at him. Again he said nothing.

'Do you work here?' I asked.

He nodded.

'Well, how much is it?'

'4000 pesos for a dorm.'

I eyed the tent over in the corner.

'Can I camp?'

'Of course,' he replied. '2500 pesos.'

'Right, I'll camp then,' I decided out loud. 'Can I pitch my tent anywhere?'

'Yes, except on my car.'

This was going to be an interesting place.

Beat and his wife Claudia owned and ran the hostel. They both came from Switzerland and were accomplished cyclists. They had ridden in many countries around the world, and the many pictures hung around the hostel testified to that. Despite his unusual behaviour at the entrance Beat had actually proved to be quite a nice bloke, just as dry as the Atacama Desert when it came to humour. Of all the places they had been to, they loved this the most and returned to start up this hostel. With the arrival of their newborn it would be a while before they undertook another long cycling trip.

With my temporary home erected I trotted off to indulge myself in the totally selfish need to lie on the beach and do nothing but soak up that sun. However halfway down I realised that I needed desperately to do some washing. I popped my head in the nearby laundrette, but they wanted 3500 pesos. So instead I bought a small packet of washing powder for 250 and did it myself in the outside sink at the hostel. As I soaked and scrubbed the clothing under the running water, Beat stopped by, cocked an eye and warned: 'Don't waste water!' This was something he was most concerned about, judging by the many signs posted around the hostel. The rules were one shower per day, per person. In an area with such an abundance of lakes, I wouldn't have thought water shortage to be a problem. Or maybe he was just tight?

I finally made it to the lake to catch the late afternoon sun. The lakeside was crowded with holidaying Chileans. Children swam in the shallows of the deep blue water as the huge shadow of the volcano on the other side of the lake loomed across the water. I found a nice quiet spot, laid down and put on my headphones to drown out the noise of the kids, then spent the next couple of hours doing nothing else except work on that so far non-existent tan. I'd waited a long time for this, and bloody earned it too.

That evening I sat outside in the hostel garden and dined on two-minute noodles and bread rolls. From now on I was cutting back on expenses. It was so nice to be back in the warm again. In the distant darkness I could see a flickering red glow emitting from the crater of the still active Volcán Villarrica. The town lies on the western side of the huge Lago Villarrica. So the town, the volcano and the lake were all called Villarrica; a distinct lack of imagination on some-one's part, I'd say. On the eastern side of the lake lay the town of Pucon. This was reputed to be even more touristy than Villarrica, due to its closer proximity to the volcano. From there left the guided tours that would take you up to the 2847-metre summit. Quite a sight I should imagine. But I stuck to my desire to save the forty dollars.

I was soon joined by Jason and Klaus. Klaus was from Germany and cycling around the Lake District. He was the owner of the tent next to mine. Jason told me he was from Canada and, up until recently, had been travelling with a friend from home. However they had split and now gone their separate ways.

'I'm not bothered anymore, I'm having a great time without him,' he told me.

'His name isn't Richard by any chance?' I asked, the story sounding extremely familiar.

'Yeah, how do you know that?' he replied, a look of total surprise having just appeared on his face.

'I just left him in Temuco.'

This did come as a surprise to Jason because when Richard went he left a note saying he was going horseriding with a girl he'd met.

'Well he was alone when I met him,' I replied.

Guess it didn't work out.

We sat and discussed many things, including the relationship between Canada and the US. The majority of Canadian backpackers travel with a Canadian flag sewn onto their backpack. Some say it's so other Canadians can identify them, and others say it's because they do not want to be mistaken for Americans.

'Some Americans are so arrogant,' said Jason, 'I met this one guy and we had an argument about how America is so much better than Canada. He said to me, 'Hey man, we can annihilate you in *five point three seconds!*' 'Huh! You couldn't annihilate me in five minutes!' I said, 'let's go round the back and see who can annihilate whom!''

He wasn't taken up on the offer.

That night was the first I had spent in a tent for a long time where I wasn't freezing my nuts off. I awoke in the morning and poked my bleary eyes outside to the sight of grey sky and rain. For a split second I thought I was still down south. Bang goes my lazy day on the beach, I thought.

I had got up too late for the hostel breakfast, so had to

make my own. Klaus had already packed away his tent ready to set off, when it started raining. So he decided to stay one more day in a dorm. Jason was off to Pucon today to cancel his river-rafting trip. As the rain had spoiled my plans to lie by the lake all day, I decided to take a short walk along the lakeside instead.

I followed a rough trail past a group of locals camping wild, and into a forest. Soon I found myself in swampland. I remained there for a moment, staring out across the now grey lake. The mighty Volcán Villarrica was barely visible through the thick mist that coated the horizon. Yesterday it had been a prominent feature of the landscape. It must be amazing to live near such a spectacle. Imagine having a soaring snow-capped volcano as the view from your back garden.

The weather was getting worse so I decided to head back. I emerged from the undergrowth and followed a back-road. A group of children were playing further down the road. As I approached I felt something on my hand. I glanced down to find a wasp crawling over it. I shook it off, then felt one on my neck. I swiped it, then turned my head in time to see a huge swarm about to engulf me.

'Holy shit!' I shouted, and broke into a sprint, arms flailing in the process.

The group of children screamed and dispersed rapidly in all directions as I ran straight through the middle of them, bringing this swarm of wasps with me. Fortunately I managed to escape unscathed.

After another warm night's sleep I awoke to discover I had fifteen minutes left before breakfast ended. I threw on some clothes and wandered scruffy and bleary-eyed into the common area where I was helped to my seat by the people already sat there, and given a strong cup of coffee.

Sitting across from me were the blurred figures of a couple from Santiago. They both worked for one of the Chilean newspapers. We soon got on to the subject of Pinochet. It seemed that many of the Chilean people were tired of it all.

'He is old and will soon be dead,' said the guy, 'we all just want to forget about it and get on with our lives.'

They believe that he is already suffering because he believed that he was untouchable wherever he went, but that was proving to be untrue. He is running out of places to hide. Life under Pinochet was total hell for a lot of people. They were never allowed to express an opinion or challenge anything. If your neighbour suddenly disappeared you were not to question it. Today they have the freedom they were denied for a long time. But old habits die hard and still the people are not used to standing up for themselves or voicing their own opinions. Change will be a slow process for many of them.

Also at the table was a middle-aged German couple. They had been out to a festival on Easter Island. The guy suspected that he might have picked up psychic powers whilst there. More like he'd picked up some local fever that was causing delirium.

The sun had returned today and so once again I spent the day on the beach. Upon return to the hostel I found Jason sitting with a very attractive Dutch girl. Nathalie smiled and offered me some coca tea. She had recently come from Bolivia and had with her a bag of coca leaves. Although it was illegal to bring them into Chile, she had managed it by feigning innocence at the border.

'Oh I'm sorry, I didn't know you weren't allowed to bring

them in. I just use them for tea.'

'You're from Holland, no?'

'That's right.'

'Okay, go on,' replied the customs officer with a grin.

I discussed with them my plans to go hiking in a nearby national park. Jason was leaving for Santiago that night. However Nathalie was keen on the idea and agreed to come along. Just north of nearby Pucon lay the Parque Nacional Huerquehue. A hiking trail leads through a series of lakes and up over a mountain, ending at a campsite near some hot springs. Just the tonic we'd need after all that hiking. I figured we could hike it in a day. We could travel northward from there. Nathalie only had a week before she flew back to Holland, so she would have to make her way up to Santiago from there.

So the next morning I got up early, much to the surprise of the others at breakfast, and packed up ready to go. Nathalie and I had discussed our strategy the night before. We stocked up with food and then caught the bus as far as Coroillo. From there we took a minibus to the entrance of the park. At the minibus we met Emily and Holger, who were about to embark on the same hike as us. Naturally we joined forces. Emily was from London and over here for a short trip only. Holger was from Germany and travelling around in-between studies. They had both left most of their stuff back in Pucon because they planned to hike back. Nathalie and I had everything, my pack being the heaviest. Nathalie's was so light I began to wonder what was inside.

The packs were loaded on the roof and we were taken to the park entrance. It was well into the afternoon by this time. At the northern end of the first lake was Camping Olga. Its owner was stood at the entrance touting for business. We decided to pitch camp there and start the hike first thing in the morning. The campsite owner led us down a narrow track to the lake edge. He explained that he usually takes people over by boat. However once all the packs were loaded there was no room for us, so we had to walk.

We found a nice little sheltered spot and pitched camp. Emily and Holger had a one-person tent each. Together they looked like a whole tent cut in half.

'That looks like a good tent,' I said to Holger.

'Yah of course, it is German!' he replied, with a sardonic grin.

German people have a wonderful sense of humour, so unlike their stereotype.

We spent the afternoon swimming in the lovely clean water of the lake and lazing on the beach. In the evening I built a fire - a skill I'd perfected with the aid of Nick - and we cooked our meals. We then played musical chairs round the fire as we ate, to avoid the line of smoke. We were blessed with a full moon this night and ventured down to the beach. The entire lake was bathed in a sea of liquid silver, and the volcano was once again glowing in the blackness of the distant horizon. It was beautiful: a perfect setting. We stood and gazed at the picture perfect scenery for a while before heading off to bed. We had an early start the next morning.

'Ian, Ian,' whispered the soft angelic voice in my head.

'Hmm… Yes dear what is it?'

'It's six o'clock,' said Nathalie.

'Uh!'

I awoke to the realisation that I was still in my tent and not on that desert island with Andrea Corr.

'It's six o'clock,' repeated Nathalie.

'No it's not.'

'It is, look,' she said, showing me her watch.

I didn't hear the alarm, I thought.

'It can't be, it's still dark. Your watch must be wrong.'

'No it's not!' she insisted.

Now that I was heading north the days were getting shorter. I was used to waking at five to blue sky. I fell back to sleep. The sun came up at seven. Even then I couldn't get up. Neither could Nathalie. Eventually we heard Holger moving and we unzipped the tent and poked out our heads. He was sat at the opening to his tent rubbing his eyes.

'What happened to six o'clock?' he asked,

'It was a bit dark,' I replied.

We wanted to tackle the hardest part of the trail before the heat of the sun set in. We had some breakfast and watched the morning mist rolling over the lake, then set off around nine. The first part of the trail wound its way up into the mountains from 750 to 1000 metres. From each viewpoint the volcano dominated the scenery. You couldn't have got away from the bloody thing if you tried. It was pretty tough going with the full weight of my pack. Holger, being only twenty and having hardly anything in his pack, was always up front. Once again I was at the back, closely superseded by Nathalie; who I felt hung back mostly for moral support. After all the hiking I had been doing things should have been getting easier. I was getting fitter, but was also increasing my load each time and tackling harder trails. How stupid am I?

After an hour and a half we passed the shimmering Lago Chico and then came to Lago Verde. We must have spent over an hour there. It was so beautiful. The area is dominated with the strangely named Monkey Puzzle Tree. The branches spread out and bend and twist into all sorts of shapes, making it resemble a maze. That explained the puzzle, but where does the monkey part come in? It was quite obviously beyond my cranial capabilities to figure it out, so I trudged onward trying not to let it occupy my thoughts too much.

From there we passed another lake and then took a steep climb up to a plateau lying at 1320 metres. Here we branched off to see the disappointingly muddy Lago Huerquehue. It seemed strange to think that the national park was named after such a dismal-looking lake, when there were others so much nicer.

The sun was high in the sky now, and I was knackered. After a short rest we continued on. The trail now led out of the forest and along the edge of a steep valley that rolled off across a landscape scattered with fallen trees and dry wood. Without the shade of the trees the going was extremely hot. Also we were making our way downhill on a trail made mostly of gravel. The weight of my pack was forcing me down faster than I wanted. I was constantly in danger of losing my footing. Our halfway point and planned lunch spot was the refugio. As I stumbled and slid my way downhill we soon re-entered the shade of the trees. Shortly after that we broke out into a clearing where stood a rotting hut that we could only assume to be the refugio.

We selected a nice shady spot and had lunch. I removed my pack, and collapsed gratefully on the floor. It was now three in the afternoon. A group of passing hikers had informed us that there was one more 250-metre climb then it was all downhill from then on. I wasn't sure which was better. The descents with the pack were proving quite difficult.

What made it worse was the terrain being so dry and gravely. Still we had got the worst part out of the way. It shouldn't be much longer now.

We made it a short lunch and then set off. The climb was made in the full heat of the sun. The heat was making me short-tempered, and each slip of the foot was met with a stream of profanity. Once over the pass the trail led continuously downhill until we came across a farm. We approached the gates to the sound of two barking, snarling dogs. This had totally unnerved Holger - who up until now had been the first to jump to his feet and encourage us to get moving again - and now he was stood at the gate hesitating. However we had no choice. The trail led through the farm and there was no other way round.

During my entire trip so far I had encountered many barking dogs. However in my experience they are all bark and no bite. When I had been taking a walk in Ushuaia once, I was spotted by a huge white dog. The instant he saw me he came bounding down the hill barking and snarling. I didn't move, feeling that running would only excite him the more. He came right up to me, skidded to a halt and then just sat there while I stroked him. So with that in mind I figured these two ahead of us were more than likely just warning their owners of approaching hikers, and so I encouraged the others to go on. Holger remained at the back this time.

As I suspected they never bothered us. After another two kilometres we thankfully arrived at the campsite. The one thing that had kept us going was the thought of soaking our aching muscles in the hot springs. So with extreme impatience we all made camp and made for the pool. The springs had been piped through to the campsite pool.

As I gently lowered my body into the piping hot water,

each aching muscle sizzled with delight. It was like taking a huge bath. A carton of wine was cracked open and we celebrated our victory over the mountain. The only thing missing were the bubbles. However I felt that after the wine had been consumed there might well be a remedy for that problem.

9

<u>Nathalie</u>

The truck sped along the dirt road, the four of us clinging on to whatever secure object we could find. The track rolled out ahead of us like a sea of huge rippling waves. Enquiries at reception had proved that the nearest form of civilisation was 40 kilometres away in the town of Cunco. We were now sitting on the back of the owner's pickup, huddled together against the back window while our legs fought to find a space amongst the pile of backpacks, luggage, a pot plant and a very funny middle-aged Chilean woman called María. The others were seated on two large bags, while I sat one cheek on the wheel arch and the other suspended in mid-air; Nathalie's shoulder proving to be very supportive indeed.

We arrived at Cunco in very high spirits, mostly thanks to María's joking. The Lake District has a very large German population. For this reason the local delicacy is the German cake known as kuchen. We had seen many signs advertising this, but strangely no one had any left when we enquired. So we went off in search of some here while we waited for the bus to Temuco. We split up, tackling different places each, but all came up empty. Very strange!

Holger and Emily had decided against hiking back and planned to get the bus to Pucon from Temuco. Nathalie and I planned to take the overnight train to Santiago. There wasn't a whole lot of difference in the price, and I fancied a change from the bus. So once in Temuco we exchanged e-mail addresses and headed off in different directions. The train wasn't due to leave until nine that evening, so we bought the tickets, put our packs in storage and headed off to spend the day in Temuco.

We bought some food and relaxed in the plaza. We found a nice spot on the grass, removed our shoes and eagerly licked our lip in anticipation of our upcoming feast. However this was delayed somewhat by the approach of the park attendant informing us that he was about to turn on the sprinkler system, and could we move. We gathered our stuff and headed for the next section of grass, which was already wet. We tried the next. Wet. So we tried the final section. This was dry, so we positioned ourselves in the sun, lay out our food and began to eat.

As we ate the sun was suddenly obscured by an overweight gypsy woman. I looked up to see her staring hard-faced at us. She then plonked herself down and leaned forward, her unwelcome display of an unsightly large and droopy cleavage suddenly suppressing my appetite.

'You two are lucky, I can see that you are going to have good fortune come your way. You pay me and I will read your fortune,' she told us.

Or at least it was something to that effect.

I politely refused her offer. So she shoved her hand out to me.

'I said no,' I repeated.

'Moneda!' she insisted.

Again I said 'no', but with a stare that hopefully conveyed to her that her presence was no longer required. As she was about to open her mouth again, the park attendant approached.

'Let me guess, the sprinkler system?'

He nodded.

Grateful for the distraction we gathered our things and started to walk, closely followed by our gypsy woman who was beginning to get a bit aggressive in her demand for money. It's times like this that I wished I knew some rude words in Spanish. But Instead I just ignored her and kept walking. As we walked on she shouted something at me, which I can only assume was either an insult, or she had just put a spell of bad luck on me. With all that had happened so far on this trip it seemed I already had one, so one more wouldn't make much difference. Therefore I replied with the international hand-gesture, made behind my back, that she could go stick her ugly mug in her own bubbling cauldron.

We eventually found a spot where we wouldn't be bothered with the sprinkler system, and passed the rest of the day discussing places for me to go in Bolivia and sharing opposing views on the nearby art gallery. Nathalie was a Graphic Designer and quite naturally had attended art school. Therefore she was quite appreciative of the paintings on the wall, while I thought that most of them were a pile of crap. How can you pass off something that looks like an inflated version of your four-year old's first painting as an expensive work of art? It's something I don't, and possibly never will, understand.

*

Up until now I had been impressed with the quality of the public transport here in Chile. That is until we approached the train waiting on the platform. It looked more like it was bound for the scrap heap, not preparing to whisk passengers northward to the nation's capital. We boarded, found our seats and then sorted out what we needed for the overnight trip before hauling our packs into the overhead rails. The upside was that the seats were wide and spaciously arranged for plenty of legroom. We removed our shoes and stuck our feet up on the seats in front. Then we spent the next few hours talking endlessly about all sorts of things. I was finding Nathalie to be a very good and easygoing travel companion. She was very funny and would constantly take note of my English slang and my pronunciation of *water*, using it whenever she felt that I wouldn't understand her.

Peaceful sleep on the train was inhibited by the constant stopping and getting on and off of the passengers throughout the night. We should have arrived in Santiago at nine the next morning, but were delayed until eleven. I don't know what the problem was, but we kept stopping for long periods on the outskirts. Nathalie was going on to Valparaiso, while I had planned to stop in Santiago. However not only was I enjoying Nathalie's company so much, but also didn't have the energy to face a city after a long night on a train without sleep. So I decided to go with her.

After a short rest and something to eat, we boarded a bus and were in Valparaiso two hours later. I had been recommended the *Hospedaje Juan Carasco* by Frank back in Temuco. It was a good choice, although the walk to it made me doubt that at times.

Valparaiso is a port town, and also Chile's second largest

city with over 100,000 residents. However the opening of the Panama Canal in 1914 caused a massive downfall in the local economy because most shipping began avoiding the treacherous Cape Horn route. Now its main industries are food processing, mining and fruit exports; and of course it's an important base for the Chilean Navy. Thankfully it hadn't surrendered to tourism to keep the economy afloat, like neighbouring Viña del Mar.

We trudged our way wearily through the traffic-choked streets. It was funny to think that only a couple of days ago we had hiked for eight hours over a mountain, but were finding a short walk to the guesthouse much more difficult.

Valparaiso sprawls its way from the waterfront and up into the surrounding cliffs. Once away from the centre the area turns into a maze of narrow, winding cobblestone streets, occasionally bursting out to a magnificent view of a harbour littered with giant container ships. After asking directions we made our way to the guesthouse by means of a large circle, only afterwards discovering that we could have avoided it by taking the flight of steps we had passed much earlier.

Juan Carasco was in a large ornate building situated in a dead end street perched high up on the hill. Once again there was no sign on the front to indicate it was even a guesthouse. The door was answered by a smiling old lady who ushered us in and proceeded to show us the rooms she had available. We chose the twin at the back for 5000 pesos each. There was ample space and the two big double windows allowed in plenty of daylight. The old lady gave us a rundown of the facilities in very long and slow sentences. I wasn't sure if this was for our benefit, not being fluent in Spanish, or that she talked that way normally.

Nathalie and I were so exhausted from the journey that all we managed to do that day was drop our laundry off, buy some food and cook it in the guesthouse kitchen. One of the other guests was a Frenchman. Jean-Marc was waiting around in the hope of getting a ride to Easter Island with the Chilean Navy. They were due to leave in three weeks time, but the families of the officers were to get priority over him. Therefore he would have to wait until the last minute to see if he could go. The entire trip would cost him around $200 and take about a week. His plan was to travel across the South Pacific islands, but he wanted to do it totally by boat. The idea being that to truly experience the romance of the South Seas then you had to cross it by ship, just like they used to in the old days. I couldn't agree more.

The old lady had told us that the guesthouse has a rooftop terrace, which provides a fantastic view of the surrounding area. I decided to check it out that night. So whilst Nathalie got ready for bed I ventured up there. With both pairs of jeans in the wash I had no choice but to wear my shorts. I put on my fleece, figuring it would be quite cold up there, and made my way up the stairs looking like a complete American tourist.

On the top floor I found a small set of stairs leading up to a small room with a sofa, a bookshelf full of reading material and a set of table and chairs, all with a window view of the sparkling harbour lights. I noticed a ladder leading up to an open hatch, so I climbed up and emerged onto the terrace to a full panoramic view of the harbour and city lights. Patio chairs had already been laid out. I sat down, lit a cigarette and immersed myself in the sights and sounds of the surrounding city. Not many hotels provided this for ten dollars a night. In the distance I could see the flickering lights of

Viña del Mar: a playground for the rich Chileans, and also a preferred home for the more affluent citizens of Valparaiso. I for one didn't have much interest in seeing it. As far as I was concerned it would be no different from Mar del Plata.

The next morning Emily arrived. I had told her about this place and she decided to come check it out. Holger had gone off cycling. She spent a good part of the day sleeping while Nathalie and I took a walk through the city's many hilly streets.

The next day we all took a bus down to a place called Isla Negra (black island), so-named by the famous Chilean poet Pablo Neruda. It's situated 80 kilometres south of Valparaiso. However the name is slightly misleading, it's not an island. Pablo Neruda built a home here along the beach. Looking out from his window, the black rocks lining the beachfront gave him the illusion of being on his very own desert island; hence the name. However I wondered what he would make of it now. His home had been turned into a museum housing his entire collection of bowsprits, nautical instruments, ships in bottles and hundreds of other memorabilia he had collected from his travels around the globe. Each day flocks of tourists pour into town to visit his place.

For five dollars each we got a personal guided tour by a thin, blonde-haired woman with a strong South African accent. It was the only way to see inside the house. Pablo Neruda had this house built in the shape of Chile. The interior was designed to resemble the inside of a ship, as he considered himself a *marinero de la tierra* (sailor of the land). We were guided through a room full of statues and art from all around the world and up some steps into one of his bedrooms. We stepped through the door into a giant room with polished wooden floors and a king-sized double bed situated at a forty-five degree angle. It faced the rear of the room. The two adjacent walls had been constructed entirely from glass. The bed looked out to the golden, rocky beach being pounded by choppy waves coming in from the sparkling ocean. It was perfect. What a view! This is my kind of place, I thought. So open and free. I fell in love with it instantly.

'I'll take it,' I said to our guide, as I stood staring out the window in awe.

Unfortunately for me it wasn't for sale. Oh well, I couldn't afford it anyway. Maybe one day though.

Once the tour was over we were allowed to spend as much time as we wanted on the grounds or go to the beach. We chose the beach. We returned to Valparaiso late that afternoon. Unknown to us at the time there was a hostel at Isla Negra. It would have been nice to spend the night there.

Emily was due to fly home the next day and Nathalie the day after, so we went out for a goodbye meal. Café Turri, at the upper exit of Ascensor Concepción, is reputed to be the best place to eat, and also offers a panoramic view of the harbour from your table. However it proved a bit too expensive for our meagre budgets, so we found a more appropriate restaurant. We were seated upstairs in a room full of arty pictures of topless women plastered all over the wall. The food was good and the prices very reasonable. A much better choice all round.

Nathalie woke me early the next morning so we could watch the sunrise over the distant cliffs from the terrace. Emily went straight to the airport and we left for Santiago shortly after. Nathalie knew of a hostel called Scott's Place. We walked to the main road and hopped on one of the many large yellow local buses. We then clung on for dear life as the driver hurled the bus through the streets at a speed not too far off from breaking the sound barrier. It seemed that these buses ruled the roads here in Santiago. Any cars had no choice but to swerve out the way, if they wanted to live. We were going so fast that we overshot our stop and had to walk at least 500 metres back.

Scott's Place was located in a residential area outside of the city centre. We were ushered in by his assistant Claudio and were soon sipping tea and chatting with Scott himself, who turned out to be American. He told us of his plans for Chilean domination, of the environmentally friendly kind. His grand plan was a massive project that would build and link up thousands of hiking trails throughout the Lake District. His most ambitious plan was to build an entirely new town that would be totally environmentally friendly; of which I'm sure he would be Mayor.

Scott was an extremely nice guy and would go out of his way to help, but he struck me as a bit of a control freak. He gave us a guided tour of the hostel and outlined the rules. Water was to be boiled and put into thermos flasks, so as not to waste any. When we showered we were to wet ourselves down, turn off the water, soap up and then rinse, with as little wastage as possible. When washing our hair the process was to be repeated. The pantry was full of food. We were welcome to help ourselves to anything we wanted, but to note what we take, add it up from the price list on the wall and note it on the board out front next to our name. Upon departure it would be added to our total bill. The best part about all this was that we didn't have to do our own washing up. Scott instructed us to put everything into a big green container and explained that one of the staff would wash everything when it was full, to save on hot water.

Scott had married a local woman and they now had a one-year old daughter. The little girl was running around the hostel as Scott scooped her up.

'Meet the future president,' he announced, beaming from ear to ear as she stared at us with snot running from each nostril.

He went on to boast as to how intelligent she was and that she never cried.

'From the day she was born she has been as good as gold,' he explained.

He waffled for ages about her many great accomplishments in her one year on this planet.

'She learns so quick, knows exactly what she wants and how to tell me,' he said proudly. 'She's so smart.'

If she's so smart, I thought, then why is she still sitting in her own shit?

A slightly overproud father, I think.

Klaus, the German cyclist from Villarrica, was staying at the hostel. He was due to fly home the next day also. We brought each other up to speed and then headed out to a nearby park for a walk. It was a warm night and the streets were full of children playing. This is something you rarely see back home. Most children are locked away after dark for fear of weirdoes and perverts hanging around. Obviously this wasn't a problem here. I wondered why that was? Was this country free from that sort of thing? Or was it just that there was less hysteria about it? Families sat on their front doorsteps watching them and talking to each other's neighbours. It was almost how I remembered my own childhood. My mother would be chatting with the neighbours while we all played. We knew the people that lived around us. Nowadays we are all so absorbed in our own lives that we don't have the time for others. When I was a child people didn't have all the things that we have now. Everybody is immersed in the delights of the modern age. So much so that we lock ourselves away for fear of others seeing and trying to get what we have. We are wary of strangers and tend to stick in our own little safe circle of friends. At night we pull the curtains for fear of prying eyes.

I wondered what the people of these lesser-developed countries would think if they saw this. They would undoubtedly think we were all so well-off: a nice house, a new car or two, new TV and video, state of the art stereo and our very own home computer. To them we would appear to be basking in prosperity. But for a lot of people it's all a glossy surface really. It's a fake prosperity. How many of these people actually own these things? If you looked beyond the surface you would probably see a pile of debts and a family slowly being torn apart by the stress of having to work all hours to make those repayments. They live under constant fear of losing their jobs and having all they own being taken away. Their lives are being controlled by the banks and finance companies that give them all this money. All for material gain. The whole thing is all about image. Everyone wants to be better than the next man, or feels that he ought to have these things to keep up with his friends. The more money they earn the more things they want, and consequently the more money they can borrow. Thus the competitive streak that has fuelled the prosperity of the country has boiled over into our everyday lives. The burning question is, is it really worth it?

However walking through these streets I seemed a million miles away from that. Children played on old bicycles and the families sat on rickety old chairs in front of their homes. Now Chile is by no means a third-world country. There is a major difference. But it was almost like England was twenty years ago. I hoped they wouldn't lose the little things that many of us have lost along the way. Mind you saying that, I'll be the first to confess that I'm only talking about my own experience in the south of England. Perhaps it's different elsewhere? Some tell me it is up north. But I have never seen anything of my own country. Something I plan to remedy sometime in the not too distant future.

With that thought in mind, we all returned to the hostel and turned in for the night, our sleep being hampered by the future president crying her eyes out in the next room.

Nathalie woke me at 9.30. She was a great alarm clock. Over the past week she had constantly threatened to pour water over me in a bid to get me up in the mornings. This wasn't my strong point. Any thoughts she had about making this a parting present were inhibited by the fact that others were in the dorm. She sat on the side of my bed talking to a Dutch couple in the next bed, as I shook the sleepiness from my head and rubbed my eyes.

Nathalie was leaving today. The realisation hit upon me that I didn't want her to. I was enjoying her company and could quite easily have travelled the rest of the way with her. But her time was up. She had been travelling for five months, starting in Ecuador and making her way down here. She had been on quite an adventure, and had a lot of guts in my mind. For a girl to travel alone for five months in South America was quite brave: and good for her too. But as she explained, you just have to trust your instincts.

Upon her arrival in Ecuador the plane had been diverted due to the eruption of the volcano near Quito. She had therefore arrived somewhere else at night and didn't quite know where to go. In the airport she was befriended by two local men who expressed their concern over her wandering the streets at night looking for a hotel. The men, two brothers, insisted that she come and stay at their house for the night, after they had seen off their friend; which was their reason for being at the airport. Nathalie went with them. Now you could say that was a very stupid thing to do. After all, Ecuador is reputed to be one of the more dangerous countries in South America. She didn't know these men and was alone with them. Who knows what could have happened? But Nathalie explained that her instinct told her that these two were good people. Nothing about them seemed to suggest there was an ulterior motive. They were two kind and extremely considerate men who just wanted to help her, nothing more. Quite simply she felt that she could trust these two, so she took them up on their offer and spent a great night with them and their family, and gained an insight into the life of an Ecuadorian family. A perfect start to her trip.

We had breakfast with Klaus before he left, then spent the day in the city. Santiago had the cheapest Internet access in all of Chile. Whilst e-mailing I received a new message there and then. To my surprise it was from Tom and Donna - from way back in Buenos Aires - telling me that they were in Santiago at the moment. Instantly I mailed them back and told them where I was staying. It seemed that they were planning to move to that hostel today, so I would see them later. I looked forward to it.

Nathalie bought some presents for people back home and then we wandered off in search of a coffee. As the food is often expensive in coffee shops we bought something in the panadería around the corner and tried to sneakily eat it when the waitress wasn't looking. Although when she brought our coffees she laid out a couple of serviettes in front of us. Guess we weren't all that sneaky.

'We have to leave each other,' said Nathalie, as I sipped my coffee.

'Don't,' I replied, 'I hate goodbyes.'

This was one I really wasn't looking forward to. And it seemed that Nathalie was feeling the same way too. In our week together there hadn't been any romance. I don't know why that was. I did quite fancy her. But there had been no spark of romance, until now. In our week together we had developed a strong friendship that could, I felt, have grown into something more. In the past week we had hiked a mountain together, camped rough and taken a fourteen-hour ride on a cold, noisy train that afforded hardly any sleep. But through all that we had never argued, always understood each other, laughed a hell of a lot and had many great conversations. Never before had I known such a perfect travel partner. I was going to miss her.

I wanted to buy her a little something to say goodbye, so while she was buying some bread I shot off to a nearby shop to buy her a bar of chocolate to eat on the plane. I had to be quick before she started wondering where I had gone. Due to an illness she'd had a while back, she couldn't eat sugar. I relayed this information to the assistant, who then showed me the ones they had. I chose one and shoved the money in his face. He calmly told me to go pay at the cashier. Bloody stupid rules, I thought to myself as I dashed over and joined the slow moving queue. I paid the man, snatched the receipt from his hand and rushed back to get the chocolate. He hadn't even got it out from behind the counter. He took my ticket, smiled and casually made his way to the rear of the counter, removing the chocolate and asking me if I wanted a bag.

'Forget it!' I replied, grabbing it from his hand and rushing back out into the street.

I found Nathalie standing there looking around for me.

'Oh, I thought maybe you left because you didn't want to say goodbye,' she said as I approached, her face lighting up when I showed her my reason for disappearing.

The Chilean system for purchasing something can be quite frustrating at times.

A few hours later we found ourselves trotting along the road to the bus stop. Nathalie had given away a lot of her stuff and now carried a pack that was lighter than her daypack. To me she had given her bag of coca leaves. Quite naturally she couldn't take them home with her, especially flying into Amsterdam. As we stood at the bus stop our intimate moment was made rather awkward by the constant interruption of an approaching bus. We had to check each one to see if it was hers. Plus the large backpack made it difficult for me to put my arms around her. Time was ticking and there was no sign of the bus. The airport was a long way from the city. She was beginning to worry. Eventually she had no choice but to take a taxi. I flagged one down and we loaded her stuff in the back. With an impatient taxi driver watching us we kissed goodbye rather quickly and sloppily. Not the perfect ending I had hoped for.

As I trudged off down the road back to the hostel, Nathalie's bus came hurtling around the corner. It seemed we had been waiting at the wrong bus stop.

Back at the hostel I sat outside and smoked a cigarette. It started to rain on me, a good reflection of my mood. I finished my cigarette and wandered moodily into the dorm to get my packet of two-minute noodles for dinner. Ellen, one half of the Dutch couple, entered as I was about to leave. She spied the noodles in my hand.

'What are you doing?' she asked.

'I'm about to have dinner,' I replied.

She snatched the noodles from my hand and tossed them across the room. 'You are not eating that rubbish!' she snapped, 'You will eat with us.'

I didn't feel I had much choice.

'Well if you insist,' I replied, silently chuckling to myself.

After dinner we played a crazy game with a bunch of other guests and then I got slowly drunk on wine as I chatted with Tom and a few others outside. My spirits were once again lifted.

It's hard to remain sad when you're on the backpacker trail.

___10___

The Long Walk Home

I had to get up early the next morning. I promised Tom and Donna I would have breakfast with them before they left. They were making their way over to Rio de Janeiro for the carnival. A friend had offered them a flat for a couple of weeks while he went away.

'Come with us,' they said, 'you can stay at the flat, it won't cost anything.'

It was a thought. But I was bound for Lake Titicaca and this would be quite a large diversion. Plus the travel fund wasn't all that plentiful. But it was a tempting offer: lots of partying, alcohol, gorgeous girls and lots of sun and sand. On the other hand: lots of money, hangovers, AIDS, and sand in places you never knew you had. The one downside to the beach is that after a day working up a sweat by basking in the heat, and running in and out of the sea, you often end up walking away looking like a sugared gingerbread man. And no matter how hard you try you can never get it all off, and it stays with you for days afterwards. So after weighing up the pros and cons, I declined their generous offer.

I planned to head north to a town called Copiapó. The journey would be long and taken overnight, so I spent the day here in town. I decided to go visit the city cemetery. Unexpectedly I got a personal guided tour by Edgar, one of the security guards whom I had questioned as to the whereabouts of Salvador Allende's grave. I was wandering in the direction he had sent me when I heard a whistle blowing. I turned to find him running after me. He then proceeded to take me there personally, and also on a tour of the graveyard itself.

It's enormous, and the architecture is out of this world. The family burial tombs are more elaborate than houses - some even resembled mini cathedrals. The tomb for Salvador Allende stood as high as a house. It was a featureless slab of rock - quite unfitting for one of Chile's former presidents - that towered high above the rest. It was shaped like the head of a pitchfork. At the base was a raised platform. Inscribed on the tomb just in front were the words:

SALVADOR

ALLENDE

GOSSENS

1908 - 1973

The rest of the tomb was blank. I couldn't understand this. I had walked through row upon row of elaborate architecture to get here, and it wasn't a patch upon the rest. According to the guidebook his grave was visited by many pilgrims, so he was obviously a well-revered man.

He was elected president of Chile by a narrow margin in

1970. During his time in office Allende brought about many social reforms, which benefited the poor immensely. He increased the speed of land reform, breaking up large estates and giving land to poor farmers. He nationalised many businesses, and also froze prices, raised wages, subsidised milk, and made medical care and education available to children.

However this nationalisation wasn't met with approval by all. The US government opposed his socialist policies and began discouraging new private investment. I had also read that the CIA secretly sent $10 million to Chilean groups that opposed Allende. The resulting pressure and Allende's policies contributed to problems in Chile's economy, which suffered from high inflation. The country was also suffering from food shortages.

On September 11th 1973 his government was overthrown in a violent military coup led by Augusto Pinochet Ugarte. During the coup Allende was offered safe exile, but chose to remain in the presidential offices. The offices were attacked and besieged by Pinochet's troops. Allende was found dead, riddled with bullets. Official reports state that Allende committed suicide, but many assert that he was assassinated by the invading soldiers. What followed then was two decades of military rule under Pinochet.

Edgar led on down a lane containing the graves of all the ex-presidents. Further along we passed the grave of the Pinochet family and ended at the memorial for the people who had disappeared under General Pinochet's two decade reign of terror. Edgar and I shook hands and parted company here.

In front of me, rising high and stretching wide, was a giant wall commemorating all the people who disappeared during the dictatorship. The wall was full. There were over two thousand names. Either side of this memorial stood the graves of the few that were actually found. At least their families could mourn them properly knowing what had actually happened, and that they were truly dead. It was pretty certain that all the others were, but without a body you cannot actually accept this for sure. Never knowing the truth behind what really happened must only serve to increase the agony.

Before coming away I hadn't really paid much attention to the situation with Pinochet. I had heard snippets on the news, but was far more preoccupied with other things to really care. But after travelling here and experiencing the immense kindness and friendliness of the Chilean people, it was hard not to care. It was quite shocking to think that this monster had butchered all those innocent people. The man was a cold-blooded murderer and should be treated as such. He should be made to pay the price for what he did. If not for the people whose names I now stared at, then for their families and friends. I longed for the day when his name would be added to the Pinochet grave in this cemetery.

On that sour note I left the cemetery and wandered back down the road to the city centre. I was in the northern part of the city. It was quite rundown in comparison to where I was staying. The bottom of the road was abundant with flower stalls. Ambitious hawkers were mobbing the approaching cars of grave visitors in an attempt to drum up some business.

I got myself a can of coke from a nearby machine and sat by the river. Santiago is situated on the Río Mapocho. It was a pitiful excuse for a river. What water was running looked extremely filthy. Strewn along the northern side of the river were row upon row of market stalls. The area south was much more inviting, with beautiful plazas and interesting architecture, so I decided to take a walk through there. I finished my drink and threw the empty can in the bin. It went straight through the bottom and bounced across the pavement. I peered inside to see the entire bottom of the bin was gone. Sharp jagged edges were all that remained. It almost looked as though the bottom had been blown away by a bomb. Further investigation revealed that all the others were the same. I wondered what it was all about?

I took a walk through the area just south of the river before returning to the hostel. Later that evening Scott was visited by a friend who owned a research station down in Antarctica. It was a non-profit organisation that studied survival and the impact of pollution. He was looking for someone to work down there voluntarily on a six-month project. It would involve collecting and analysing the litter that washed up on the shores of the peninsula. The collection would be made once a week and analysed in-between. He said it would be during the winter months, therefore you would be pretty isolated. The only other people to talk to would be in an Argentinean base a few miles away. Even if you could walk there, what would you talk about?

'Hey guess what guys, some lovely rubbish washed up today!'

Six months as a dustman in Antarctica, I must admit I've had better offers.

Sitting on the bus that night I realised that I had forgotten to get in touch with Marcelo. A pity, it would have been interesting to have tried that Joté. But there was nothing I could do about it now. By morning I would be 800 kilometres north of Santiago, and I'll be damned if I'm going back just for a drink. My travel companion was Lawrence from La Serena, a town halfway between Santiago and Copiapó. He told me he was a Fishing Engineer. Further enquiries proved this to be someone who monitors and controls the area's fishing, to make sure everyone gets a fair chance and that the stocks are not depleted.

Chilean buses always have an onboard steward. On the few buses I had taken so far they had come round every now and then with a snack or a tray of sweets. Our steward for this overnight bus came in and formally introduced himself, welcoming us aboard and laying out the itinerary for the evening; all this being done with the zest of a Sergeant Major drilling his new cadets. First of all we were going to play a game of bingo. Now I can honestly say this is the first time I've ever played bingo on a bus. Still it was a good way to practise my numbers in Spanish. One game was played - rather hurriedly, it seemed - with no apparent prize, and then the boards were whipped away from us. He then marched down the aisle handing out blankets and pulling the curtains. I hate that. Closing the curtains always makes me feel hemmed in. I like to see the outside world go by. So I reopened mine.

We hadn't been going all that long and already we were in the desert. The Atacama is the driest desert in the world, stretching 363,000 square kilometres and forming the majority of northern Chile. Although, we weren't quite there yet. The section we were entering is called Norte Chico (little north) and is a semiarid transition zone from the Atacama to the Valle Central. It's also known as the region of 10,000 mines. The land is rich with copper and nitrate and most of the cities owe their existence to at least one of these minerals.

One of the things I love most about the desert is that it's the greatest place in the world from which to view the stars. The Southern Hemisphere contains more stars than the north. I remember once I was camping in the outback of Australia, near to Ayres Rock. Our tour group was sat around a roaring fire, slowly digesting the contents of a huge barbecue. As the evening progressed people trotted off to their tents, eventually leaving me sat there with just a few Danish guys. The fire had burned down and was now a large mound of glowing coals set against the most awesomely bright starry sky I'd ever seen. The stars were so prolific that it was hard to make out any of the constellations. This image will always represent the desert in my eyes.

As the bus rolled on into the night, I sat and stared at the starry sky. The headlights of the bus cast a small pool of light, dimly illuminating the desert sand as it whizzed past the window. Large shadowy sand dunes stretched off into the distance. All I needed now was my Doors tape to perfect the moment. Unfortunately that had mysteriously gone missing whilst camping back in Tierra del Fuego, along with another. I still find it hard to believe that someone would break into my tent and just steal two cassettes. But nothing could be done about that now, so instead I put on my Sarah McLachlan tape and drifted off into a mild state of euphoria. That is until Sergeant Major came and closed my curtains again. Git!

I was rudely awakened in the morning by a sharp shove in the shoulder. I prised open my eyes to see a roll being held under my nose. I took it and was then passed an empty cup. It wasn't even light yet. I sat up and allowed the cup to be filled with coffee, then looked out the window at the approaching lights of La Serena. Lawrence had got off way back to visit friends before heading home, so I now had the two seats to myself. I was beginning to get used to sleeping on buses. Normally I sleep very badly, but once Lawrence had got off I had been able to curl up on the two seats, wrapped up nice and snug in a blanket.

I unwrapped my breakfast, bit into the roll and was left with a mouthful of plastic cheese and dry bread. I needed the coffee to help it slide down my throat. We still had quite a few hours to go before arriving in Copiapó, so I forced the rest of it down and returned to slumberland.

The bus pulled in to Copiapó at eleven. I disembarked and made my way to the tourist office where I obtained a map of the town. The guidebook said that there was a hostel in Juan Antonio Rios Street. When questioned as to whether the hostel was still in business, the girl behind the counter pulled a face that resembled a squeezed out teabag.

'There is no hostel there,' she replied, in a loud voice that was directed partly at me but also as a question to her colleague who was busily typing away in the corner.

'No, there is no hostel there!' replied the other girl, spinning around on her chair to emphasise this fact.

'No there is no hostel there,' repeated the first girl, just in case I hadn't quite understood.

'Are you sure?' I asked.

They both nodded.

She then shoved a handful of leaflets in my hand, which I deposited in the bin outside and went off in search of the hostel.

It wasn't that I didn't believe them you understand, but I wanted to be sure. I know the guidebook had been letting me down on this sort of thing in the past, but I was prepared to give it one more chance. A big mistake. It was a bloody long walk and the heat of the desert sun was causing me to pant like a dog and leave behind a trail of sweaty residual. After all that I was directed to a building that looked like some sort of youth centre. A woman inside expressed surprise at me thinking this was a hostel.

Bloody guidebook!

I found a room in one of the cheap hotels. Copiapó is a dusty desert town with not a whole lot going for it. However it did have a nice plaza where I had lunch and enjoyed the sunny day. The next morning I caught an early bus to Chañaral, a small town on the edge of the Pan de Azúcar National Park, and two hours from Copiapó. The park entrance was at least another thirty kilometres away. The tourist office was closed so I decided to just find the road and hitch hike. Being in South America this possibly wasn't the safest option. Mind you it isn't anywhere. Yet it can have its rewards. I had done a bit of hitching in Ireland the previous year with no problems, and I met some great people. Sten back in Río Gallegos had hitched all the way down and had no problems. The American, Tim, had been hitching and apart from one worrying incident he'd had no problems.

This one particular incident was with his first ride in the north of Argentina. The guy seemed friendly enough, but after about an hour he asked Tim a question:

'How big is your penis?'

At first Tim couldn't quite make out what he was saying, and asked him to repeat.

He repeated the question.

Understandably disturbed by this sort of question, Tim pretended not to understand. He figured that as long as the car was moving the guy couldn't do anything. However at the next town, he made his excuses and got out. He hitched on from there without incident.

The area around Chañaral is startlingly beautiful. The town is a tiny dilapidated mining port situated on the edge of the Atacama. The main road ran along the coastline and split at a point just outside of town. The right fork continued inland while the other went off into a landscape of blinding white sandy beaches and distant mountains. This road led to the national park, and was deserted.

As I stood on the desolate road that ran off into the shimmering heat of the lonely desert, I wondered if this was such a good idea. In the desert no one can hear you scream. I wondered how many bodies were buried in deserts around the world. I mean, it's the perfect place to kill somebody. Think about it for a moment, if a psychotic madman drove these desert highways picking up lone backpackers like myself, it would be quite easy to murder them and bury the body out here. Who would ever find it? More to the point, who would ever come looking for you? For example if I was to go missing during my trip, it could be ages before someone gets concerned that they haven't heard from me for a while, and even then it could be months before anyone starts looking. Plenty of time for this madman to have taken my body miles from any form of civilisation, and buried it deep inside a sand dune. It was a disturbing thought, and one that preyed on my mind as I stood there with my thumb poised ready to attract the attention of the next passing car.

After a while it became quite apparent to me that I would have a long wait. This didn't seem like the sort of road that would be choked with traffic. So I lay down my backpack and plonked myself on top of it. Sweat oozed from every pore as I sat there foolishly dressed in black jeans and a tee shirt. It was unbelievably hot, as deserts are apt to be.

After about half an hour a car turned off the main road and came my way. I stuck out my thumb as it approached, but there was no room. The driver shrugged as he passed and drove off into the distant heatwave. I continued to sweat as the vultures began to circle in anticipation of an upcoming meal. From the distant haze emerged two cyclists. I watched them approach and waved as they passed. They both ignored me.

'Sod you then!' I shouted after them.

Ignorant bastards! I thought.

The heat was beginning to get to me. I was sorely tempted to run off across the sand and dive into the nearby sea to cool off. However, for reasons that were to become evident later, it was lucky for me that I didn't.

My saviour came in the form of a small van bearing the words *Los Carbineros*. The window wound down to reveal two uniformed policemen.

'Where are you going?' asked one of them.

'The national park,' I replied, wondering where else they thought I might be going. This road only went to one place.

He looked at his colleague, who in turn nodded, and stepped out to open the back door. I threw my backpack into the rear of the van and climbed in the back seat. They then happily chatted to me as we drove to the park.

And who says hitching isn't safe?

Carlos and Pedro very kindly dropped me off at the campsite where I secured a spot for the extortionate price of $10 per night. Mind you I was given ten litres of purified water and all the firewood I could burn. As I set up my tent I noticed a beat-up red Toyota pickup park beside me.

Through the cracked windscreen I could see a buck-toothed young man wearing a baseball cap. On the side of the truck was a sign advertising penguin tours.

At least give me a chance to put up my tent, I thought.

Rodrigo did just that. In fact he even helped me. The ground was far too hard for the pegs, so Rodrigo came up with a great suggestion. Using the many large rocks scattered around the area, he fixed the guy rope to the bottom of the pole and then secured it by tying the string to the rock. Thus the process was repeated with the other three corners. He wasn't as stupid as he looked.

He then managed to sell me a boat trip out to the tiny barren island just offshore. From where I was camped it looked as though someone had just dumped thousands of tons of dirt and rock from the nearby mine out in the middle of the bay. There were no trees, and it certainly didn't look as though it could support an abundance of wildlife. But Rodrigo assured me that I would see penguins, sea lions and much bird life. Now call me stupid, but I was in the desert here. And even I know that penguins and sea lions like the cold, not the heat of the desert. Either this was some sort of elaborate con trick, or another idiosyncrasy of nature. Either way I intended to find out and paid him the 2500 pesos.

The boat trip wasn't until 12.30 the next day, so I took a short walk and then relaxed on the beach for the day. Upon entrance to the park it had become cloudy. The clouds remained for the rest of the day. In the evening I wandered to the office for some firewood, and ended up chatting for ages with two of the guys who worked there. They had me in hysterics as we discussed the many important things in British culture such as: Robin Hood, Cero Cero Siete (or 007 as we call him) and John Lennon and his ugly wife. Now before someone slaps a lawsuit on me for slander, I must point out here that it wasn't me who called her ugly. I might agree with them, but that's completely different.

Naturally the conversation got on to Pinochet. They thanked me on behalf of the Chilean people for having Pinochet in my country. They said that Chile is now a much more peaceful place without him. They didn't want him back and said that England was welcome to keep him.

'We don't want him either,' I replied.

It seemed the country was divided three ways on this subject. Some didn't want him back; some wanted him back so he could stand trial for his crimes; and others worshiped him, believing that he was the saviour of Chile - the latter being mostly the rich who lived well under him. Many say he brought a lot of money into the country and created a better standard of living for everyone. But at what price? Was it really worth all those people dying for it? I don't think so. But that is for the Chilean people to decide, not me.

The conversation ended with an offer from Pepe to take me into the interior of the park the next morning. Without transport of my own this would have been impossible, or at the very least difficult. I gratefully accepted the offer and agreed to be ready early in the morning. With that I returned to my tent, built my fire, cooked my two-minute noodles and drank coca leaf tea.

I rose early the next morning, re-started the fire and made breakfast. Today was the start of March. I now had only one month left. I had hoped to visit Peru and hike the Inca Trail to Machu Picchu. However if I did that then I would be rushing to do two countries. I don't like to rush. I'd rather spend more time in one country and miss out on the other.

Plus Lake Titicaca was my second focal point, and, to all intents and purposes, the end of my trip. So I wanted to spend a lot of time there. Therefore I decided to leave Peru for another day. After all, it wasn't going anywhere.

At 9.30 Pepe pulled up in his truck and asked if I wanted more firewood. I already had plenty.

'Are we still going to the interior today?' I asked.

'Of course, we are going with them,' he replied, indicating the tent across from mine.

Parked next to the tent was a large pickup truck. I assumed we were going in that. At ten I made my way to the office and waited. Pepe informed me that the couple were still having breakfast. So I sat and chatted with him while we waited.

Pepe was quite knowledgeable on the area. He explained that *Las Onas* and *Los Alacalufes*, the indigenous races that once inhabited the southern regions of Chile and Argentina, are now extinct. Their culture has been completely wiped out. A race called *Los Changos* once inhabited the Pan de Azúcar region, but are now also extinct. Pepe pointed out a distant mountain near the entrance to the park called *Cerro el Elefante*, and explained that behind there is an old Indian burial ground. In the early 1800s this region was discovered by the English who mined the area for copper, which they exported back to the UK. They established a port right around the corner from where we were sitting, but it was destroyed by a Tsunami in 1823. The area is now a large beach with a row of dilapidated huts, owned by a few families that run tours and restaurants.

Two hours passed and still they hadn't come. My boat trip was due to leave in half an hour. However Pepe urged me to wait for them. 'The interior is much more interesting,' he insisted.

'But they said they would be here over two hours ago,' I replied. 'What's going on?'

'Hora Chilena (Chilean time),' he explained. 'In Chile if someone intends to be prompt, they say, 'hora Ingles (English time)' otherwise it's hora Chilena.'

So I had no choice but to wait. They arrived shortly after and apologised for their tardiness. It seemed they had been up all night with bad stomachs, something to do with dodgy empanadas.

Pablo, Evelin and their young son, who proudly introduced himself as Juan Tomas, were kind enough to allow me to join them on their excursion. Pepe it seemed was acting as tour guide. We stopped at the office to explain to Rodrigo what was going on and he booked me on the four o'clock trip instead. With that we headed off. Soon we left the paved road and found ourselves bouncing along a sand and gravel road that led through an arid valley. We got about ten kilometres into the interior when all of a sudden the engine died.

'¿Qué pasó?' exclaimed Pablo.

After many attempts at re-starting, it was obvious there was something seriously wrong.

For the next couple of hours the car was pulled apart in search of the problem. In the end it was determined that the fuel pump wasn't working. Pepe had the bright idea of removing the wiper wash container and using that as a temporary tank to get us back to the campsite. So he set about removing it and siphoning petrol from the tank. I stood there quietly smoking a cigarette and wondering if I was beginning to jinx others now with my bad luck. Or perhaps that gypsy had put a curse on me after all. Maybe if these kind people hadn't taken me with them they would be happily cruising along observing the wildlife. However I felt it best to keep these thoughts to myself.

Pepe's idea didn't work.

'I hate these modern machines!' he exclaimed, referring to the fuel injection system.

There was no choice but to wait for someone to come our way and help. But first we had to turn the truck around. Not an easy task in the narrow road and the heat of the day. However after much effort and a fifty-point turn it was soon facing the right way. All we had to do now was wait. Three cars passed us going the other way, but didn't even stop to ask what was wrong. Minutes turned into an hour and still nobody had come to our rescue. Pablo had tried his mobile phone, but we were out of range; not surprising really considering we were in the middle of the desert. Finally Pepe suggested that he and I walk back to the campsite, where we could get help. Not a problem. After all it was only ten kilometres of wild barren desert.

We had half a litre of water between us. With my limited Spanish conversation was difficult, but not impossible. During the gaps we just walked in silence, listening to the sound of our feet crunching on the gravel road. It was here on this remote desert road halfway across the world that I discovered the most outrageous theory on the death of Princess Di, or the Lady Dee as Pepe called her. A story was spread through all the Chilean papers that she was pregnant by Dodi Fayad, and that the Royal Family arranged for her to be killed because this would bring shame upon the family. I've since learnt that many of my friends back home had heard of this theory. Is it really possible that people think we are still living in medieval times? 'Off with their heads!' I find this sort of thing hilarious. It seems there is no limit to people's imagination when it comes to gossip. Are we really that desperate for scandal to liven up our lives? If so then heaven help us.

We walked for an hour without a single car passing us either way. This surprised Pepe. 'Usually there is lots of traffic on this road,' he said.

'What even during the week?' I asked.

He nodded.

I suspected that this might be another symptom of my jinx. I wouldn't have been surprised if when we stumbled into the campsite half dead, a fleet of cars passed us bound for the park interior. We trudged onward, every turn promising a change of scenery or some hope of being rescued. But all we found was an unchanged landscape and the next turning far in the distance. The desert was deathly silent, other than the occasional shriek of a bird or the call of a guanaco high up on a nearby mountaintop. It can't be much further, I thought. The surrounding landscape looked treacherous and forbidding. The mid-afternoon sun beat down upon us. My mouth was as dry as the landscape around me. I stopped to take a photo of Pepe, who stood in front of me dressed in jeans, a tee shirt, shirt and brown tank top. Yet there wasn't a bead of sweat on him. On his head sat a large yellow baseball cap - the kind you'd expect to see on the assistant at a gas station in some small southern town in the United States. He stood there with a big grin on his face, showing none of the concern that I felt at our predicament.

We continued on. All of a sudden I was snapped out of my delirium by the sound of a tooting horn. We both turned to see a white pickup approaching at high speed with arms flailing from the windows. They skidded to a halt next to us. Pablo's car was being towed behind.

We were saved!

We arrived at the campsite gone four o'clock. I figured I had missed my boat trip, but as I was taking down my tent Rodrigo pulled up and explained that they had waited for me. So I jumped in his beat-up truck and he took me to the launch spot.

As we all waited for the boat to be prepared, I sat and watched the muddy barefoot children playing. It seemed like a very isolated life for them and their families. There wasn't much in the way of facilities here. I wondered what kind of schooling they had? The day before Rodrigo had asked me if there was any sea in England. I was surprised to find he had no idea that England is an island. The only other time I had been asked such a question was by a young Indian girl in Mexico. I hadn't expected it here.

The boat was brought to the shore and we were rushed on before the next wave hit. It was in surprisingly good condition. I had expected an old wreck. I watched the pile of dirt and rock that was claimed to be an island, actually turn into one as we got closer. And sure enough it was abundant with penguins, sea lions, cormorants and pelicans. It seemed so strange to be in the desert, not too far from the Tropic of Capricorn, and be looking at Antarctic marine life. The reason for this is because the Antarctic current that flows up this coast goes as far as Peru and keeps the ocean cold right into the tropics. Thus it's possible for this type of marine life to survive in the otherwise unsuitable climate. It was all quite bizarre.

Our guide wasn't very talkative. I pointed out some plant

life on the island and asked him what they were called.

'Plants,' he answered.

Obviously he went to the same school as Rodrigo.

Back on dry land I walked back to the campsite and finished my packing. I was offered a lift into town by Rodrigo who was going to tow Pablo to a mechanic. They were in a rush because it was getting late and the mechanic would be closing soon, and urged me to hurry. However I was interrupted by Tomas, who had pitched camp nearby earlier that day and chose this time to befriend me.

'Are you a photographer?' he asked, having seen me taking lots of pictures earlier.

I tried to be polite while he launched into his life story about working in a bank and taking his holiday here alone to relax and think about what he wanted to do with his life. I had no choice but to interrupt him in mid-sentence and tell him, in a diplomatic way, to piss off because I was in a hurry. When Rodrigo arrived I hadn't finished packing so I just threw everything in the back and we sped off to town.

In town I bade farewell to them all. Pablo wished me luck.

'I think you'll need it more than me,' I told him.

I had been dropped off at the rear of a restaurant. As I packed my stuff a short, dumpy old lady came out of the back door. Upon spying me she yelled out an over enthusiastic greeting and came over. She told me that I was wonderful and beautiful and that she loved me, then proceeded to show me the toilets.

'They are beautiful, no?' she exclaimed.

'Err yea, they're very nice,' I replied.

'You want to use them?'

'No thank you, I don't need to right now.'

I think the desert air had dried up her brain. She then waffled on about being born here and that the ocean around this part is very dangerous, it had killed four of her brothers. A good thing I hadn't gone for that swim to cool off.

I managed to get away from her in time to watch the sunset. I sat myself down on a sand dune by the side of the road, and looked out across the huge expanse of white sandy beach at the sun sinking into the Pacific Ocean far off in the distance. My only company was the many packs of wild Dobermans sitting on the surrounding sand dunes. For obvious reasons I decided not to hang around once the sun had gone down.

11

¡Bolivia! ¿Es posible?

I took another overnight bus to Calama, where once again I was woken in the morning with a prod and another plastic cheese roll held under my nose. Overnight I had gone from sea level to an altitude of 2700 metres. The morning air was decidedly chilly in comparison to Pan de Azúcar. The guidebook listed many cheap places to stay, including the interestingly named *Residencial Splendid*. I opted for Residencial Toño.

It was early in the morning as I trotted up to the narrow double doors and rang the bell. A little old man answered and proceeded to open one of the doors, beckoning me in. I felt I really ought to point out that my own bulk plus that of my backpack wouldn't fit through. He insisted that I could. So for the next five minutes he helped me wriggle and squeeze my way through a gap that was half the width of a normal door, instead of just opening the other.

I felt like I had entered a scene from Alice in Wonderland. The toilet and shower doors were so small that I had to bend down to enter. The sinks came up to just above

191

my knees, and I had to crouch down to see myself in the mirror. Also everything worked backwards. The door to my room was upside down, and opened from the left hand side. The little old man had diligently shown me how the door handle operates upwards to open the door, and that the key goes in upside down and had to be turned towards the lock to unlock it, as opposed to normal. It was all very strange, and I half wondered if I was still asleep in the bus, locked in some strangely surreal dream induced by the intake of too much coca tea.

But it was all very real. I passed a quiet and fairly boring day here and headed to the bus station the next morning. I planned to head to San Pedro de Atacama, an oasis village 120 kilometres to the southeast. It was also slap bang on the Gringo Trail. It sits at the northern end of the Salar de Atacama, a vast salt lake. In the early 1900s it was a major stopover on the cattle run from northern Argentina to the nitrate mines. However the building of the Salta to Antofagasta railway soon put an end to that era. Nowadays it thrives on tourism, offering excursions to the many nearby attractions. My reason for going there was that it was the starting point for a three-day tour across the Bolivian Altiplano, ending in the town of Uyuni. Many backpackers had recommended this tour, and the fact that it starts in Chile and ends in Bolivia made it a good way to start a new country.

I arrived at the station at 9.30 to find that the next bus didn't leave until eleven. I had confidently assumed they would be more regular. So to kill time I found a little café and had breakfast. As I sat down I noticed everyone was glued to the television with blank expressions. I couldn't hear it very well and could only make out that someone of importance was flying somewhere.

'¿Qué pasa (what's going on)?' I asked the guys at the next table.

'Pinochet is being returned to Chile,' replied one of them, as they both got up.

'When?'

'Now,' they both replied, and walked out.

For the next half hour I ate my breakfast and watched as the plane flew in. I wondered what the others in the restaurant were thinking. When the plane landed, an elaborate display of helplessness was put on show by the man himself as he was helped into a wheelchair, lifted off the plane and wheeled to the waiting congregation, who cheered and chanted his name. It was shocking to see that such a man could be given a hero's welcome. It seemed the peace that Pepe and the two journalists so cherished was about to be shattered.

An hour or so later I was cruising into San Pedro de Atacama. The village is gifted with a row of snow-capped volcanoes as its backdrop. It was a magnificent sight. San Pedro wasn't the tacky tourist town I had envisaged, but a small village made of adobe houses and dusty streets. It was almost like being transported into 19th century Mexico. It would have been much more appropriate to have entered on horseback.

You could tell I was back on the Gringo Trail, the bus contained backpackers other than myself. Three Canadian girls got off and were persuaded to follow a woman to her hostel. Nathalie had recommended me a hostel here, so I trotted off to find it.

Ahead of me walked a very thin guy wearing a baseball

cap and carrying a backpack half the size of mine. I caught up with him at the tourist information board. The map wasn't all that helpful, so I decided to try the tourist office. I invited Arjen to join me. He happily agreed.

Arjen came from Holland and, as it turned out, had been in Pan de Azúcar the same time as me. He had camped wild in the mountains using just his sleeping bag. When wandering one day, he came upon the wreckage of a light aircraft. That is one of the unique features of the desert, there is always some burnt out wreck to be found somewhere. Often they are left to rot like the carcass of an animal, almost like a symbol denoting how cruel this land can be.

We found the tourist office in the main plaza and obtained a map of the area, and directions to the hostel. At the door we were greeted by a short, skinny woman with a mop of bobbed red hair - it looked more like a straw-thatched roof than a head of hair - and a large mole on the side of her face. She resembled a scarecrow. She spoke in Spanish but with an accent that made it plainly obvious she wasn't from around these parts. In fact she was from the Czech Republic. She had married a local man and settled here to run this hostel. She showed us to a very spacious dorm whose only other occupant was a tall German. Stefan was sat at the table just outside the door. Arjen and I joined him. He had been here for a few days and was finding it quite relaxing. I sort of had the feeling that this village could have that effect. I had intended to arrange the tour and head straight off. But now I was beginning to feel like I could spend a few days here.

The Sonchek Hostel was a small adobe building with a restaurant attached. Like San Pedro it was a tranquil place, perfect for relaxing in the heat of the afternoon sun. However that tranquillity was broken in the evening by a run-in with the scarecrow's husband, a thin, wiry man with a thick mop of jet-black hair - they obviously used the same hairdresser.

Arjen and I were relaxing outside our dorm when he decided to go make a coffee. Upon arrival we had been informed that the kitchen cannot be used after ten at night. The kitchen was separate from the owners' house. Whilst boiling the water the gas ran out, so Arjen used his camping stove as it was already late and he didn't want to bother anyone. Soon after, the kitchen door burst open and the owner started ranting and raving at him about it being ten and that the kitchen was closed. It seemed it was he who had turned off the gas. Arjen apologised, saying that he didn't realise the time and that he just wanted to boil some water, pointing out that he was using his own gas. This made no difference.

'You are in my house and will obey my rules!'

He then told him to leave the hostel.

'I'm not leaving,' replied Arjen, 'I've already paid for the night, and it's late.'

'I'll return your money and you will leave! If you don't I will call the police!' he shouted, and then stormed off.

Arjen had no intention of leaving, especially when Stefan pointed out that it was actually five to ten. He proceeded to tell the scarecrow this. The guy returned, slapped the money down on the table and stormed off again. Arjen remained where he was. At the back of the hostel was a set of tables for the restaurant. We both took our part-cooked coffees and sat there. A short while later our psycho friend wandered past, mumbled an apology, and slumped off into the darkness to play his ukulele. A very strange man indeed.

The next morning his wife politely asked Arjen to leave. She felt it best considering what had transpired the night before. So he grabbed the money that has been slapped down on the table the night before, packed up and left; happy in the knowledge that he'd got a free night's accommodation out of it all. He decided that he would wander out into the hills that evening and pitch camp there.

As it was Saturday I decided to spend the weekend here. It was such a nice little village and I wanted to see some of the surrounding area. Stefan was also planning to take the Uyuni tour. There were many different companies, all leaving on a daily basis, so we decided to leave on Monday.

Many people had recommended Colque tours, saying that they were the best of a bad bunch. There were many stories circulating of vehicles with no brakes, or vehicles breaking down and being stuck high on the Altiplano. Colque was recommended as they were the biggest company and had more vehicles. Therefore there was more hope of being rescued. I wasn't sure if all this was true, or just one of those isolated incidents that are taken and blown completely out of proportion each time the story is told by another backpacker. However just to be sure we took the Colque tour.

Later that afternoon myself and an English couple from the hostel decided to join Arjen as he hiked upriver to find a good spot for camping. The surrounding landscape was an amazing contrast of arid sandy mountains, snow-capped volcanoes and lush green vegetation, quite obviously irrigated by the melting snow on those volcanoes. We walked a good eight kilometres before taking a rest by the river. Here we left Arjen and headed back. Halfway we were offered a lift by a passing local.

Julio told me he owned two houses in San Pedro, along with an expensive hotel, and although having travelled to many other countries, he loved it most here in San Pedro. I have to admit that I couldn't blame him. This was such a beautiful area: peaceful and open, with breathtaking views. It was also the sort of place to make you very lazy. The afternoons are so hot that you never feel like doing anything. Many just hang out in the plaza, or wander aimlessly through the dusty streets. Secreted away in the backs of these red-brick buildings that line the streets are many little café bars and restaurants. Although this is a prime tourist destination, it didn't feel like it. And I liked that.

For $70 we got ourselves booked on the Monday tour - all except Arjen who got back too late and lost his seat. He had to go with one of the other tour companies. We wished him luck. With a day to kill I decided to take the evening tour out to El Valle de la Luna (valley of the moon). We stopped at many other sights like the Valley of the Dead - so-called because the ancient Indians used to go there to die, like the elephants - and headed through valleys running through undulating hills of sand and rock coated with salt. From the distance you could be forgiven for thinking it was snow. The jagged, sandy rock is said to resemble the surface of the moon, hence the name. Well I couldn't really make the comparison, not having been to the moon myself. But it certainly was spectacular.

The entire trip was planned around watching the sunset from a certain lookout point. Everything leading up to it had been just to kill time, or so it had seemed. Our guide drove us to a point where all the other tours met and everyone hiked up a giant sand dune and along to the sharp ridge of a nearby mountain. Here we all set up our cameras and patiently waited for the sun to go down. When it did I began shooting. After three pictures my camera decided to die on me. I couldn't believe it. The night before a three-day tour across some of the most spectacular scenery in South America, and my camera packs up. I was fuming.

There was nothing I could do about it now, except hope it was just a dead battery. I followed everyone back down the sand dune to the waiting bus. The sunset hadn't been all that spectacular, but as we made our way out of the park the entire valley was bathed in a soft, deep crimson colour. The surrounding landscape had completely changed. I regretted not hiking out here with my backpack and camping the night, like I'd intended. But the park is fifteen kilometres from San Pedro and what with the heat of the desert sun, I just hadn't been able to get motivated for the trek. Come midday I would be back at the hostel for a siesta.

Fortunately for me Stefan had a spare battery that fitted my camera. Once inserted the camera worked once again. I heaved a huge sigh of relief. At eight that morning we wandered down to the office to catch the bus that would take us to the Chilean border. Upon arrival we checked out of the country and then drove from an altitude of 2440 metres to 4400, along the longest section of no-man's land yet, to the Bolivian border.

The border was nothing more than a lone hut high up on a vast open plateau, and manned by two guards bundled up in warm clothes to protect them from the chilling winds that were howling across the open mountaintop. There were no trees or anything to protect them. This was possibly the friendliest immigration I had ever come across. Not surprising really. I'm sure being stuck up here in the wilderness would make anyone welcome visitors with open arms.

From the border we drove to Laguna Blanca where we had breakfast in a lone building set aside a lagoon stretching out before us like a giant mirror. The mountainous backdrop was perfectly reflected in the water. Pink flamingos dotted the shoreline. The morning air was crisp and pleasant. There was no sun, and the clouds hovered just above the snow-capped mountains. It wasn't really that cold though. I perched myself by the lake and surveyed the rocky land-scape stretching out before me. It seemed quite barren and lifeless. However looks can be deceiving. This part of South America is littered with volcanoes, both active and extinct. This area was alive with geysers and hot springs. It was going to be an interesting trip.

It seemed that all the tour groups followed the same path and stopped at the same places. Our group was split into two jeep loads. My half contained Stefan, a German couple called Martina and Oliver, and a French girl called Pascale. Our guide was Vicente, a short, thin, grubby-look-ing man. He was dressed in a greasy blue jumper and dark jeans, and sported a thick mop of wild, spiky black hair. Permanently squinting eyes sat on a roundish dark, weath-er-beaten face with high cheekbones that seemed to be there to accommodate his huge grin. That grin would become a familiar sight over the next few days. We also had our very own personal cook. Veronica was a short, dumpy fifteen-year old girl, who was doing this job in-between her stud-ies. It seemed that the people in this part of the world are definitely vertically challenged - for want of a more politi-cally correct turn of phrase.

Vicente pulled up in a beat-up silver jeep. The other groups had got into equally beat-up jeeps; our other half having had to jump start theirs because the starter motor was broken. We loaded our backpacks and all supplies on the roof, which Vicente covered with an old piece of tarpaulin, then clambered aboard. For the next three days Colque would be providing all our food. All we'd needed to bring was our own water. Just to be sure we had all brought five litres each. Each of us then waited, fingers crossed, as Vicente started the car, and were relieved to find that it started first time. It looked as though we had got the better end of the deal. Vicente turned and grinned us a confident grin.

One of the women who had made us breakfast came to see us off. She was dressed in a large gypsy-style skirt, with many undergarments making it puff out like a lampshade, and a plain green jumper. She looked like she had once been tall, but had fallen into her arse. However I suspected that underneath all those layers she wasn't as dumpy as she appeared. Draped around her neck and hanging loosely from her body was an old apron, and perched right on the tip of her head was a black bowler hat. She happily posed for a photo and waved us off as we started our way along the bumpy gravel road.

Our first stop was at Laguna Verde, yet another large shimmering body of water providing mirror images of the surrounding landscape. At a lookout point high above the lake was a section where stones had been neatly piled on top of each other to form an array of towers overlooking the lake. We discussed the possible significance of this. Maybe this was a sacred Indian burial ground where the spirit could rest eternally overlooking the beauty and splendour of the lake? Or perhaps it was where the ancient Indians used to come to worship the gods? As we wandered back down to the jeep we questioned one of the Indian women from the other jeeps.

'It's for the tours,' she replied, 'to indicate that it's a good viewing point for the lake.'

Oh!

From there we drove to some hot springs and had lunch. My shorts were in my main pack, so I didn't bother going in. It was here that we seemed to mysteriously pick up another passenger. I don't know where he came from, but he would prove a valuable assistant to Vicente in the days to come.

After lunch we continued on our journey. As we started to ascend a hill the jeep began to struggle and splutter and eventually come to a complete stop. A few hours into the trip and we had already broken down. We all got out and stretched our legs. We were in the middle of nowhere. The rest of us stood around looking slightly worried while Vicente's little legs dangled from the side of the bonnet, the rest of him buried inside the engine trying to determine what was wrong. Somehow I imagined that being stranded out here on this barren, unsheltered mountain wouldn't be a whole lot of fun. The landscape was an amazing array of rolling hills - that looked like they had been airbrushed with many different subtle colours - vast open desert and snow-capped peaks. The air was thin but clean and crisp. Fortunately I hadn't suffered any altitude sickness. At break-fast we had been encouraged to drink coca tea, as this is an effective antidote for altitude sickness. This was the highest I had ever been for such a long period. The highest point of the trip would be later today, at an altitude of 4800 metres. If we ever make it that far.

Vicente managed to get the car going and we all dived back in. As we drove on up the hill he explained that at these high altitudes it was necessary to widen the gap between the contact points. I'd never heard that one before.

Vicente continued on through more stunning scenery, whilst probing me for new words to add to his small vocabulary of English, until we arrived at Laguna Colorada. We came over a hill to the sight of a large deep-red lake. A herd of llamas grazed on the adjacent hills. At our request Vicente pulled over so we could take some pictures.

We spent the night here, in a small settling built mainly for the tours. Whilst our cook set about preparing our dinner we checked into our room. It seemed we were definitely in the land of the munchkins now. The doors were low and the beds short. Six beds were crammed around a table in a dark room with dirty brick walls. A lone dusty old light bulb swung precariously above the table. An old wood furnace stood by the door. However it wasn't all that cold so there was no need to use it. I selected my bed. There was bedding provided but I lay out my sleeping bag underneath as extra warmth.

I stepped outside to the sight of Vicente working hard on the jeep. The poor bloke hadn't stopped all day. All the other groups were here also. Arjen emerged from the building. He wasn't happy. His jeep was so filthy that he couldn't see anything out the window. He also suspected that the brakes were not so good.

Dark ominous-looking clouds were gathering on the horizon. A few of us took a walk down to the lagoon. The water apparently changed colour at different times of the day, something to do with the alkali content; hence the name Coloured Lagoon. We started along the water's edge with the intention of getting a closer look at a distant salt deposit, but the approaching storm drove us back to the shelter of the lodge.

The night was long and very uncomfortable. Due to the shortness of the bed, I couldn't straighten up and thus felt quite cramped. I had the sneaking suspicion the others were having the same problem. Something to do with the amount of tossing and turning and creaking going on in the night. Pascale occupied the bunk above me and was especially fidgety. At regular intervals a torch would come on and someone would make their way through the darkness to the toilet outside, myself included. When morning came I felt like I hadn't slept at all.

Outside the rain had stopped and the sky was clear once again. The air had that unique freshness that often follows a storm. I wandered down to the lagoon. The water was no longer red, but crystal clear and glistening in the morning sun. Fresh snow covered the surrounding hills and light fluffy broken clouds drifted past the jagged peaks. This was without doubt the most awesomely beautiful place: so peaceful and serene. Feeling as tired as I was, I could quite easily have laid down by the lagoon and gone to sleep. But I had another day of travelling to do.

The journey was long, slow and quiet. I think everyone was tired just like me. Our first stop was at El Arbol de Piedra (tree of stone), a rather pathetic excuse for a tourist attraction. It was just a rock that could have looked like a tree - if you were imaginative enough. Then it was on to the more impressive sight of the geysers. Large holes in the ground contained bubbling and spitting cauldrons of grey sulphurous liquid. A hideous stench of rotten eggs came with it. We continued on through more desert land and across muddy salt flats, where the distant sky looked to be melting onto the horizon, and pulled up at an army base in the middle of nowhere.

Our passports were checked by a young boy in his teens wearing a uniform many sizes too big for him. I thought it was some kind of joke, but Vicente told us that due to a lack of volunteers boys as young as fourteen are allowed to enlist in the Bolivian Army. They could at least provide them with a uniform that fits. How could you take seriously an elite fighting squad that came charging towards you with guns taller that they are, and soldiers constantly tripping over the hems of their trousers?

An hour later we arrived at San Juan. Tomorrow we would be going across the Salar de Uyuni, but first we would spend the night here. San Juan was actually a village and not a purpose-built settlement for the tours. The accommodation was a bit better this time. The room had windows and felt a bit more spacious. The beds were wider and not in bunks, yet they were still short. And the toilet had a seat - a luxury on the trip so far. I dumped down my pack and collapsed on the bed. Fortunately there was nothing at the bottom of the bed and so my feet were able to hang over, affording me the luxury of stretching out.

I dozed for a while, until Vicente came in asking for change. I knelt up on the bed in order to check in my pockets. With a loud bang a portion of the bed collapsed and my knee was sent crashing to the floor, much to the amusement of the others. It appeared there was an ill-fitting slat of wood underneath.

It was carnival time in Bolivia and San Juan was staging its very own. We wandered off in search of the procession. San Juan was a small village made up of light brown adobe huts and dusty streets. A lone church sat just on the outskirts of town. Little brown-faced children dressed in muddy clothing rode around on old beat-up bicycles and played in the dirt.

In the distance we could hear the faint sound of music. As

the music grew louder, the quality grew worse. It sounded more like a Salvation Army band on acid. Drums were being banged out of time and flutes and whistles sounded like the wailing of cats that had been staked out in a row while someone ran back and forth across their tails. We rounded a corner to the sight of the town's Indian residents staggering drunk through the street, coloured streamers tying them together and dangling from their clothing. Flour was splattered over their clothing and faces. Their eyes were sunken and glazed with the effects of so much alcohol coursing through their veins. Their children wandered next to some of them, literally acting as support.

It was clear that they had been partying most of the day. The majority of them didn't look a day under sixty. I was impressed that they were still standing, just. The women were dressed in traditional coloured skirts and shawls; bowler hats perched on the tips of their heads. The men were dressed in simple trousers or jeans, and jumpers. As they approached Pascale shot off a couple of pictures. This triggered the attention of the three up front.

Two old ladies with rotten and missing teeth staggered and swayed their way up to us, whilst supporting a short fragile-looking man in-between them.

'¡Tienes que pagar (you have to pay)!' they shouted, referring to the photos. '10 bolivianos!'

Ten bolivianos is equal to one pound. They then dragged the man back and forth as one swayed the opposite way to the other. Pascale sniffed at the idea of paying so much for pictures she already had, and walked off.

'¡Tienes que pagar!' they shouted again. '¡Diez bolivianos!'

And then the two women broke away from the guy and

205

lunged at me, one pulling from behind at my daypack and the other from the front at my camera. As I fought to get them off me the old man stood in front swaying back and forth like a bowling pin about to fall over, whilst displaying a toothless grin and rolling eyes.

'I haven't taken a picture!' I shouted in Spanish, arms flailing to fight them off.

They grunted and broke away in time to catch their companion before he did topple over. They hoisted him up and the three of them then staggered off to rejoin the others, muttering something as they went. I remained where I was for a while, chuckling to myself. It's not everyday you get mugged by toothless, drunken old ladies in bowler hats.

After having dinner and resting a while, Stefan and I went to the local pub, in actuality a tiny corner shop that served beer and had a table in the corner where you could sit and drink. Benches lined the back wall also. The entire place was no more than five by three metres in size. We walked through the door and spotted Arjen sat on a bench next to a local campesino (the name given to a man who lives and works in the countryside). He wore a dirty brown puffy jacket and sat hunched up, clutching an empty beer glass. His sunken eyes revealed the amount of beer he had already consumed. Permanent saliva trails were etched into his chin. Stefan and I ordered a couple of bottles of the local beer. As we poured out a glass each the campesino immediately stood up and leant forward.

'Hola, me llamo Alfredo,' he announced.

We greeted him and introduced ourselves.

'¿Tomar, es posible (is it possible to have a drink)?' he slurred, pointing his empty glass at our bottles.

We filled it for him. He smiled and lifted the glass,

'¡A Bolivia!' he toasted.

'¡A Bolivia!' we all repeated, clinking glasses and taking sips.

The campesino downed his in one, eyed his empty glass for a moment, and then pointed it our way.

'¿Es posible?' he asked.

We all laughed.

There was a good crowd in this makeshift pub. The Uyuni tour ran the opposite way also, and crossed at this point. Therefore many groups were in town. We chatted and drank as the evening went on - the campesino interrupting every now and then to salute his country. '¡Bolivia!' he would cry, raising his glass and then pointing it at one of us. '¿Es posible?' It amazed me how these people managed to drink themselves to the point of no conversational skills whatsoever, other than, '¿Es posible?' and still manage to remain on two feet. Throughout the evening others staggered in with their own handcrafted wind instruments and offered us the mouthpiece, freshly dripping with saliva, for us to have a go. We politely refused. They were all coming from the party next door, where the campesino eventually disappeared to after running out of people to scrounge beer off.

Stefan and I left shortly after and fumbled our way through the pitch black streets to our room. Luckily it wasn't far. I went to the toilet, smoked a cigarette, went to the toilet again and then to bed. I was nice and snug in my sleeping bag when ten minutes later I needed to go to the toilet again. I hauled myself out of bed, put on my boots and tiptoed out to the toilet and then back in again. I climbed back into my sleeping bag and settled down. Ten minutes later I needed to go again.

Shit! What do they put in that beer? I wondered to myself as I put on my boots and tiptoed out to the toilet once again.

Upon return I wriggled into my sleeping bag and lay my head down. Everybody turned in their beds at the crashing sound of wood hitting the floor. That piece of wood had fallen out again and my arse was now wedged in the gap.

Not wanting to disturb people more I climbed out, fumbled around for my torch and, lifting the mattress, attempted to replace the piece of wood in the small pool of light emitting from the tiny torch. Once achieved I climbed carefully back into my sleeping bag and settled down. The lump in my back told me that I had put it back wrong.

'Bollocks!' I muttered under my breath.

I had no intention of getting out again, so left it. Ten minutes later I needed the toilet again.

I did eventually get to sleep and was woken in the morning by the others moving around, and the familiar sound of wood hitting the floor. I lifted my head in laughter at the sight of Oliver sat across from me with his arse sunk in the bed and legs up in the air.

'Serves you right for laughing at me!' I said.

I got dressed and wandered outside to the familiar sight of Vicente's legs hanging out the front of the jeep. He was fitting a new part. So it seemed we would be leaving a little later than the others.

I took a walk around town. All was quiet. Not a single adult was to be seen. Some children played in the streets. I heard the ringing of bells and spotted two young boys herding llamas on the outskirts of town. Somehow I suspected that San Juan was suffering a major hangover.

This was without doubt a whole different world from the

South America I had so far seen. The poverty was apparent in the condition of the children's clothes and in the humble dwellings that lined the dusty streets. Yet the village was set aside rolling green hills, free from the encroachment of the modern world. No paved roads choked with lorries and cars, no ugly towering buildings dominating the skyline, just a small rural community set aside the beauty of the landscape that nature had created. The air was free from pollution. Whatever they lacked in material possessions was made up for in natural beauty.

We left around ten and headed out of town along a dirt road that had been ravaged by heavy rains. Portions of the road had fallen away leaving large holes and deep crevices. Vicente constantly manoeuvred the jeep to avoid them. The roadside was lined with fields of Quino, the local produce. An hour out and the jeep began to splutter and cough. We managed to chug our way as far as another army camp where our passports were once again checked - they probably didn't have anything better to do - and we remained there while Vicente and his young assistant drove to a nearby pueblito (small village) to make more repairs.

The six of us sat on a wooden bench by the main office, a small building at the entrance to the camp. The hot sun beat down upon us. Flies buzzed around us. In the background we could hear the soldiers on their daily workout. This was possibly the quietest army camp around. I wanted to take some pictures, but after what had happened at San Juan I didn't want to take the chance: these people had guns. So I just took one sneakily.

I desperately needed the toilet. So I wandered into the reception building. Inside was a bed, table and chair, and lots of empty space. Sat on the chair behind the table was an officer. I asked if there was a toilet here.

'You want the toilet?' he replied, looking somewhat disturbed.

I nodded.

He got up and cautiously walked out of the building and up the road, almost as if he suspected this was some sort of trap. I followed. He stopped and called over one of the cadets, and then shuffled nervously as we waited for his arrival.

'Where are you from?' he asked, obviously trying to break the awkward silence.

I told him and then attempted to get some small talk going. He wasn't listening. I looked around the camp. The soldiers were jogging around a large open plaza surrounded by the barracks. At the far end of the camp stood a row of dilapidated trucks and jeeps. It looked more like a scrap yard than an army vehicle depot. Nearby two young cadets were busy tripping over their trouser hems. It seemed that the Bolivian Army was indeed not a formidable force.

When the cadet arrived he was ordered to take me to the toilet. As we walked across the camp he reluctantly answered a few questions for me. Fifty people lived in the camp itself. Some with families. The two children playing nearby confirmed this. Others had families in the nearby pueblito. We entered yet another big empty building, passed an old man mopping the floor, and on to the toilet. There were two cubicles. He looked in one and then pointed me to the other. I entered, lifted the lid and was engulfed by a swarm of flies. The basin was piled high with a wide selection of turds. I wasn't about to add to the collection, so I just took a piss and got out quick.

Vicente returned an hour later and we continued on. We

stopped just short of the salar to stuff quino plants into the front of the engine. This was to protect it from the salt. At the edge of the salar we stopped and had lunch at some apparently deserted buildings. A lone dog lay outside. By the look of him he was well fed and in a good state of health, so I guess he had an owner.

We all sat outside the front of the building. A solitary Indian lady walked along the edge of the salar and off into the distance. Vicente and his assistant were busy fitting a tarpaulin to the underneath of the engine while Veronica prepared the food. It was amazing how hard this guy had worked since we left, and for such little money. Veronica had told us that they weren't paid much. I figured we should take him out for a few beers upon arrival in Uyuni.

Once the work was done and everyone was fed and watered, we continued on. We entered the Salar de Uyuni, a giant saltpan at an altitude of 3653 metres. It stretches over an area of 12,000 square kilometres and was once part of a prehistoric salt lake that covered most of southwestern Bolivia. When it dried up it left a few puddles and saltpans. We entered via a manmade dirt road and drove along it for about twenty minutes or so. A blindingly white, flat landscape stretched out before us, ending at two skies. The horizon was perfectly mirrored in the glistening salt. Then, to my surprise, Vicente left the road and drove onto the salar itself.

The water was about a foot deep. Obviously this was the reason for the tarpaulin. After a while the water subsided and we continued on a hard compact layer of salt. We were heading for the curiously named Isla de Pescadores (fishermen's island). I shouldn't imagine there was much fishing to be had here. We broke down twice along the way. Each time we got out and stood surrounded by nothing but Persil-white ground and deep blue sky. A passing tour guide gave Vicente some spare contact points and a condenser, which he believed to be the cause of all the trouble.

Isla de Pescadores is a tiny arid island laden with cacti, sitting alone and forlorn-looking in the middle of this huge expanse of salt. It really is the most unusual sight. Vicente let us off at the edge and we walked around the island, clambering over the rocks until we spotted the jeep parked by a lone hut at the edge of the island.

In this hut lived a man and his two boys. A couple of llamas wandered about nearby. The mother lived elsewhere with their baby. He didn't say where, or why. The island's other inhabitant was Alberto, a lone kestrel who had arrived once with a flock and remained when the others left. A few of us were sat on a rock on a the nearby hill when Alberto came trotting round the corner, passed us with complete indifference, and made his way to his nesting place. At first we thought he couldn't fly, but he proved otherwise later on. After a short rest he trotted down and happily posed for photographs whilst rummaging through my backpack and pecking at our shoes.

We remained on the island for a few hours while Vicente, assisted by Oliver, fitted the new parts. Once that was done we headed off for the 76-kilometre drive to the edge of the salar. We had lost a lot of time and it was already very late. However the upside was that we were fortunate enough to be viewing the most amazing sunset in the world. The entire salar was bathed in a sea of deep red. It seemed to last for ages also. We could almost have been on the planet Mars.

When the sun set the jeep chugged and spluttered to a stop once again. Things were looking very bad indeed. The darkness was looming upon us and we were still miles from the edge of the salar. We were also starting to hit water. Vicente removed his shoes and jumped out, taking a sharp intake of breath as his feet splashed in the icy cold water, and proceeded to work on the engine. His assistant had deserted us back at the island and jumped on a passing jeep to Uyuni. Oliver grabbed a torch and joined him, while the rest of us remained silently inside.

The engine was fixed and we continued on. The jeep's dim headlights cast a pitiful pool of light on the land ahead. Vicente lent out the window while he drove. Believe it or not, there was an actual road to follow. Vicente needed to see the tracks left by the other vehicles in order to follow it. Everyone was beginning to get a bit worried now. Personally I took my mind off it by watching the lightening on the distant horizon. Vicente explained that if we were not in Uyuni by nine then someone would be sent to look for us. However they would not come out on the salar at night, so we had to get to the edge.

We broke down once more. This time it took longer to get going. The batteries in the torch were running low and they were having to work in the dark. The jeep was started again, just. The engine was barely running. Vicente chugged on, head out the window, while Oliver expressed his concern that the engine was in a very bad way. None of us relished the idea of spending the night cramped here in this jeep on a cold saltpan high up in the Andes.

A light flickered in the distance. It was the Hotel Playa Blanca, which was situated on the salar and constructed entirely of salt. After what seemed like an eternity, each minute lived in fear of us breaking down again - Oliver didn't feel that the jeep could be started if it broke down again

- we finally arrived at the hotel.

Here the panic began because Vicente wanted to continue on. 'It's not much further,' he explained.

Everyone else wanted to remain at the hotel for the night, Martina was especially scared. The arguments began. A frustrated Vicente pointed to the horizon at a flashing light. It was the rescue party. However they would not come out on account of there being many roads between here and the edge, and it was too dangerous. Our only hope was to get to them. He started to drive on, and was forced to a stop by the shouts of the others. Irrationality was starting to set in. Martina was shivering with fear; Oliver was arguing that the engine couldn't last much longer and Pascale that it would be safer to spend the night at the hotel and head out in the morning. Stefan and I just sat there looking pensive.

I for one was scared, but we had made it this far. Each time we had broken down Vicente had got us going again. He had worked his arse off on this trip and I felt we owed him a lot. Without him we possibly wouldn't have got as far as we had. So I felt we ought to put our trust in him to get to the edge of the salar.

'Look everyone,' I interrupted, feeling that someone ought to make a decision. 'The guy has got us this far. He knows what he's doing. He'll get us there. Have faith in him.'

They all turned and looked at me.

'You are sure?' asked Pascale.

'Absolutely. Look, if we can see a car's headlights from here, then it can't be much further. We can make it!'

I had tried to sound encouraging.

They all nodded to each other in agreement and murmured, 'okay.'

'¡Vamos!' I shouted to Vicente.

He heaved a huge sigh of relief and continued on.

A deathly silence fell over the jeep. I continued watching the light show on the horizon, hoping that I was right about all this. If not then I could die a horrible death at the hands of some very angry backpackers.

The jeep chugged along in the pitch-black night, Vicente's head out the window and eyes firmly fixed on the dim pool of light in front of us. How he could see those tyre tracks was beyond me. The light on the horizon kept vanishing and reappearing. After half an hour we stopped. Vicente got Veronica to hold down the accelerator while he wandered off into the night. We thought he was lost as he stood there surveying the area around him. The tension in that jeep could be felt by everyone. Shortly after, Vicente returned and took up the reins once again. He turned in the direction where he had been stood and soon we felt a bump. I looked out the window to see the reassuring sight of a dirt road. We had made it.

The jeep erupted in sighs of relief and we all thanked Vicente wholeheartedly. He turned and grinned his boyish grin that had been such a familiar sight over the past few days, but not so for the last few hours. The light we had seen from the hotel was now moving towards us. We were saved. A short way down the road the jeep died for the final time. But we didn't care now, we were safely back on land and help was on its way.

___12___

Bad Roads

As the youngster loaded our baggage on the top of the bus, we all shuffled on and took our seats. Everyone but Martina and Oliver was here. Although their destination was the same, they were going with one of the many other companies lining this muddy, rain-soaked street in Uyuni. Many other familiar faces from the other tours filled up the bus, including the Canadian girls I had seen get off the bus back in San Pedro. However, in a bus full of backpackers I happily found myself seated at the back with a group of Bolivians, including a youngster carrying a puppy in a cardboard box.

We had spent the night in Uyuni for free at the tour company's own hotel. A saving of three dollars. When the rescue jeep had arrived we had transferred our bags over and jumped in. As we sped off down the road, I realised that we had left behind Vicente and Veronica. I had thought they were coming with us. Thus none of us had said goodbye. I felt awful, and so did the others. As we sped off towards the lights of Uyuni in a jeep that worked, he was still working his arse off in the cold night. We had no idea what time he would get back, so the chance to buy him a few beers went out the window. The next morning Pascale tried to find the Colque office to leave him a note, but couldn't. Upon arrival at the bus station the other groups were relieved to see we had arrived safely, they had been very worried.

'Vamos a acompañar (we are going to travel together),' said Lucio, the man seated beside me.

Along from him sat a slightly nutty-looking Indian woman hugging a pile of dirty clothes and a filthy plastic container. I had been told that the journey to Potosí would take five hours. It took eight and a half. The road was unpaved and full of potholes. It wound its way over mountain passes and along ridges where large pieces had fallen away into the steep valley below. A slight cause for concern. Twice we had to get out and walk across a floodplain, the reduction in weight lessening the risk of the bus sinking into the mud halfway across. At the first crossing we spotted Oliver and Martina sat on a hill, along with a group of others. Their bus had broken down. That was all they needed, considering the events of the last few days.

Just under halfway we passed through the village of Ticatica, which was in the midst of its carnival procession. The residents here however, weren't pissed as farts. The music was in tune and the people marched proudly through the streets dressed in a vast array of colours; coloured streamers flowing behind them in the process. It was a pity we couldn't have got off. However soon I was to decide that maybe this wasn't such a bad thing. The Bolivian carnival tradition is to throw water bombs at each other, something the children took great delight in; especially when a bus full of gringos came down the street. Arjen poked his head out the window and got one smack bang in the face. I curled up laughing, safe in the knowledge that my window was firmly closed. But my laughter was soon quashed as I felt something hit me on the head and a stream of water run down my face and soak my front. It seemed it had come through the window on the other side. I had to admit their aim was good, the little sods.

We arrived in Potosí late at night. The city's backdrop is dominated by *Cerro Rico*; the immense silver mine to which the city owes its existence. Situated at 4070 metres, Potosí also holds the title of world's highest city - a fact Arjen and I were reminded of as we walked up the very steep Avenida Independencia. Being seasoned travellers we had refused to take a taxi with the others, electing to save the money by walking. It started off well, what with all the hiking I'd done recently I had gained a moderate level of fitness. However this hadn't been at such a high altitude where oxygen wasn't so plentiful. Halfway up we began to regret our choice. Energy was waning. Three quarters of the way I stopped and took an asthma attack break, before completing the last leg.

The streets were lined with tiny kiosks from which more short, dumpy women served a variety of foods. I grabbed a bite to eat, hoping it wouldn't cause frequent dashes to the toilet that night. It's always a risk in the third-world countries, but the way I see it you just have to get on with it. Some people warn you not to eat from these sort of places. But not only are they the cheapest, they also represent a way of life for the country you visit. If the locals can eat it, then why can't you? Sure you might run the risk of a bout of diarrhoea, but that soon passes. When travelling Mexico I found myself struck down by the food on occasions, but it didn't last long, and never really stopped me from doing what I wanted. Often I meet people who have been struck by the bug and are

218

pouring diarrhoea tablets down their throat all day in the hope of a quick cure. Now I'm no doctor but in my experience that defeats the object. The reason you have this symptom is so your body can flush the bug from your system, and at the same time build up immunity and allow your body to adjust to the new food. Popping pills to stem the flow, so to speak, only prolongs the agony, as I have witnessed with many people. It's much better to just let it all out, and keep yourself from dehydrating by drinking plenty of water and nibbling on salted crackers. It worked for me once in Palenque, Mexico. But that's another story.

We stayed in a nice little guesthouse called *Casa de Huéspuedes María Victoria*. It was in the guidebook and so all the other backpackers were there. The next morning the majority of them went on the city's main attraction, the silver mine. Potosí was founded in 1545, following the discovery of silver in Cerro Rico. The veins proved to be so rich that the mine soon became the world's most prolific. Because of this the city blossomed and by the end of the 18th century became the largest and wealthiest in Latin America. For two centuries labourers were put to work extracting the ore, in conditions so appalling that many died in considerable numbers, either due to accident or disease. The boom didn't last though. At the turn of the 19th century the silver production waned and decline soon followed. It was only the demand for tin that rescued Potosí from the threat of obscurity and brought about a slow recovery.

Silver extraction continues, but on a smaller scale. However working conditions have remained unchanged. Some of the labourers are young teenage boys. All the work is carried out by hand, using primitive tools. Working temperatures range from below freezing to a stifling 45 degrees centigrade in the depths of the mountain. The miners, who are exposed to all sorts of noxious chemicals, normally die of silicosis pneumonia in ten years of entering the mine. Working conditions are dangerous. It's been said that the mine itself is structurally unsafe.

But for the bargain price of $5 you can enter the mine and be taken on a guided tour through the tunnels. You can watch these people slugging out their last remaining days for little money, to extract a mineral that will make others rich and prosperous. You can talk with them, take photographs of them and help ease their pain with the friendly offering of cigarettes or coca leaves. This was what the others were off to do, while Arjen and I wanted no part of it. I felt sure that the miners saw none of the profit being made by these tour companies. Judging by how our friend Vicente had worked so hard on our tour across the Altiplano, for such little money, I doubted this would be any different. The one difference here though, was that these people were being exploited. Five hundred years ago they were being used as slave labour to the advantage of the Spanish monarchy. Now at the turn of the Millennium this was still happening, only to the advantage of the tourist industry. It seems as though some things haven't changed all that much in some places.

So the Dutchman and I remained in town. First thing on the agenda was to get some local currency. Here the currency is bolivianos. You get six to the US dollar. I had to change my Chilean pesos. Arjen was having trouble with his visa card and I was rushing around trying to find somewhere that would accept Chilean currency. Thus we went our separate ways for the day. After much walking I found somewhere that did accept Chilean money. Whilst in the queue I was mobbed by three grubby-looking children all wanting to polish my boots. As they tugged at my clothes I told them that I had to change money first. They patiently waited as I did this, then converged on me once again. I selected one and he did an amazing job of cleaning off two months of accumulated dirt from places as far away as Tierra del Fuego, then buffed up to a shine that rendered my boots as good as new. He charged one boliviano. I gave him three. I know, I'm all heart.

It was nice to be in a country where everything was cheap. A good thing too because money was tight, and I still had three weeks left. Internet access here was cheap also. And there was a surprising number of Internet places around. Back home we take having our own computer for granted. The majority of people have Internet access in their own home. But here it was a different story. I queued for ages to gain access to a computer room full of locals doing a variety of things from homework to surfing the web. So far Internet access had been expensive, three to four dollars per hour. Here it was eight bolivianos per hour. So I spent two hours online, instead of one. Kind of defeats the object a bit really.

My Chilean pesos hadn't amounted to that much, so I decided to get more money out. The rate for traveller's cheques was quite bad here, so I used my visa card. It sometimes amazes me how much technology has advanced in the last century. Years ago someone like me who needed to get money from home, would have to have it wired across and then wait weeks for it to arrive. Yet here I was at the turn of the Millennium in a third-world country halfway across the world, and all I had to do was pop a piece of plastic in a machine and draw money from my account back home, all in an instant. I wondered what it would be like when I have grandchildren and they grow up and start travelling. I expect they won't have money then. In fact, I expect that when they go travelling, it won't be around the world, but around the solar system. Could you imagine saying to your friends: 'Hey guess what? I'm talking a year off and going backpacking around Mars!' It might sound funny, but it could be closer to the truth than we realise.

The two young boys shining shoes nearby looked on with longing and awe as I drew 300 bolivianos from the machine and stuffed the notes into my wallet.

'You want your shoes shined?' asked one of them, eyes twinkling.

'They are already clean!' I pointed out.

'I'll clean them more,' he replied eagerly.

I had no choice but to decline his generous offer and set off for a look around Potosí.

I spent the day wandering the markets before sitting in a café for two and a half hours writing my journal. Now I was in Bolivia I intended to stock up on artisans. I love the Indian textiles. However there was a severe lack of them here in Potosí. The markets consisted mostly of stall upon stall of consumer products, food and large pots of coca leaves. I still had plenty of coca leaves left from the bag Nathalie had given me. (It was amusing to think that she had taken a considerable risk sneaking them out of Bolivia, only for me to bring them back.) I did however buy a couple of small hand-woven blankets. The woman displayed impatience at my indecision.

'¡Llevatela gringito (take it)!' she kept saying.

I returned to the guesthouse and relaxed for a bit. All the showers I had seen here in Bolivia so far had been heated electrically; a large open fusebox with wires running precariously down to it was fixed to the wall nearby. A cause for concern and a short shower. I stepped into the one at the guesthouse and noticed a sign on the wall informing guests to only use the shower for six minutes per day. I wondered from where they plucked that figure.

The Dutchman returned later that evening. He had decided to go walking on Cerro Rico and met an Indian woman who was walking along with her son and nine-month old baby. He waved to her and she returned the wave, then sat down to wait for him. She explained that she was going up the mountain to visit her sister for the first time ever. They chatted for a while and then she continued on, giving him an apple as a parting present.

I got up at seven the next morning in order to catch a bus to Sucre. Arjen intended to remain another day. I took a slug-gish half-hour walk to the bus station. The night before we had all gone out for a meal and danced in an empty night-club until late; that is until they put on the Karaoke. During the meal I had finally got talking to the Canadian girls I had seen so many times since San Pedro de Atacama; well one of them. Erin was from Vancouver. It was funny that I had first seen her over a week ago, but hadn't spoken to her until now.

I checked in and also had to check my bag. This time I made sure I was right about it. My pack was taken and low-ered onto the bus from above. The bus then left without three of the passengers. We stopped outside a tyre factory while they caught up and some maintenance was carried out on the bus. During this time I watched an Indian woman preparing her baby for transport. Using a blanket like the one I had bought she lay the baby out, crossed her arms, bent over and curled up the edges. She then scooped up her child and swung it around onto her back, tying the corners into a large knot across her chest. The baby remained there perched happily on her back as she strolled off down the road. It certainly was a handy way to carry your children. It seemed that most parents, mothers and fathers alike, carried their children here. There had been no sign of a pram anywhere. I suppose when you think about it, there is no better way to bond with your child.

After a three-hour ride on one of Bolivia's very few paved roads we arrived in Sucre. Officially Sucre is the capital of Bolivia, but most of the governmental power has been moved to La Paz, making it the de facto capital. I took a long walk to the centre and found a bed in the Alojamiento Turista. For 16 bolivianos I was given a shared room with an American. He wasn't there when I checked in.

I spent the afternoon dodging the rain and ate in a Chinese restaurant. I'd had no idea it was Chinese. The sign out front advertised typical Bolivian food, yet when the menu arrived all it contained was Chinese food. So I ordered a huge plate of chicken fried rice for 8 bolivianos.

Upon delivery I questioned the waitress as to where I could find an artisan market.

'Err, Mercado Negro,' she replied, somewhat dimly.

'Where is that?' I asked.

'Err!'

'Well which street is it in,' I continued, pulling out my map in a vain attempt to ease her obvious pain.

'Err!'

This wasn't getting us anywhere.

'Is it far?'

'Err, you have to take a taxi.'

I thanked her and allowed her to go, not wanting to overload her only brain cell.

Outside I followed directions obtained from a guy on the street. I came across what I thought was Mercado Negro, only to find evidence to the contrary. I asked a stall-holder.

'It's further up the road, but we have many things here,' she replied.

'I'm looking for artisans,' I informed her.

'Oh you won't find any there,' she replied.

'But I was told otherwise!' I exclaimed.

She shook her head.

'Stupid waitress!' I mumbled to myself, as I headed back down the street.

I had heard that the trains in this part of the world, although slow, travel through some of the most spectacular scenery around. I figured it would be a good idea to take the train to my next destination, so I trotted off in search of the station in order to find out where I could go to from here. Time was short though. Although I had just under three weeks left, I wanted to spend a good portion of that at Lake Titicaca; after all it was my second focal point. Also I wanted a good few days in La Paz to take care of a few things before flying out. Therefore I had to head in that general direction.

I found the spot where the station was indicated on the map, but found only a large derelict building, at the end of which stood an open gate. I wandered down and through to find the remains of what was once a train station. A lone derelict freight train stood on tracks that were now over-grown with grass. The station was now occupied by dogs, tramps and, strangely enough, students doing their homework. It seemed that the Sucre line was no longer in operation. I was to be told later that Bolivia's rail system had been sold to Chile, who in turn used it for their freight purposes, but didn't really bother with the rest of it too much. Consequently much of it was left to rot.

Upon return to my room, I befriended two Dutch girls. They were fortunate enough to have been given the best room in the place. Two big double windows opened out to the patio terrace. I found them sat on the window ledge as I came up the stairs. I joined them and we were all closely followed by the owner's children. I often think that this sort of environment is perfect for a child to grow up in. With people from all over the world to talk to, the kids couldn't ask for a better education. The boy of the group showed no fear of strangers and happily plonked himself on my lap and peppered me with questions. I passed the majority of the evening with them before heading for a bite to eat and then back to my room.

My roommate turned out to be a tall, middle-aged and skinny man from America. Horn-rimmed glasses sat upon a pointed nose and his long, grey hair was pulled back into a ponytail. Back home he was a university professor. He'd been travelling for the past year and a half through Central and South America, and planned to go all the way down. We talked about the Uyuni tour. He was considering taking it. I told him of my experience and of the ups and downs and cost involved, before finally getting ready for bed. Upon return from the bathroom I found him lying in bed on his back with the covers pulled up to his chin. He lay there motionless, just staring at the ceiling.

I switched off the light and settled down for the night. At the point of dropping off to sleep I was jolted back by a voice from the darkness.

'So it's three days then.'

'That's right,' I replied, and returned my head to the pillow.

A few minutes passed,

'And it's 70 dollars?'

'Yes.'

More minutes passed.

'And what's the name of the company?'

'Colque!'

Eventually I dropped off to sleep.

I awoke in the morning to find him still lying in the same position as when I'd turned off the light the night before: eyes wide open and staring at the ceiling. I wondered if he'd actually been asleep. He probably spent the entire night churning over this new information in his head, and continuing to blurt out questions even though I was asleep and not answering.

The time was 6.30 am and I had a bus to catch. The evening before I had bumped into Pascale and she had told me about the Sunday market at *Tarabuco*, a small Indian village 65 kilometres southeast of Sucre. The market apparently stretches the length and breadth of the town. The two Dutch girls joined me and we rode there on a bus full of gringos. There wasn't a single local on it.

We arrived to the discovery that the market had been cancelled due to an Indian festival in a nearby village. There was dancing and music, but we couldn't get to it. Tarabuco was quiet. Apart from a few shops and a small scattering of very old and knackered-looking Indians, there wasn't much to see. We had breakfast and wandered around for a while before relaxing in the plaza and waiting for the return bus.

I spent the return journey sat next to a tall, stocky and hard-faced man with pure white hair, who just sat there clutching his backpack on his lap and staring out the window. I wondered what he had in that pack? To take my mind of it I poked my head through the gap between the headrests in front and talked to a very lovely German girl called Andrea, whom I had befriended back in the plaza. Andrea had been on the Uyuni tour also. We had seen each other but not spoken, until now.

Later that afternoon I shared a taxi to the bus station with Andrea and an American guy. They were going to La Paz; the American to get a second lot of rabies shots. It transpired that he had been bitten back in Chile. I went to find out if there was a day bus to Cochabamba. Firstly, I had found the scenery here in Bolivia so incredibly beautiful that I wanted to see it, not be stuck on a bus at night and miss it all. Secondly, as the roads were so bad here, and the fact that you had to keep getting out to cross rivers, I didn't fancy taking a night trip. There would be nothing worse than having to keep getting out and squelching your way across muddy terrain in the dead of night, and the freezing cold. But unfortunately for me there was no day bus at all.

I had been told by one of the other backpackers about a supposed public transport strike in Bolivia lasting three days. All buses, trains and taxis would be shutting down. With my time restrictions I didn't need to be stuck here for all that time. I asked at the bus station. It turned out that it wasn't confirmed but if it did go ahead then there would be no transport from Tuesday onwards.

I decided that if I was going to be stuck somewhere for three days, then I'd rather it be La Paz, or Lake Titicaca. So after another long conversation with the professor I decided

I definitely couldn't be stuck in Sucre with him for three days, and therefore made plans to leave the next day.

I rolled out of bed at eleven the next morning, took a cold shower - not by choice I might add - and said goodbye to the Dutch girls. They were heading off to Potosí. An Englishman had arrived that morning. He had lost his visa card and had no more money. The owner had agreed to let him stay and pay when his new card arrives in two weeks. He could eat in their restaurant downstairs and it would all be added to his bill.

As I packed my bag the professor was preparing to go out for the day. The goodbye was cut short due to him dropping a loud and ultimately smelly fart. He remained there awkwardly for a moment, watching as my nose wrinkled up and my nostrils sealed themselves shut, then made a hasty exit. I then stepped out of the room for some fresh air.

I left my pack at reception and took a walk to the bus station. The threat of the strike was still looming, so I decided to take a bus straight through Cochabamba to La Paz. At worst I could hitch to Lake Titicaca. For 60 bolivianos Trans Copacabana went straight to La Paz. Also the bus had heating. The Englishman had taken the overnight bus here from La Paz for 35 bolivianos, but had frozen all night. After nearly three months of roughing it, I didn't fancy another night freezing my arse off. So I figured it was worth paying the extra. After all it was only a few extra dollars.

Back in town I bumped into Erin, the Canadian girl. Travelling constantly with friends had brought her to the end of her tether and she felt she needed to get away from them for a while. When I told her I was the taking the bus to La Paz, she impulsively decided to join me. So after some rushing around she found herself seated next to me on a bus of equal comfort to those Coche Camas in Argentina. Instead of freezing we actually found it to be too hot and had to open the window.

The road between Sucre and Cochabamba was reputed to be very bad. Fortunately for us our bus took the route via Potosí. Most of the section between there and La Paz was unpaved, but the condition didn't seem so bad. I take back what I said about the scenery not being as good at night. I stayed awake until gone three watching as the moonlight cast ghostly reflections on the undulating landscape, and distant lightening lit up the broken cloud on the horizon.

I awoke on the outskirts of La Paz, Bolivia's largest city and home to over a million Bolivians - over half of Indian heritage. Bolivia is the most indigenous of all the South American countries. Fifty percent of the inhabitants are of pure Indian blood, and many still retain traditional and cultural beliefs and ways. I wondered if that included getting blind drunk and attacking backpackers?

We approached the city via the suburb of El Alto, a grey poverty-stricken area sprawling with derelict-looking houses. People packed the muddy roadsides going about their everyday business, trying to eke out a living as best they could.

Soon we hit paved road and in a matter of minutes found the landscape to the right of us drop off and spread into a large valley sprawling with a vast array of buildings. The canyon is shaped like a bowl and the city centre sits 400 metres deep. The canyon itself is five kilometres in diameter. The city is so huge that buildings fill the entire canyon and spill over the edges. The day was clear and we could see the snow-capped triple peaks of *Illimani*, lying at 6460 metres and dominating the background. It was a magnificent sight.

As the bus hit the rim and slowly made its way down the steep, twisty streets that ran down the side of the canyon, Erin and I watched wide-eyed as the city's many colonial buildings grew larger before our very eyes. Arriving in La Paz is without doubt a most memorable experience.

____13____

__Final Destination__

La Paz was without doubt the craziest city I'd ever been to. Traffic was prolific and minibuses choked the streets, each with a young kid leaning out the open side door yelling the bus's destinations at the top of his voice. Each word was totally incomprehensible. People filled the streets and dodged traffic as they tried in vain to cross the busy roads. It was impossible to simply wait for traffic and cross because the traffic never ceased. First you had to walk past the row of parked minibuses and taxis for a view of the road ahead. Then slowly crawl your way across the lanes like a hedgehog until you reached the other side.

I did this with the utmost impatience as I hurriedly made my way back to the hotel to collect my backpack, the morning after arriving in La Paz. The day before had been quite an eventful one. I had discovered that one of the guests in my hotel was Jason, the Canadian from back in Villarrica. He was still having lots of fun without his friend. I had also bumped into Pascale and Andrea in the street, and Erin had met up with a friend from home. All of us had arranged to meet in the main plaza later that night, and had then gone for a meal. I took along a very lovely Peruvian girl I had befriended back at the hotel; with whom I had spent an hour and a half talking in Spanish. (My brain hurt considerably afterwards.)

I had just tried to change the direction of my return flight so I could stop at Mexico City, but British Airways wouldn't allow it. I was supposed to meet Andrea at her hotel afterwards, so the two of us could make our way to the bus station and catch the bus to Copacabana. The threat of the strike had not yet materialised, and so I decided to take the opportunity while the buses were still running. I had already been to the main bus station and found the times. Ironically, the company I had come to La Paz with, Trans-Copacabana, didn't go to Copacabana. However I found one that did and the next one would be leaving at midday. As I rushed back from the British Airways office I found Andrea had already left. It was 11.30. I wasn't sure I would make it in time.

This was one of those times when paying when you leave is a pain in the arse. I grabbed my bag and announced I was leaving. The receptionist didn't have any change. The subject of change had been a very significant one in Chile and Bolivia. Basically people hated parting with it. The correct money was always preferred. Large denominations were often frowned upon and followed with the question, '¿No tienes cambio (you don't have change)?' More often than not, if somewhat reluctantly, it could be changed. But on occasions I would have to put back my desired purchase and go in search of change. However this time I couldn't put back my purchase, I'd already used it. I waited impatiently as he ran off in search of some, and upon his return rushed off up the street to the bus station. Attempting to run at just under 4 kilometres above sea level with a large weight on your back is not the easiest of tasks. I thought I was going to die as my heart pounded against my chest and my lungs fought for oxygen to fuel the demand being made by my overworked leg muscles. I stumbled up to the ticket office just in time and bought a ticket. I then followed the guy out to the road and was taken by car to another bus station elsewhere in the city.

As I got out I spotted Andrea about to get on a bus. I called out to her. Fortunately it was the same bus as I was about to take. The only other passenger was an old man, so the trip was cancelled and we were transferred to another service, which left at one. There were a few more people on this bus.

We watched as the women walked up one by one with their belongings bundled into one of those Indian blankets tied onto their backs. They deposited them and waddled on to the bus. Our bus looked set to fall apart at any given moment. The low tread on the tyres was especially worrying. We soon hit the shore of Lake Titicaca and stopped just over halfway by the water's edge. Most of the passengers got off here. The bus was then driven onto a barge just wide and long enough for it to fit. As I peered out the window I was amused to see this heavily laden vessel being powered across the lake by a tiny outboard motor.

I wondered what had happened to all the passengers? I couldn't see them crossing elsewhere. As we drove off at the other end, I spotted another barge bearing the name *Titanic*. A brave naming on the owner's part. I for one was glad we weren't travelling across on it.

We stopped in the plaza and picked up the others. I had

no idea how they'd got across, or why they got off the bus. Three and a half hours after leaving La Paz we arrived in the sleepy town of Copacabana. Lake Titicaca straddles the border with Peru to the west and Bolivia to the east. However Copacabana is situated on a peninsula that juts out from the Peruvian side of the lake. The peninsula however, belongs to Bolivia. Hence the reason for us having to cross the lake to get here.

Although the town was very much on the backpacker trail, like San Pedro it didn't seem touristy. Andrea and I took a room in the *Alojamiento Aroma* for ten bolivianos each, chosen because it had a terrace overlooking the lake. That, as it soon turned out, was its only endearing feature.

We had a bite to eat and then made our way down to the lake in time to watch the sunset. Lake Titicaca is over 230 kilometres long and 97 wide, according to the guidebook. Yet an Internet search brought about two differing sizes. Whatever it's exact size, it's bloody big. It's the world's highest navigable lake and sits in a depression on the altiplano at an altitude of 3820 metres. It's a remnant of the ancient inland sea known as Lago Ballivián, which once covered most of the altiplano before geological faults and evaporation caused the water level to drop.

We wandered down the muddy, dusty streets, lined with tour companies and artisan shops, until we came to the lake's edge. The giant body of water shimmered in the evening sun. The shoreline was dotted with fishing and tour boats. We watched as a group of backpackers and a couple of Indian women returned from the nearby island, *Isla del Sol*. A small number of canoeists were scattered between the moored boats. All of these became perfectly silhouetted against the large orange ball now sinking ever closer towards the distant waterline. Scattered clouds on the horizon reflected the sun's rays to produce a bright orange horizon as it eventually sank into the lake. It was magnificent.

Well I had finally made it. This was my second focal point and, in a sense, the end of my journey. However I wasn't about to make the same mistake as I had back in Tierra del Fuego. I still had two weeks before I flew out of La Paz. Now there were many things I could do here in Bolivia. Back in La Paz I had considered risking the death-defying bus journey to Coroico. I had to admit that the idea of falling 3000 metres into a giant canyon in just 80 kilometres held a certain morbid fascination. As well as an intense adrenaline rush, the scenery must be out of this world. But on the flip side there was the very high risk of being sent to an early grave by a runaway bus. I know that many people might say, 'When it's your time to go, there is nothing you can do about it.' That's fair enough, when it is my time to go I'll gladly submit. But what if it's the driver's time to go, why the hell should I go with him? I had also heard stories of drivers being drunk. I don't know how much truth there was in that, but it was a cause for concern. Even if they weren't drunk, there was the problem of fatigue. I had seen how hard Vicente had worked on our trip across the altiplano. He and many of the other drivers had been made to drive from Uyuni to the Bolivian border overnight in order to take us on our three-day tour. They'd had no sleep. (One of the other groups had to keep waking their driver.) Also since Sten had told me way back in Río Gallegos of the Dutch girls being killed on one bus, I had heard of yet another going down and killing a group of Israelis, along with all the other passengers. All of these ingredients made for a potentially lethal cocktail. Was it worth taking the chance?

However the choice had been made for me. The road to Coroico was closed. Bus drivers had blockaded the entrance in protest for better roads in Bolivia. So I couldn't if I wanted to.

There were many other places on the backpacker trail to visit. Peru was just a few miles away. In fact I could even see it across the lake. It's always tempting to try and see as much as possible, but that only leads to rushing through and taking pictures. The same applied to all the other places I could have visited in Bolivia. Thus I decided to spend most of my time here and soak up the atmosphere.

The air grew decidedly chilly with the setting of the sun. Not surprising considering the altitude. Andrea and I wandered off in search of a cheaper Internet place than the one in the plaza. A sign in the street directed us to a café bar called *Sol y Luna*. Just up the road from Plaza Sucre stood the very posh *Hotel Gloria*. Sol y Luna was attached to this. We stepped through the door to the sight of two very surprised Englishmen sat at the bar. They both knew Andrea from further back on their travels. The barman was English also. Tom was looking after the place for a month while the owner was away. He was originally from Southampton, but had been travelling around South America for over a year. The others were from Marlborough. Both towns are near to where I come from.

Sol y Luna no longer had Internet access. But it did have cheap beer and a great atmosphere. Lit by candlelight it made for a very relaxing place. Along with the drinks and food, the menu also listed a choice of music to go with your purchase. We ordered a bottle of beer and chatted with the Englishmen. John and his wife had been travelling around the world for a few years when visa problems sent them both back home for a while. Upon return to travelling they persuaded Dave to quit his job and come with them.

After a couple of bottles we headed back to the hotel. The room was freezing. I attempted to do some writing, but my hands were too cold. The bed was cold too. Being a gentleman I had given Andrea my sleeping bag, so I threw on as many layers of clothing as possible. While Andrea drifted snugly off to sleep, I tossed and turned for a couple of hours before finally falling asleep myself.

In the morning the room had warmed up somewhat. Andrea had a flyer for the hotel *La Cupula*. It looked really nice and she and Pascale had wanted to find out how much it cost. We both decided to find another hotel. I could accept having a cold room, but not a cold bed. After depositing our backpacks at reception we wandered off in search of *La Cupula*. It was situated at the edge of town on the lower bank of Cerro Calvario, one of the two hills the town is set between. Although it wasn't high the climb at this altitude seemed to deprive you of all oxygen. Upon arrival at the front gate we were blown away by a breathtaking view of the sparkling blue Lake Titicaca down below.

The hotel was in a newly built colonial-style building with whitewashed walls and beautiful pinewood-framed windows. Just below us was a small garden with tables, chairs and hammocks. I liked the look of it already. We questioned the receptionist as to the prices and were offered a twin room for $6 each. An absolute bargain. The room was spacious, bright and decorated with bamboo furniture. So we took it.

It was a beautiful sunny day. Before collecting our bags we went for breakfast in one of the many cheap restaurants lining the streets of Copacabana. We found a nice little place with seating on a patio. Andean panpipe music played in the background, adding to the atmosphere somewhat. However it soon became apparent that it was the only tape they had. The Indian waitresses seemed very young. In countries like this the children are often made to work from a very young age; especially in restaurants and hotels, as they are often a family business.

Upon settling the bill I had no choice but to produce a 100-boliviano note. It was all I had. For the next five minutes I observed the waitress darting back and forth across the restaurant before finally reappearing with a handful of coins and dumping them on the table with a smile. It was almost as if she had raided everyone's piggy bank. Not wanting to be weighed down with silver I offloaded them to a woman in a nearby shop. She was glad of it. She explained that it was always difficult to get change here in Bolivia.

Pascale arrived later that day and got a double bed in a giant, well-lit room to herself for $7. We spent the days lazing in the hammocks and taking walks along the lakeside, and the evenings in Sol y Luna. La Cupula had its own kitchen, but it was so cheap to eat out that there was no need for it. Pegrey and trucha (kingfish and trout) were the specialities here, both fresh from the lake. Andrea had expressed a desire to swim in the lake. At this altitude the lake was not really warm enough for swimming.

'You must be mad!' I exclaimed, as she got ready to go in.

Pascale and I sat and watched as she slowly shivered her way in.

'It's nice once you get used to it!' she called out.

I wasn't about to find out, at least not yet.

*

At night barking and snarling dogs surrounded the lane to our hostel. After what had happened to the American, the girls were afraid. I however, had developed an indifference to them over the past three months. Okay so there was more chance of catching rabies here in Bolivia, but again the dogs were all mouth and no action. So I strolled past and ignored them. This always worked, apart from one night.

Coming back from Sol y Luna with Andrea we were challenged by a solitary dog. Instantly she stiffened. I told her not to worry and guided her past, keeping myself between her and the dog. However this one had guts. To my surprise he bounded up and clasped his jaws around my leg. As quickly as he did this he removed them and backed away a few paces, assuming a challenging position. Guess he didn't like the taste of me. Somehow I managed to keep my cool and continue walking, possibly the amount of alcohol inside me. To have retaliated would only have antagonised him the more. Although it was tempting to turn and kick the little shit down the street, he had the advantage of me: to inflict a potentially fatal disease. It didn't feel as though he had pierced the skin and upon return to the room I discovered he hadn't even pierced my jeans.

Wimp!

After a long day walking along the lake, in which we were adopted by a friendly stray dog, we spent the evening in Sol y Luna drinking with Tom. Although he was working he drank nearly as much as we did. The place wasn't exactly busy so it wasn't really a problem.

Just like Doris, Andrea had insisted that I look her in the eyes when we said cheers.

'Why is it that you Germans are so insistent upon that?' I asked.

'Because if you don't, then it means seven years bad sex,' explained Andrea.

'Hmm, well seven years bad sex is better that seven years no sex, I suppose,' I thought out loud.

Andrea laughed.

She then proposed a toast. We clinked glasses and her soft brown eyes looked directly into mine. I stared back.

'Prost!' I said, hoping to impress her with my limited knowledge of the German language.

She smiled. Guess it worked.

The smile remained and her eyes suddenly seemed bigger and deeper. A warm light emanated from within, almost as if she was telepathically trying to convey me something. I found myself being drawn to them. How is it that women can do that? Does their mother teach it to them at an early age? Or does it just come naturally? Even so it's very unnerving that they have this power over us men that we simply cannot, and never will, understand.

'One for the road,' announced Tom, as he looked at our empty bottles.

The two of us had been giving the girls lessons in English slang. 'One for the road,' was possibly the one they will remember most. We had many for the road and eventually staggered back very late and very drunk, leaving Tom the problem of working out our final bill in his intoxicated state.

At the hostel Andrea and I wandered up to the balcony for a nightcap - cigarette in other words. The stars twinkled above us and the now very dark lake formed the backdrop. A gentle breeze rustled the leaves on the nearby trees. The hotel was silent, but the night air was filled with the howling of stray dogs. I couldn't help but notice Andrea's eyes looking at me, conveying that telepathic message once again. Am I reading too much into this? I thought. I couldn't be sure. It wouldn't have been the first time. If I'm wrong then it could be very embarrassing for us both. Still, there was only one way to tell.

The night was cold. I stubbed out my finished cigarette and took her in my arms. She didn't resist, and there under the starry night nearly 4000 metres above sea level, in a place I'd dreamed of travelling to for years, we kissed. It was a long, lingering kiss, eventually broken by the annoying sound of barking dogs.

Preferring to get out of the cold, we made our way hand in hand downstairs and into our room, closed the door and pulled the curtains.

___14___

The Land that Time Forgot

Well you didn't think I'd tell you what happened next, did you?

A couple of days later I found myself wandering down to the lake with the intention of catching the boat to Isla del Sol (island of the sun). The island is an hour or so by boat from Copacabana. Of the forty-one islands on the lake, Isla del Sol is the largest at 14.3 square kilometres. It is credited as the legendary site of the Incas' creation. It is said that the first Incas were born there, along with all sorts of other important entities, including the sun itself. The Aymara and Quechua Indians accept these legends as history and the island remains sacred to them.

Pascale had taken a boat over the day before and returned this morning, somewhat redder than usual. She and Andrea were now heading off to Peru to hike the Inca trail. I questioned her as to what the island was like.

'Putain!' she exclaimed - this being a regular phrase of hers - 'it is beautiful! But there is nothing much to do once you have hiked the island. You can only spend one day there. And you can't buy anything on the island.'

Well I was about to see for myself.

Andrea came down to the pier to see me off. As we chatted I was suddenly aware of a little old man appearing next to me.

'You want to go to Isla del Sol?' he asked.

'Yes,' I replied, 'I'm going to take the boat.'

'I have a boat, I can take you,' he offered.

The price was the same, ten bolivianos, so I agreed and followed him down to where his boat was moored. I said goodbye to Andrea and hauled my backpack in to the rear of the boat.

I was pleasantly surprised to see that I was not embarking a tourist boat. The old man was ferrying supplies to the island, along with many of the locals. I was the only gringo on board. I talked briefly with a toothless old man, who I couldn't understand, and then had to dash back to the hostel to return my forgotten key. There really had been no need to run though; we didn't leave for over an hour.

I spent most of the time listening to the mix of Aymara and Spanish being spoken around me. I was soon to learn that most of the Indians spoke in Aymara. But due to some of the language being lost since the Spanish domination, and the fact that there weren't any Aymaran words for many of the things in the modern world, these words are now supplemented with Spanish.

The boat wasn't exactly the most powerful on Lake Titicaca, so we made slow progress across to the island. However I was in no hurry. I disembarked at the southern end and was approached by a nine-year old boy offering to take me to a hostel, where I could get a room for ten bolivianos.

The hostel was in the hilltop village of Yumani, about 200 metres up from where we stood. I followed the boy as he led me up a steep and long flight of steps and then continuously uphill along a winding track. The boy took confident strides while I puffed and wheezed along behind with two backpacks.

'¿Cansado (tired)?' asked the boy.

I nodded.

'Let me carry one of your bags,' he offered.

It was a nice offer, but I couldn't expect him to do that. So I soldiered on.

Halfway up we met his five-year old sister, the cutest little Indian girl I had ever seen. She was dressed in the traditional way. The two of them conversed in Aymara and then she joined us for the final stint of our hike uphill. The girl spoke Aymaran and very little Spanish. After much insistence from the boy I let him carry my daypack. The two of them shared the burden between them. I joked with them about taking my big pack.

'I can take it,' offered the boy, seriously.

'No I think it will be too heavy for you,' I replied.

He was adamant that he could carry it though, but I couldn't let him.

We finally made it to Posada Ñustas, which was owned by the children's aunt. Perched on the very brow of the hill it afforded an all round view of the island. The children eagerly followed me into my room and sat watching me unpack.

'La Propina,' said the boy, holding out his hand.

I should have guessed. It was only fair though, so I gave them a couple of bolivianos each. As I unpacked I remembered the inflatable globe I had brought with me for just such an occasion. So I pulled it out and ventured back outside to find them.

'¿Regalame?' asked the boy, his eyes alight.

'It's for you both,' I explained, as I helped them to blow it up.

The boy instantly recognised it as the world and pointed out the school he goes to along with eighty-five children, before joining his sister in using it as a football. Kicking it down the lane he shouted back, 'It will be good for school!' instilling in me the hope that it might actually help improve their knowledge of the world, as well as make a great football.

As I followed them down the street other children ran up to me - after hearing of my gift to the boy - shouting: '¡Regalame!'

'I don't have anything else,' I replied.

We passed a teenage Indian girl who was trudging up the hill with a large bundle on her back. She stopped and picked up the globe, studying it with fascination.

I wished I had brought more.

As the sun went down I trudged back up the hill and over to the other side in order to watch the sunset. I joined an Australian couple already there, and we sat and watched the locals slowly trudging their way up with the day's produce and supplies from the mainland. Heavily laden donkeys helped carry much of the burden, but the men, women and children all carried their share. The years of hard physical work was etched into the adults' faces. There were no vehicles on the island and no machinery to work the land either. All farming was carried out totally by hand and foot. Despite this they remained some of the friendliest Indians I had come across yet. As they passed us they all responded to my greeting, and some even stopped for a chat. One of the women told me that most people on the island speak Aymara. There are some that speak Quechua, but very few. They had just returned from Copacabana, where they went every weekend to visit friends or relatives and to stock up with supplies. This was the only way they had of carrying the supplies up from the harbour.

After the sunset I wandered back up the hill to the sight of the full moon rising from behind distant snow-capped mountains on the other side of the lake. I took a short walk through the village and was accosted by children asking me for sweets.

'Regalame, caramelos,' they all said.

I didn't think it was such a good idea to give these children sweets because they had no dental hygiene. On the boat over I had seen many of the adults scoffing on sweets with the few bad teeth they had left. Also it's not good to encourage children to beg, even if they are poor. They must learn that these things have to be earned, and that in order to receive something they must give something in return. That's how the world works. You cannot blame them, it's us that cause it. Tourists who take pity on these cute children and give them handfuls of sweets often don't realise the damage they are doing. Although it's hard to say no to these children, you have to be cruel to be kind. It broke my heart to see their faces drop when I said no, and it was even sadder to see them following me up the street putting on these sad faces and begging for sweets. But they had to learn.

That night I ate in the restaurant next to the hostel. This was also a hostel. I found a table by the window and was brought a candle by the owner. Outside the window I could see the moon was now high in the sky and casting a long pool of soft light across the surface of the lake. For 18 bolivianos I dined on fresh trout and washed it down with a bottle of cold beer. I had the feeling I was going to like it here.

It was after ten when I returned to my hostel. The door was locked. I tried the one around the corner. Locked. So I returned to the rear door again and banged loudly. The night air was cold, and the thought of being stuck out here for the night sent an added shiver through me. Then I spotted someone coming out the door at the other end. I rushed over. It was one of the guests coming out for a cigarette. While he did this I ducked in and went to my room. For some reason my light didn't work. I was to find out later that the electric was only switched on for a few hours in the evening. My room was of adequate size for one person. It was pretty basic - two beds, bare walls and a window - but was all I really needed. I placed my sleeping bag under the covers already provided and crawled into the welcome warmth of my bed.

The next morning I arose bright and early, had breakfast next door and then headed off on a hike across the island. A network of walking trails linked the other villages on the island. Locals used these trails as well as tourists. Obviously as there were no vehicles on the island, the inhabitants either walked or took a boat. Most visitors either took a day tour from Copacabana that takes in all the typical sights, or the more adventurous got dropped off at the northern end and hiked the trails to Yumani, where they either spent the night or caught the boat straight back.

From behind the hostel a trail led north along a ridge and past farming plots. It seemed that the entire island was built on ridges, and each one had been sectioned off and farmed. A short way along I bumped into the Australian couple, but soon lost them as I inadvertently took a different route.

I came over a hill to the sight of the village of Challa down below. A lone Indian woman was herding sheep along the slope of the hill. She made a perfect figure against the surrounding landscape. However the instant I took out my camera she sat down with her back to me. I put my camera away and walked over, apologised and said I wouldn't take a picture if she didn't want.

'¡Tienes que pagar!' she shouted back.

I chuckled to myself. At least she didn't attack me.

It seemed I had lost my way a bit.

'Where is the path?' I asked her.

She kindly directed me back onto it and I continued on.

In the village below stood two large buildings. The woman had told me that it was the colegio central (central college). The trail led into a forest, which provided shelter from the light rain that had now started to fall. I came across two young women herding bulls along the trail and wisely got out of the way. They chuckled and greeted me as they passed. The trail led on through the forest and down the side of the mountain to the northern town of Challapampa. Here the locals seemed less friendly. I suspected this was because boatloads of tourists stopped here daily.

Contrary to Pascale's belief that you couldn't buy anything on the island, I found a little shop by the harbour and bought cigarettes, a snickers bar and a bottle of fizzy drink. During my entire trip through Chile I had been unable to buy any decent chocolate bars. They just didn't seem to stock anything like snickers or mars bars. Yet here in this remote part of the world, where the people lived a life that belonged more at the turn of the last millennium, these tiny shops were filled with them. It was one of the very few luxuries these people had. It's a pity that toothpaste wasn't one of them.

I took a short break and continued onwards. The trail led across a beautiful sandy beach running down to the deep blue of the lake - I could almost have believed I was on a Mediterranean island. I continued back uphill, passing a group of Americans I had talked to the night before, and then ventured on until I came across a small shop in the middle of nowhere. It was way outside of town, but at one of the many listed attractions on the route.

'¿Comprame (buy something from me)?' asked a little old lady stood behind the counter, looking longingly through a diary containing pictures of other archaeological sights around Central and South America. She said it was a present from a passing tourist.

She then directed me to the nearby attraction, *La Piedra Sagrada* (sacred stone). It was a stone. Personally I failed to see the attraction. The old lady explained that wrong doers were killed upon it. The three sins were to steal, to lie, and the other I couldn't understand. She then produced a dirty shopping bag full of broken pottery and explained that her daughter had found it buried in the mountain. She said it was very old, before the Incas. But somehow I doubted that. Her daughter was apparently suffering with arthritis and they were waiting for a doctor to come and treat her, but as yet he hadn't arrived. The old lady wouldn't tell me her name. When I asked she became all shy and nervous and said it was an indigenous name and that I couldn't pronounce it. She made me laugh. In the end I bought a couple of pieces of the broken pottery from her and headed back off with a Dutch couple that had come along while we were talking.

After a short visit to the Chincana Ruins, situated at the

northern end of the island, I took the main route back over the mountains and arrived back in Yumani around five.

I took a short rest to ease the headache that had now set in - caused by not drinking enough water - and then played football with the small boy of the family who ran the hostel. He didn't have a ball so we made do with an empty mineral water bottle. This became a daily occurrence.

That evening I ate in my hostel's restaurant. It didn't have the candlelit atmosphere of the other place, but it did have the company of two very nice girls. Vanessa was from Peru. She had gone to school in Switzerland. There she made friends with Veronica who had now come over to visit her. Thus Vanessa spoke fluent French as well as Spanish. The two of them had been working in a small village on the Bolivian side of the lake, researching and photographing the life there. Normally the people would demand money for photographs, but when they explained that it was for their college studies the locals happily obliged. Upon arrival in La Paz Veronica had tried to take some finishing pictures, but had been bombarded with potatoes. Due to living in a rural area for the past week or so their staple diet had been potatoes. They were sick of the sight of them. So being pelted with them was not a fitting end to their studies.

I had breakfast with them both the next morning and they informed me that they had made an on the spot decision to go Ecuador.

'We are fed up with the cold,' explained Vanessa.

I could relate to that. So I said goodbye to them and took a walk to the neighbouring village of Challa and the beach I had spotted the day before. Yumani and Challa pretty much run in to each other.

'This is the border,' explained Joakin, a local man I had

befriended as I had made my way through the village.

A tiny narrow lane ran down the mountain, denoting the division between the two villages. We crossed over into Challa and continued on.

I liked it here. There was no noise, no pollution and the locals lived a relatively simple life. Although they didn't have much. I had spotted many men carrying beat-up old radios they had somehow managed to lay their hands on. It seemed they relied a lot on gifts from visitors. They worked hard however. That was apparent each evening when I would watch families traipsing up the hill loaded with the day's produce on their backs. Agriculture and tourism are the island's only sources of income, along with the occasional chance for some real estate.

'Do you want to buy some land?' asked Joakin, after I had told him how much I loved this island.

He had some land in the north that he wanted to sell.

'You can build a house and find a nice local girl to settle down with,' he told me.

Not an offer you get everyday, especially at the cost of ten dollars per square metre.

I declined his generous offer though, explaining that I didn't have the money. We parted further up the hill and I made my way along a winding trail to the beach far below.

As I emerged from the undergrowth I was greeted by a pig. Livestock ran freely by the water's edge. A small rowing boat was moored nearby. As I shot off a few pictures I was approached by a middle-aged couple.

'You want to take a picture of us by the boat?' asked the man.

'Very kind of you,' I replied.

So I shot off a picture of two smiling locals stood by their boat.

'Muchas gracias.'

He nodded and held out his hand. 'La propina.'

I should have guessed.

I gave him a few bolivianos and then he started to push the boat out to the water.

'You want a lift to the next village?' he asked.

I declined for fear of another unexpected cost. As I watched them row off into the lake I shot another picture, intending to get my money's worth.

I then wandered off along the beach. The beach was at the end of a large green valley. A small stream ran from the mountains, along a large open field and out into the lake. Donkeys and pigs grazed around it. I followed the stream inland and headed towards the village. On the way I met Joakin again.

'Are you going swimming?' he asked.

'No, it's too cold,' I replied.

'If you go around to the next bay it is warmer,' he explained.

I told him I'd think about it.

I headed up a path, through the village and over a hill that took me down to another beach. It was also the colegio central. On the walk down many children had stopped and asked me for sweets.

'It's rude to ask for things,' I had told them.

The village had been quiet. Most of the youngsters were at school, it seemed, and the adults were out working in the fields.

I crossed the beach and made my way up over the cliffs and found a nice secluded spot by the water. I had decided to take Joakin's advice and go for a swim. It was a beautiful day and the shimmering clear blue water looked so inviting. I felt that I couldn't leave here without having swum in Lake Titicaca. But most of all I needed a wash. I hadn't showered since arriving at the island. There was a shower in the hostel, but it was provided from a dirty big container that caught the rainwater and channelled it to the showerhead. Feeling there was a good chance that the water would make me dirtier than I already was, I decided against using it. Lake Titicaca is so clean that it would be a much better way to cleanse my body.

There was one drawback though; I hadn't brought my swimming trunks. But there was no one around, and I was in a wild and untamed land, where people probably washed this way daily, so why not go as nature bore me?

My decision made I stripped off and dived in. As my body hit the freezing cold water the air was instantly ripped from my lungs as my body tensed from the shock, and I surfaced gasping for breath. If this was the warm part of the lake then I'd hate to think what the cold part was like. Instantly I began swimming in rapid circles in a desperate attempt to get the blood circulating once again. It took ten minutes of vigorous exercise, but I finally acclimatised to the water. Once that was achieved I happily swam around in some of the freshest water I'd ever had the pleasure of being immersed in, and then climbed out and passed the rest of the day sunbathing.

Walking back I took a different route up into the mountains and along the dusty, stony paths that ran along the edge of the hills. Down in the lush green valley I spotted an Indian lady sat by a tiny meandering stream washing her beautiful long, jet-black hair. Her son played in the dirt nearby. Her hair glistened in the evening sun as she sat and brushed it: a shining glossy black like the feathers of a crow. I continued on through the valley, passing the odd group of young Indian girls sat on a nearby hill, and made my way to the top, where I took a rest.

Whilst sat there I was greeted by a local guy wearing a trilby hat. Mario Quispe Mendoza, as he introduced himself, was on his way to visit a friend, but found time in his busy schedule for a chat. He pulled from his pocket some freshly picked awa, the local produce - along with potatoes and other vegetables. It was very similar to a runner bean. He was eating them raw, so I felt inclined to do so; not wanting to offend local custom. Actually, they tasted quite nice. Mario explained that it only grows on the island and is exported as far as France and Germany.

'Do you want a place to stay?' he asked, using the only bit of English he knew.

In response to this I pulled out my English-Spanish pocket dictionary and gave it to him as a gift, explaining that he could use it to help learn some more English. I was near the end of my trip and felt sure I could do without it for a few days. I could buy a new one when I returned to England. I wrote a message in both languages on the inside and he gratefully accepted.

Mario was forty-six and had been born on the island. He had three children: one working in Brazil, another working in Argentina and the last at school here on the island. He had no intention of leaving the island, this was his home. He also had a boat and offered to take me to Isla de la Luna, a nearby island.

'Could you take me on to Copacabana?' I asked.

He nodded. 'When do you leave?'

I wasn't sure of this. Contrary to Pascale's belief that you could only spend one day on the island, I was enjoying myself. I liked the tranquil atmosphere, the friendly locals and the ancient way of life. I felt like I had travelled back in time and didn't have a care in the world. I could quite easily have stayed here for a few weeks. However I didn't have a few weeks to spare. I had a flight to catch in a week's time and things to do in La Paz.

I sat and thought for a moment. Today was Tuesday, my third here. I wasn't ready to leave just yet, so I decided to stay one more day and leave on Thursday. Mario agreed to come see me at the hostel and make arrangements to leave. With that we shook hands and went our separate ways.

I followed the path back to the hostel and came across a perfect photo opportunity. A solitary llama stood on a ridge overlooking the lake. Next to him was also a solitary sheep. With the soft light of the evening sun shimmering on the surface of the lake far below it made a beautiful setting. I pulled out my camera and set about shooting off some pictures. As I concentrated on lining up a shot I felt something touch my leg. I looked down to see the sheep had wandered up and was now nuzzling my knee. Once he'd attracted my attention he looked me straight in the eyes and lifted his paw.

'La propina.'

I should have guessed.

Clouds had drifted in later that evening and remained throughout the night. As I ate my breakfast the next morning I debated whether I should leave today. There was always the chance it might clear up. Then I suddenly realised just how English I was being, moaning about the weather. We always complain about the bad weather, yet when the sun does come out we all moan that it's too hot. Outside it was cloudy and windy, but it wasn't raining. So I decided to stay and experience the island on one its bad days. After all, I'm sure it isn't sunny and hot all the time. If it did rain, great! These people needed the rain in order to make a living. So with that in mind I finished my breakfast and took a walk to the southern end of the island.

There was no one around. The locals were far below working their plots. The wind dropped around midday and the thick layer of cloud broke into scattered clouds providing sunny spells. It warmed up so I found a spot on a mountaintop and sat and watched the locals at work.

Laboriously they went about their everyday tasks, using hand tools only and moving everything by foot. It looked to be backbreaking work. I wondered if maybe I ought to have let that boy carry my large backpack. It would have been good training for the work he would undoubtedly have to do when he grows up. It was a tough life for them, and it showed. I felt sure that many of them were a lot younger than they appeared. It's a life I certainly didn't envy them.

Later that evening, as I was wandering through the village, a young girl approached me. Dora asked if I wanted to take a photograph of her.

'How much?' I asked.

'50 centavos,' she replied.

She was cheaper than the old couple with the boat had been.

'What are you going to buy with the money?' I asked her, knowing full well what the answer would be.

'Galletas (biscuits),' she replied.

Here was my dilemma. I would much rather give her some money in return for posing for a photograph. At least that way she would be learning the value of having to give something in return. Much better than begging for sweets.

Although I wouldn't be giving her the sweets, she would still go and buy them, but will at least have earned them.

Yet the problem still remained that without proper dental hygiene her teeth would rot.

'How do you clean your teeth?' I asked her.

'Like this,' she replied, rubbing the tip of her finger across the surface of her teeth.

'Yes, but what do you use?'

'Saliva!'

I went on to lecture her that she must clean her teeth very well after eating sweets. 'Sugar is very bad for your teeth,' I said.

She nodded her head. 'You take a photo of me now.'

I wondered just how much of this she was taking in. I took the photo and then gave her one boliviano. I know, I'm too kind.

I wandered back up to my hostel and sat outside the Hostel Templo del Sol next door. This was where I had been eating. I preferred it to mine, as I liked the candlelit atmosphere. María, the owner, joined me and we chatted.

On the adjacent hill stood a building still under construction. María explained that it was going to be their second hostel. They had owned this one for four years now, and business was good. It slept forty people. January and February were busy months with lots of Argentines; June and July also. We talked about the lack of work here in Bolivia and the poor standard of living. I told her a bit about England.

The people of these third-world countries often have the mistaken belief that all us foreigners are rich. It's perfectly understandable really when they see us with so much money to spend. And in their countries we are rich because everything is so cheap to us. But in our own it's a totally different story. We may earn more money but the cost of living is so much higher. And everyday things often cost so much more. Where I come from real estate has reached ridiculous proportions, and petrol is unbelievably expensive. I agree we have a much better standard of living than these people do, which goes without saying. But the problem is that many only see the riches and therefore want to come, believing that they too can live such a wonderful life. They see people like us flashing lots of money around. They see our television programs and everyone living this life of luxury. But the sad truth is that when they do come, most have no skills and cannot get good work. Many end up begging on the streets, or working in menial jobs with very little pay. Either way they are still living the same lifestyle they had in their own country, but they now have the added envy of living next to people with much more than they do; and have to suffer racial prejudice. Most would have been better off in their own countries.

The biggest problem here is the lack of decent education. The ones that are able to leave and get a good education, in the US for example, invariably don't want to go back. And who can blame them? But if they did go back they might be the ones who could help pull the country out of its economic depression. Many people say that countries are often third-world because they are landlocked. But you only have to look at Switzerland to see that it not true. Switzerland got rich on its banking system, so there is always an answer. Many years ago Bolivia had access to the sea, but lost that land to Chile. It has also lost land to Brazil and Paraguay over the years. It hasn't had much luck really. Ever since that the Bolivian people have refused to accept their landlocked status and continuously voice their demand for access to the sea. Personally I think they should accept this status and set about finding other ways to improve the economy.

Hoping to dispel the myth that we are all filthy rich I told María about the cost of things in England and gave her an example of how much a house would cost to buy.

'Most people cannot afford to buy outright,' I explained, 'they have to borrow the money from a bank and pay it back over 25 years with interest. If they lose their job they cannot pay.'

María was quite surprised to hear this. With a bit of luck this news would spread around and these people might see us in a different light. It made me sad to think that many of them view us as nothing more than a vending machine for money and sweets. And it was our fault this was happening. Tourists, who passed through here in a day and never got to know any of the locals, made this worse. It was something to think about. When little Maria Teresa asked me if I wanted to take a photo, I did so and then talked with her. She was happy of the company and remained with me, even though I had already given her the money she originally wanted.

As darkness fell I talked with an Argentinean girl who was staying in my hostel. The little boy I had been playing football with each day was now wandering around in circles nearby, singing at the top of his voice, '¡Bonitas muchachas (beautiful women)!' It seemed that they learned quick on this island. I had enjoyed my stay here and would be sad to leave in the morning. I was also glad that I had opted to stay longer than just one day. I felt sorry for the people who just passed through here in a day, because they had missed so much. On the surface it seems like there is nothing much more to see.

But there is. María had told me that if I come back next year, I could work for her in the new hostel. Not a bad offer. If I was able to come back, I might just take her up on it. For it's not everyday you get to travel back in time.

_____15_____

A Good Deed

Stood on the quayside the next morning I waited while Mario trotted off to prepare his boat for the journey to Copacabana. With me were two English guys from the hostel, who had wanted to come along also. More money for Mario. The two Englishmen had made their way to the island via the village of Yampupata, which is just across the strait from the island. They had hiked the trail from Copacabana to Yampupata and then paid one of the locals to row them across.

We looked across the harbour wondering which of these magnificent boats we would be riding in. Then, to our dismay, Mario came out from in-between them rowing a tiny sailing boat. This would be an interesting trip.

We embarked and he set off rowing the boat for ages to get around the shelter of the harbour. Then he continued rowing around a smaller island until we reached the open lake. Isla de la Luna sat directly ahead. However the wind was against us, so we couldn't take the direct route. As the other way was a lot longer we decided to forget the island and go straight to Copacabana. Relieved to hear this, Mario pulled

in the oars and set about putting up the sail, while we drifted perilously towards the small island we had just passed.

Our boat was not much bigger than a standard rowing
boat, and the sail was fitted to an old fashioned wooden
mast. It was all quite a fitting end to my time here on Isla
del Sol. Once the sail was in position we set off.

A gentle breeze sent us gliding across the lake in perfect
harmony. During the breaks in conversation, all that could
be heard was the gentle rushing of water as the tiny boat cut
through it. This was my first ever time sailing, and where
better to have my first experience than on Lake Titicaca.
Once again it was a beautiful day and we sat back and
enjoyed it. I chatted with Mario as I watched the island
shrink off into the distance. I had the feeling that if I
returned in years to come, nothing much will have changed.
However Mario explained that by next year the island
would be powered from the mainland. Power will be cabled
across the strait from Yampupata. I winced at the thought of
large ugly electricity cables stretching across this beautiful
lake. But it's progress for the people, I know. And something that was painfully needed by the locals. But it did kind
of kill the romance of it all.

We soon hit the shelter of the mountains and had to pull
down the sail and start rowing. Figuring I would help
reduce the workload for Mario, I offered to row. However it
was considerably more difficult than it looked, and we
weren't making rapid progress. Frustrated by this, Mario
insisted that he took over.

The sky had been without a single cloud all the way, but
a thick layer drifted in as we approached the mainland.
There was a good chance that the main storm would pass us
by, and we would just get a light shower. However we

weren't about to take any chances. The three of us pulled out our raincoats and put them on. I watched as Mario pulled out an old worn and tattered jacket and put that on. It would give him no protection against the rain.

'You don't have a raincoat?' I asked him.

'No,' he replied, 'there aren't any here. In La Paz perhaps, but not here.'

For him La Paz was a million miles away. He eyed my raincoat curiously. 'You sell me yours?' he asked.

I thought about this for a moment. It had been useful, certainly. But this guy possibly needed it more than me. Mario was a fisherman who fished the lake in the dead of night. Now I knew full well just how cold it got here at night. To get caught out on the lake in the rain at night must be hell. I only had a week before returning home, and I had been thinking about buying another anyway. I wanted one that allowed my skin to breathe. So I struck a deal, which definitely favoured Mario, to give it to him in part exchange for the boat ride.

Fortunately the rain held off. Mario dropped us off in a potato field at the back of town. I had promised to take some pictures of him sailing away, and send them to him. But the onset of thick cloud had ruined any chances of a good photo.

We sorted ourselves out, paid him and then I removed my jacket and handed it to him. Obviously extremely grateful for this, he clasped my hand, bent down and kissed it. '¡Muchas gracias por tus regalos (thank you very much for your presents)!' he exclaimed, then got back in his boat and I photographed him as he sailed off, proudly clutching his new raincoat; obviously hoping he would be the envy of the other fisherman.

I felt an overwhelming sense of well-being at this selfless

act I had just performed. I had given up my *only* means of protection against the rain, in order that a poor fisherman could fish Lake Titicaca at night and remain dry and warm. I had helped improve the quality of his life. This is what travelling is all about for me. These brief encounters with the people of the country I travel, serve to add something to mine and their lives. I had gained knowledge and insight into the life of some Titicaca Indians, and they had gained an insight into mine. As long as I live I will always remember this place. The fact that at the turn of the second Millennium, when many of us were immersed in the delights and comforts of the modern world, there was a relatively large population (I'd had many conflicting reports as to the actual amount) of Indians who still lived a very meagre existence.

I thought about this as I waded across the potato field in fear of getting shot by the owner. Once I reached the road I rejoined the others and we trotted off towards Copacabana, just as it started to rain.

Now there's gratitude for you.

___16___

A Most Bizarre Tour

I passed a couple more days in Copacabana, lazing during the day and propping up the bar for Tom at Sol y Luna in the evening, then got on a bus back to La Paz. As I sat in my seat waiting for the bus to leave I got talking to an old man seated at the adjacent window. Juan was very enthusiastic about things, including his desire to speak English. He spoke it fairly well. He seemed quite knowledgeable on the area, so I questioned him about the fact that many of the local Indians seemed to have gold in their teeth.

'Is it real?' I asked.

'Oh yes, very real,' he replied. 'Each gold filling costs $1000 US.'

I gulped.

He told me about a man he once knew who had $10,000 worth in his mouth. 'It's a status symbol,' he explained, 'the amount of gold in your teeth shows how much money you have. There are no poor people in Bolivia. They all work for themselves.'

That may have been true, but the past few days had

proved to me that not everyone was that fortunate. The people he talked about were the many stallholders around the country. I didn't doubt that many of them were fortunate enough to earn good money from this business. You could pretty much buy anything you wanted from a stall in La Paz. The streets were crowded with them, and they sell everything from food and clothing to stationery and consumer technology. I once saw a woman selling miniature televisions. I wondered where they got this stuff. People bought it though, which shows that they really can make a lot of money. But I think the problem is that they lack the knowledge on how to use the money wisely, to improve their standard of living for example. As the bus rolled on down the road, I watched the lines of women washing clothes in the river. With all that money they could afford to go to a laundrette. Instead though, they spend it on gold teeth to show how much money they have. The sad fact is that they fail to realise they don't have the money anymore. It's all in their teeth.

At the lake crossing everyone got out as usual.

'Where are they going?' I asked Juan.

'They take the boat across,' he answered.

'Is it free?'

'Yes,' he replied.

Oh well, might be a good photo opportunity, I thought. As I wandered towards the boat with Juan, we stopped for a while to talk to a stallholder. She was one of the students in his English class. At the embarkation point I was shocked to discover that you had to pay one boliviano. I failed to see the logic of getting off and paying when you could have stayed on the bus.

To our dismay we found that the boat had already gone.

The next boat was already there, but he refused to leave without a full load.

'Will the bus wait for us?' I asked Juan.

'I think so!' he replied, not very confidently.

You think so!

The alarm bells started ringing. My backpack was on that bus. If they did leave without us, then there was good chance it would go missing at the other end. Travelling up through Chile I had met backpackers who talked of nothing but the fact that everyone tries to rob you in Bolivia. Well that had certainly not been my experience, quite the opposite in fact, but that didn't change the fact that it went on.

I decided that a bribe was now in order.

'How about we give you a bit extra to take us now?' I suggested to the boat owner.

'Fifteen bolivianos,' he replied.

Sounds a lot I know, but it was only £1.50. I agreed and Juan and I were ferried across privately. So getting off that bloody bus had cost me sixteen bolivianos in all! That was more than the bus journey had cost.

From the bus depot it was a long walk to the centre of town. I made my way through row upon row of market stalls, and even spotted a woman selling sheep and pig's heads. As I passed she was also skinning a dead pig in full view of everyone.

I returned to where I had stayed before, but was put in a tiny dark room behind reception. I remained there, as I couldn't be bothered to carry my pack any further. I entered the room later that evening and turned on the light. It illuminated the toothless, wincing face of an old woman with wild grey hair and an unsightly wart on her chin. She was sleeping in her bed. Not a pretty sight. I spent a restless night listening to her talk to herself in her sleep.

The next morning I awoke to find the bed next to mine was occupied by Mario and his girlfriend from Colombia. He offered me some Marijuana for breakfast. I politely refused, preferring to go get an egg sandwich. Today was Sunday. I was due to fly out Thursday morning. My plan over the next few days was to stock up on artisans. Because of all the stuff I would be buying, I felt it would be a wise idea to get a private room. Plus I felt that after three months of hard travelling, I deserved the treat. I had decided to go to Hotel Viena, where Andrea had been staying. They gave me a room for 40 bolivianos.

Once settled in I stepped outside and bumped into Desiree, to whom I had been talking the night before. She and a guy from New Zealand were about to take the San Pedro prison tour. I had heard about this tour from many an enthusiastic backpacker along the trail. The tour was led by Fernando, one of the inmates. Apparently what you were supposed to do was go to the main gate and ask a guard for him. He then comes and you are let in for the tour. It is totally illegal, and the guards are paid off. Desiree and her friend had already been there and were told to come back at 11.30. It was nearly that now, so I wandered up with them.

We made our way to the Plaza San Pedro, where the prison was located. Outside stood a long queue of locals waiting to get in. It appeared that today was open day. We joined up with a group of other backpackers - safety in numbers - and shuffled up to the front gate.

I had a picture in my mind that Fernando would be this large, muscled double-hard bastard with tattooed arms and a neck the width of a tree trunk. He would most probably be surrounded by a group of equally hard and mean-looking heavies.

As we approached the front gate we saw the crowd of people gathered behind. From the back emerged a guy pointing to the front and shouting: 'Fernando!' One of the girls in our group was trying desperately to talk herself out of this.

'You'll be fine!' we all said, encouragingly.

You couldn't blame her really, this wasn't your average tour. It didn't exactly have the tourist board's seal of approval. Yet many other backpackers had survived to tell the tale, so it couldn't be that dangerous, could it?

A few words to the guards and we were ushered in ahead of the rest. All passports and cameras were left with the guards, if you had them. I'd left it all back at the hotel. To my surprise Fernando turned out to be anything less than how I had imagined. He was of medium height, skinny and wore a polo neck sweater. He looked like your average bloke in the street, and not very intimidating.

First order of business was for each of us to pay the so-called head of security one boliviano. He didn't look very intimidating either. He and his boys would be our protection for the duration of the tour.

Fernando spoke fluent English. He led us all through an alleyway and past a small shop, one of the many businesses in the prison. We were then led upstairs and taken into his home. He apologised for the mess and said that he was just in the process of moving in. The prison was more like a small town within a city. Fernando explained that when you are first sentenced and arrive, you have to pay 25 bolivianos to enter. If you don't have it, then you must work in the kitchen for three months. This is the worst job in the prison. You then move into a cell, or a home as they like to refer to it. The whole prison is sectioned off into various communities, ranging from low to upper class. To move into a community you have to pay the allotted amount, then either buy or rent your cell. Nothing is free, you either pay or work for it. Small businesses are encouraged within the prison. Fernando planned to fix up his cell and sell it at a profit.

'It's what I do,' he explained.

As well as lead tours and sell drugs.

Once seated in Fernando's cell we each paid him 40 bolivianos for the tour. From a hole in the roof dangled the head of security who proceeded to take the money and disappear, returning shortly after with any change required. After a brief talk about the prison and his cell, Fernando then asked: 'Right, now is anybody shopping? Because I don't do business outside this cell.'

All heads were shook in the negative.

'Shopping for what?' asked the girl who had wanted to leave upon entry, and still did.

Everyone chuckled.

'You won't want what he's selling,' I told her.

We were then led out of the cell and the tour began. In each corridor Fernando lined us up against the wall, in order not to obstruct other inmates and ultimately piss them off. The prison was crowded with people, as it was visiting day. The visitors were allowed to mix and mingle with everyone. Prisoners who could not afford to house and feed their families outside were allowed to have them come live inside with them. The children go out to school daily, and the women can come and go as they please. There was a kind of code of honour amongst the inmates. All violence was held at bay until after five when all visitors had left. After that there would be a knife fight here, a fist fight there etc.

Fernando explained that his gang ruled the prison. That's why they were able to run the tours. Of the forty bolivianos we had each paid, Fernando got three, some went to pay off the guards and a large chunk went to his boss.

'Women and children are sacred in this prison,' continued Fernando. 'When anything rough is about to occur, they are ushered out before it starts. A red flag is put up to indicate this.'

He pointed out a small, round and empty swimming pool down below. 'Any knife fights that occur happen in there. That way it is contained and no one else gets involved.'

Most of the inmates carried a knife for protection. Fernando didn't. He preferred to use a couple of two-foot long ice picks. 'One look at those will usually make them think twice,' he grinned.

When a rapist was convicted and sent to the prison the swimming pool was used for his initiation period.

'Whenever a rapist enters the prison we know about it,' said Fernando. 'The flag goes up, the women and children are removed and the initiation begins. All the inmates fill this area and the rapist is brought in. He is punched, kicked, beaten and thrown through the crowd and into the swimming pool. Then everyone cheers and taunts as ten of Bolivia's hottest chilli peppers are shoved one by one up his arse. He is then beaten again and sent to work in the kitchen for six months. Chances are he won't rape again.'

He went on to explain that if the rape had been severely bloody or had been on a child, then the guy wouldn't even make it to the swimming pool. He would disappear into an angry crowd. When the crowd dispersed a limp, lifeless body with many knives sticking out of it would be the only thing remaining. When the guards come and ask what happened everyone will shrug and say: 'Couldn't see, there were so many people around. But hey, he's a rapist!' Nothing more will be said and the body is taken away and disposed of.

Fernando led us through the different communities one by one, mindful of our protection and urging us to stay together. Although we didn't always see it, his gang was keeping a watchful eye on us, and the people around us. When a creepy guy walked past Desiree and made her cringe, Fernando instantly asked: 'Did he touch you?'

'No,' she replied.

I wondered what would have happened if he had?

The tour ended in the most expensive of all the little communities. Here lived some of the richest criminals in the prison. Occupying the penthouse was a notorious drug dealer. His cell had all the latest mod cons, including satellite television. He was caught when his planeload of drugs had crashed in Peru. An apartment here cost anything up to $10,000 US. This was also the safest area of the prison. Nothing happened here, according to Fernando. The people move here because they want a peaceful life. However they seemed pretty annoyed by our presence and informed us so by whistling. This seemed to unnerve Fernando who made us turn our backs.

Back in the main courtyard we all sat on a wall and Fernando asked us if we had any questions.

'What are you in here for?' asked one of the group.

'I'm a drug dealer,' he answered.

There was no pride, no remorse or even sensationalism in his voice, just the facts. He explained that at the age of nine he went to live in New York. His mother was poor and would buy him clothes many sizes too big so he'd grow into them. He'd hated that. At the age of fifteen he was offered the chance to sell drugs. He was told quite clearly of the consequences of his actions. He could make lots of money, go to jail or be killed. The guy then sent him away to think about it.

'I didn't sleep all night,' said Fernando. 'The next day I went and got the drugs.'

He has made no excuses since. When he's caught, he accepts it and does his time. When he gets out he deals drugs again. It's the life he has chosen and is prepared to accept the consequences.

The tour ended here. We each tipped Fernando a few bolivianos and thanked him for his honesty. He told us to spread the word about the tour. 'I rely on you people,' he said, 'I cannot advertise in the paper. This is illegal, but it's not illegal.'

Once through that gate and back in the plaza we all heaved a sigh of relief. Now I for one can honestly say that was possibly the weirdest and scariest thing I've ever done in my life. But it was worth it. It was a fascinating insight into prison life here.

___17___

A Welcome Surprise

The advantage to having your own room is privacy. Your stuff is secure and not at risk of being stolen. You can spread your things around as you please, and not have to keep them in your pack. Also you have the freedom to release unbelievably smelly farts at will. Upon awakening the next morning the realisation crept into my mind that perhaps I should have left the window open.

I showered, dressed and headed out to spend the day crawling the markets. As I trotted up the street I spotted Felix, the seven-year old boy who had cleaned my boots for me when I first arrived in La Paz. He instantly recognised me.

'Amigo!' he called out, as he came across the road.

He offered to clean my boots again. They didn't really need it but I quite enjoyed talking to him. He was a funny child. He enjoyed bargaining with me over the price.

'Where are you from?' he asked.

'England.'

'What money do they use there?'

'Pounds. You get ten bolivianos to one pound,' I informed him.

A wry smile lit up his face.

'Two pounds then!' he announced.

'I don't have any pounds, I cannot spend them here,' I told him.

'Dollars then.'

'I don't have dollars either, only bolivianos.'

He then proceeded to haggle the price, the figures becoming quite ridiculous at times. He took a long time cleaning my boots. When I thought they were done, he insisted that he could make them better. I kind of got the feeling that he enjoyed the company. He was one of the many street kids of La Paz. Although when questioned about his parents, he insisted that they were nearby. But I got the feeling that wasn't quite the truth. I gave him five bolivianos for a job well done and made another appointment.

'When do you leave?' he asked.

'I fly home to England on Thursday,' I replied.

'Then I will clean your boots for you on Wednesday, so they are clean for your trip.'

And so it was settled.

The city was even more chaotic today due to a protest march up the main street. This meant that all traffic was diverted up the smaller streets. You couldn't hear yourself fart for tooting horns. The Indians were protesting about the lack of work here in La Paz, and the rising cost of things. The only thing people could do was set up a stall. But the problem was that there were more vendors than buyers.

I took a walk through a market that led uphill, and seemed to go on forever. The market was lined with stalls selling the latest fashions - Wrangler and Calvin Klein jackets for 90 bolivianos. The whole city seemed to be one huge market. I bought some things from an old Indian lady who spent her day sat crossed-legged on a table surrounded by piles of clothing.

You could buy anything your little heart desired in La Paz (except vests, which were what I was looking for). You could even make a phone call from a stall. The women who ran these stalls seemed to be there all day. Often I would walk past and find one fast asleep. Another common sight was to see their children helping out, or sat there doing their schoolwork. (Evolution in progress.) Chances are that those kids would go on to do other things.

That evening I went into an Internet place and had just finished checking a message when I received another two there and then. One was from Andrea in Cuzco, and the other from Nick and Kirsten. They were in La Paz and, unbeknown to me at the time, were in an Internet place across the road. Instantly I mailed them back and we arranged to meet at their hotel in half an hour. This is a perfect example of the irony that technology can create. I was sat in an Internet café in La Paz, and Nick and Kirsten were sat in one across the road. Yet to discover this and to communicate with each other in order to arrange our meeting, our messages had been encoded, whizzed through the air and bounced off a satellite back down to a computer somewhere in the United States. Then all this was done in reverse for us to retrieve the message. The irony of it all is that the whole process was executed in less time than it would have taken for us to cross the road to where we were sitting.

I had to rush. Unfortunately a hasty exit was hampered by the young lad with incredibly bouffant hair at the front desk. He wanted to practice his very limited English with me. I tried to be patient, understanding what it's like, but ultimately we ended up speaking Spanish. I told him I was from England.

'Ah, and do they speak English there?' he asked.

I often find it unbelievable that I can be asked this question.

'Of course,' I replied, 'it's where the language originates from.'

I rushed back to my hotel, threw down my stuff and headed off to Hotel Austria. Hugs and hearty handshakes all round, we then headed off for something to eat and some beer to drink.

'We were so worried about you,' said Kirsten. 'We heard that another bus had gone down on the road to Coroico, and were scared that you were on it.'

It seemed that the road to Coroico had been re-opened whilst I was at Lake Titicaca and yet another bus had gone down, killing more backpackers.

It was so great to see them again, and we spent the evening reminiscing and catching up. They were in town for a couple of days, so we spent them together. I couldn't have thought of a more perfect way to end my trip.

The next day we went out to the disappointing ruins of Tiwanaco, joined also by an Australian from their hotel. Kate was actually living in England with her husband, but had come over here on her own for a short break.

Upon our return from the ruins we wandered through the markets. I bumped into Felix again, who informed me that he wouldn't be in the plaza tomorrow and wanted to clean my boots now. It seemed that he had a bad tooth and had to go to the dentist. He also had a headache, a symptom of the bad tooth I suspected. He wouldn't have it though. He cleaned my boots and then Nick's. Again he took longer than needed. He seemed to enjoy chatting to us all.

'Take him home with you,' said an Indian woman walking past.

I would have loved to, but that was just impossible.

The next morning I had a last breakfast with Nick and Kirsten. Kate moved to my hotel so she could get a single room. She was being kept awake all night by two girls with chronic diarrhoea, who were getting up constantly throughout the night.

Nick and Kirsten were heading off to Copacabana. However Nick had been suffering from the effects of bad food also. Upon return that evening I discovered that they were back and staying in my hotel. Nick didn't want to chance three and half hours on a bus with no toilet. So we all went out for a meal and yet another goodbye, promising no more surprise meetings.

'This is getting a bit tedious,' joked Nick.

At least I hope he was joking.

Epilogue

A Perfect Ending (or is it?)

And so it was I found myself sitting on the plane with Nathalie's coca leaves still in my backpack. I chatted with the Canadian bloke next to me, whilst half-wondering if my backpack was in customs now with a group of dogs stood around barking at it.

The Canadian was an aircraft technician and expressed his concern about the frost on the wings.

'The plane won't take off with that there,' he said.

Fortunately it melted as we taxied down the runway and we were soon airborne, answering my previous question. However I still had to get through with them at the other end.

In the adjacent seat sat a guy with round specs resting upon a large nose. He was rocking back and forth in his seat. His face was strained and he periodically vented built up air from his large nostrils.

'You see that guy there,' said the Canadian, 'he looks like he's gonna cry.'

We discussed the possibility of him being a potential air rage nut, or someone who is trying to conquer his fear of flying and would inevitably have to be restrained.

'Are you okay?' asked the Canadian, deciding it might be best to ask him instead of just guessing.

'Yeah,' he replied, 'I left my girlfriend back in La Paz.'

We flew eastward away from the mountains. I watched as the jagged peaks of the Andes slowly disappeared and the cloud broke away to reveal the Amazon rainforest below. The plane made a stop at Santa Cruz and the Canadian got off. The other remained so I talked with him. He was English. His girlfriend was Bolivian and had been living in England for a year. That's where they met. They got engaged and he went to Bolivia to meet the family and make wedding plans. He now had to return home alone for six months until the wedding. The family was very traditional so they wouldn't allow them to live together until after the wedding.

Our conversation was halted by the arrival of my new travelling companions, the original 'we love each other' couple. They sat down and started cooing, cuddling and reading the same magazine. Not a pleasant sight for the lovesick Englishman, I'd say.

My conversation interrupted, I sat back and stared out the window as we took off. I couldn't believe it was all over. It only seemed like yesterday I was flying in to Buenos Aires. Since then I had made so many friends and travelled through some of the most spectacular scenery I'd ever seen. Okay so I'd had many disasters. But that's what made it such an adventure. And to think I had only just touched on the beauty of Patagonia. There was still so much I hadn't seen. What a perfect start to the new Millennium! I imagined my grandchildren asking me in years to come, 'do you remember the turn of the century, granddad?' I'd have quite a story to tell them.

Suddenly I realised that I didn't want to be on this plane. I wanted to be enjoying a beer in Buenos Aires with Tom and Donna. Or sat on that mountaintop in Tierra del Fuego with Nick and Kirsten. Or hiking through the Lake District with Nathalie; wandering through the desolate wonder of the Atacama with Pepe; chugging my way across the altiplano with Vicente grinning his Cheshire cat grin; lying back in Mario's sailing boat as we glide across Lake Titicaca. These were all memories to cherish, along with many more. Chances are I will never see any of these people again, but I will never forget them, or the fun we had.

I had to change planes at Miami. I was looking forward to getting back to sea level. After spending the past month at such a high altitude I was going to feel like Superman, and could probably annihilate the country in *five point three seconds*. Or overdose on oxygen. But as it was, when I did arrive I just felt tired. I had to go through the tedious process of queuing at immigration to be stamped into the country, just to go and board a plane for England. Once aboard the realisation that they were showing the same in-flight movie as the last flight sent me off to sleep.

The next morning I nervously shuffled off the plane, went through immigration and then on to collect my baggage. It arrived untouched. I hauled on both backpacks, scooped up my bag full of artisans and headed off towards the *nothing to declare* section. I casually strolled through. A couple of customs officers were already checking other people. They stared at me as I slumped through. I met their look and continued on, making it safely outside.

*

A Perfect Ending (or is it?)

Sat waiting at the bus stop, the realisation sunk in that, as the coca leaf is effectively an illegal substance in countries outside of Bolivia, I was now officially a drug smuggler.

Fernando would have been proud.

Author's note

A few years ago I began to write about my experiences around the world. I have been backpacking since 1996. However it wasn't until after an incredible four-month adventure through Mexico that I started to write down these stories. At the time it was more for myself, so I could digest all that had happened. As the years progressed these stories evolved into a series of books and I began thinking seriously about having them published. I'm not a natural writer so the road was a bumpy one, filled with self-doubt. But along the way I found people who gave me the support and encouragement that I very much needed. I would like to thank the following people for that support, their advice, for reading my books, and for assisting me in various selfless ways during the production of this book:

My Dad, Uncle Tom, Julie & Rob Murphy, John McFerren, Hans van Well, Tiffany Parkinson, Linda Ashton, Allan Hudson, Eve Brood, Nathalie Speksnijder, Andrea Becker, Doris Knoblauch, Tom & Donna, Nick & Kirsten, Ray Gilbert, Andy Newman, Chris Stott, Pascale Marion, Paul Tighe, Sheryl Fever and anybody else I may have missed out. Thank you all for believing in me.

Since its writing, two of the couples featured in this book have got married. Backpacking can be the ultimate test of a relationship: living out of bags for months on end, less than adequate hygiene conditions a lot of the time, living out of each others pockets day in and day out. These, and many more, are the things that can make or break a couple. But from the moment I first met these two couples I knew that they would make it. Therefore I dedicate this book to Nick & Kirsten and Tom & Donna. May you live long a happy lives together.